Toshié

A

Philip E. Lilienthal

■   ■   ■

BOOK

The Philip E. Lilienthal imprint
honors special books
in commemoration of a man whose work
at the University of California Press from 1954 to 1979
was marked by dedication to young authors
and to high standards in the field of Asian Studies.
Friends, family, authors, and foundations have together
endowed the Lilienthal Fund, which enables the Press
to publish under this imprint selected books
in a way that reflects the taste and judgment
of a great and beloved editor.

Toshié

A Story of Village Life
in Twentieth-Century Japan

Simon Partner

UNIVERSITY OF CALIFORNIA PRESS
Berkeley · Los Angeles · London

University of California Press
Berkeley and Los Angeles, California

University of California Press, Ltd.
London, England

Library of Congress Cataloging-in-Publication Data

Partner, Simon.
    Toshié : a story of village life in twentieth-century
Japan / Simon Partner.
        p.   cm.
    Includes bibliographical references and index.
    ISBN 0-520-23853-2 (cloth : alk. paper) —
ISBN 0-520-24097-9 (pbk. : alk. paper)
    1. Rural families—Japan—History—20th century.
2. Villages—Japan—History—20th century.
3. Japan—Rural conditions—20th century.
4. Sakaue, Toshié, 1925–.   5. Yokogoshi-mura
(Japan)—Social conditions—20th century.   I. Title.
HN723.P37   2004
306.85'2'09520904—dc22   2003058162

Manufactured in the United States of America

13   12   11   10   09   08   07   06
10   9   8   7   6   5   4   3   2

The paper used in this publication is both acid-free and
totally chlorine-free (TCF). It meets the minimum
requirements of ANSI/NISO Z39.48–1992 (R 1997)
(Permanence of Paper). ♾

In memory of Sesto Barbetti (1932–2000)
"Sempre lavoro"

Contents

Figures

Preface

This is the story of one of the most extraordinary transformations in a century of extraordinary change. In 1925, the year in which the story begins, the majority of farm families in Japan led lives of "hard labor without chains—to which one remained bound by necessity and from which only death could bring release." [1] Their lives were circumscribed by the inexorable pressure of people on the land; by a rural class system that forced them to pay heavy tribute on the land they tilled; by dirt, disease, and frequent early death; and by a community beyond which most had seldom strayed. In 1970, by contrast, those farmers who remained on the land did so with the aid of machinery that eliminated much of the physical toil of farming; they participated fully in the national economy, often as wage laborers in nonfarm jobs (leaving farming to the weekends or to women and the elderly); and their incomes and standards of living were at least on a par with those of their urban counterparts. They were, in essence, fully fledged members of the mass consumer society. In the process, several million had left the land for good, either killed in the war or absorbed into the frenetic growth of the urban industrial economy.

This book tells the story of Sakaue Toshié, who experienced those changes to the full, along with her family and the village in which she was born. [2] I first met Toshié on a field trip in 1998. During my initial research on rural Japan, I encountered a small book called *The Japanese Village in Transition,* published in 1950 by the Allied Occupation authorities. [3] The book surveyed thirteen villages in different parts of Japan, assessing their economic and social conditions before and after the land reform of the late 1940s. I decided to revisit as many of the villages as I could, to see how life there had changed in the ensuing fifty years. Yokogoshi, Toshié's home village (it officially became a town in 1995, and in 2005 it will be absorbed into Niigata City), was one of these. Assisted by the able and dedicated town historian, Fukuda Hitoshi, I met over endless cups of green tea with several groups of older villagers to discuss the land reform, animal husbandry, farm mechanization, youth and women's associations, and a host of other economic and lifestyle-related questions. Toshié sat quietly in the back of one of these meetings. She did not participate actively, but once or twice she was invited to make comments, and her words struck me. "I lost both of my brothers in the war. . . ." she began. Shortly afterward, I had an opportunity to meet with her one-on-one, and I found myself once again intrigued by her stories of economic hardship, physical labor, and loss, but also of friendship, family warmth, and new experiences. During the next three years, I traveled to Yokogoshi four more times, and met with Toshié for a total of forty hours. I continued to meet other villagers, and I worked through the town archives to find relevant materials on the history of Yokogoshi in the twentieth century. Fortuitously, Mr. Fukuda was throughout that period working furiously on the first volume of the town history, a compilation of original records that was eventually published in 2000. I benefited enormously from Mr. Fukuda's extensive knowledge of village people and affairs, and from his handsome volume when it appeared.[4] But it was Toshié's store of memories, both warm and heartrending, her willingness to share the experiences of her own life, and her quiet articulacy that convinced me to devote the bulk of my book to her.

Toshié was born in 1925 to a family of poor tenant farmers in the hamlet of Kosugi, a part of the administrative village of Yokogoshi in Niigata prefecture. In addition to farming a scattering of small fields totaling 0.4 hectares, Toshié's family members did whatever else they could— day labor, piece work, silkworm rearing, and domestic service—to patch together a living. The scale of the family farm, and the economic conditions under which the family lived, matched the profiles of millions of farm families throughout Japan.[5] Moreover, the experiences of Toshié's life—domestic service from age twelve, wartime volunteer work on the "home front", the loss of family members in the war, a long period of hardship in the years following defeat, decades of severe manual labor, and the eventual accumulation of the perquisites of a middle-class, consumer lifestyle—were shared by millions of Japanese rural family members of her generation. One of the aims of this book is to present, through the life of Toshié, a portrait of rural life and its transformations during the middle decades of the twentieth century. Rather than offer a litany of aggregated statistics, economic analyses, government policies, and macrosocial trends, this book aims to put a human face on the experience of change; to draw the reader into the hardships, the struggles, the losses, and the gains of rural Japanese in the twentieth century as experienced by an individual who felt many of those to the full.

That said, the story of Toshié's life is far from representative. No account of an individual, or even a village, can do anything like justice to the immense diversity of Japan's seventy thousand hamlet communities and thirty million rural residents at the time of Toshié's birth. With the goal of including at least the major events of Japanese rural history, I have in places filled out the story of Toshié and her family with the experiences of other members of her community, and of other rural communities. I have strayed beyond the immediate circumstances of Toshié's life in briefly covering the tenant disputes of the 1920s and 1930s, the rural depression of the 1930s, the role of the villages in war, the land reform of the late 1940s, and the arrival of the consumer economy in the 1950s and 1960s. I have included these narratives not only to fill out a portrait of rural life that would clearly be incomplete without some reference to these major events, but also to interrogate some of the intersections between the story of an individual and the larger narratives of the society in which she lives. Toshié was surprisingly unaffected by some of the great events of the twentieth century in the Japanese countryside. What does this tell us about those events and their meaning? By paying attention to the ways in which Toshié's story intersects and runs parallel to, or even contradicts, the main narratives of Japanese rural and national history, I hope to add a little to our understanding of those narratives.

The third goal of this book is to investigate the question of individual choice. In a previous work, I wrote about the arrival of the mass consumer society in Japan in the late 1950s.[6] My work focused on the intensive efforts by corporations to develop markets for new (and expensive) products, even in the face of widespread poverty. I positioned these efforts in a continuum of state and elite attempts to transform society using the technologies of persuasion. But I am left with many doubts. Can desire in fact be manufactured? Are ordinary people really so lacking in agency and initiative? Was popular support for the war effort merely the result of government brainwashing and coercion? All too often, I feel, studies of government policy or elite-dominated campaigns imply a causality between elite desires to change society in a given direction, and the actual changes that take place in society. Unfortunately, the humbler members of society—those whose lives are to be transformed—leave the lightest marks on the historical record. This study aims to redress some of that imbalance. How did Toshié make the choices she did, and where were those choices circumscribed or channeled by the actions and voices of government and other elites? Using Toshié's own memories and the available archival records, I aim to reconstruct some of the milestones in Toshié's life and to humanize forces that can seem all too impersonal and implacable.

I am indebted to many people and institutions for support in the research and writing of this book. I carried out my initial research in Japan under the auspices of a postdoctoral fellowship from the Japan Society for the Promotion of Science. During this period, I was a foreign researcher at the Institute of Social Science, University of Tokyo, where I received valuable friendship and guidance from Kudō Akira and Nishida Yoshiaki. Subsequently, I returned to Tokyo with a Fullbright fellowship. The executives and staff of the Japan-United States Educational Commission, which administers the Fullbright in Japan, could not have been more helpful or supportive. During this stay in Japan, I was a visiting scholar at Waseda University, where I am particularly grateful to Okamato Kōichi for his generous support and unflagging efforts to make my stay productive. I was also lucky enough to spend six months at Rikkyō University as a foreign research fellow, where I benefited both from the support of the university and from the valuable guidance of Oikawa Yoshinobu. I am grateful to the members of the Modern Japanese History Workshop at Waseda for valuable feedback after two separate presentations on my research, and also to members of the Kantō chapter of the Shakai Keizaishi Gakkai and the Cultural Studies Program (particularly Yoshimi Shun'ya) of the Institute of Socio-Information and Communication Studies. Also in Tokyo, Kate Nakai was an unfailing source of valuable advice and wisdom.

In Yokogoshi, I am enormously beholden to Fukuda Hitoshi, who took time out from his desperately busy life to help me with introductions, background information, sources, and any other question or practical problem I brought up. Mr. Fukuda became a good friend, and even put me up on several occasions with his family, for which I extend warm thanks. I am also grateful to Itō Bunkichi VIII, Fukuda Kiku, Haga

Yūkichi, and the many residents of Yokogoshi who shared with me their time, memories, and knowledge. Foremost among all of these, of course, is Sakaue Toshié herself.

Ann Waswo and Steve Ericson provided valuable feedback on the manuscript of this book, and the book has benefited from their guidance. My thanks also to Sheila Levine, Reed Malcolm, and Kate Warne at the University of California Press, and to my colleagues at Duke, particularly Kären Wigen, Kris Troost, John Thompson, and Gennifer Weisenfeld.

CHAPTER I

On the Banks of the Agano

On August 14, 1925, in the hamlet of Kosugi in Niigata prefecture, a child was born. Sakaue Toshié was born in her family home, a structure of wood, bamboo, and mud, on the edge of the hamlet abutting the levee of the Agano River. Her mother gave birth to her in the close, windowless room that the family used for sleeping. Her mother, whose name was Tsugino, endured the pains of childbirth lying on the floor on a cotton-backed mattress, over which were thrown several rough straw mats stuffed with ashes to catch the blood accompanying childbirth.

A birth was a commonplace event in the life of the village, but it was also a dangerous one. Tsugino could expect no assistance from modern medicines. The dangers from infection and excessive bleeding were all too real. Two out of every ten babies died in childbirth or infancy. Kosugi had no doctor; its births were presided over by Mrs. Yamazaki, the midwife. In the event of a complication, the doctor must be sent for from Sōmi, an hour and a half's walk up the bank of the Agano.

Mrs. Yamazaki was a young woman in her twenties, recently graduated from midwifery school in the nearby town of Shibata. Her husband was the priest of the hamlet temple. Mrs. Yamazaki attended virtually every birth in Kosugi, and she was usually the only medical resource available. Unlike the old-fashioned "delivery women" *(toriagebasan)*— who offered only a few herbal remedies and a supporting hand while the birthing mother clutched at a rope hanging from the ceiling—Mrs. Yamazaki was fully trained in the importance of sterility and hygiene. She no longer allowed the birthing mother to squat holding on to a rope; vertical births were now considered unsafe due to the risk of hemorrhage and the inability of the midwife to inspect the perineum. Instead, the mother lay on her back in approved fashion. But there was little that Mrs. Yamazaki could do about the dirt of the room, about the ash-filled sacks (midwifery school recommended rubber-lined futons, but few rural families had access to these), or about the dank, dark room.[1]

Once Toshié was born, Mrs. Yamazaki quickly wrapped her in Tsugino's *koshi-maki,* a cotton cloth that Tsugino normally wrapped around her hips under her kimono. It was considered most unlucky to dress the baby in its own clothes before the twenty-one-day "end-of-birth-period." The baby's umbilical cord, cut by Mrs. Yamazaki, was carefully wrapped in a piece of cloth; it would be kept for the child's entire life, a link to her origin in the realm of the gods. Kurakichi, Tsugino's husband, took the blood-soaked mats outside and threw them on the compost pile, setting others down in their place. Kurakichi buried the placenta under the earth in the toilet area to the north of the house, far from the "bright" spirit of the southern side on which the well is located. The placenta was a part of the spirit world. It must be propitiated, and Kurakichi and Tsugino would say prayers once a year to assuage its possible anger. Mother and baby lay quietly through the long day, while the unbearable heat of the summer afternoon soaked through the rough walls of the house.

Toshié was the fourth child of Tsugino and Kurakichi. Her eldest sibling, her brother Rikichi, was already twelve years old. Next to Rikichi was a sister, Kiyomi, age eight. Nearest to Toshié in age was her brother Takeharu, who was five at the time of her birth.

Tsugino and Kurakichi were poor tenant farmers. They owned virtually no land of their own—only the land on which their house stood and a tiny patch of rice field. They rented a total of 0.4 hectares (about one acre) of land, on which they farmed a small amount of rice and vegetables (mainly for their own consumption), and mulberry for silkworm rearing. They were not at the very bottom of Kosugi's social scale—that place was occupied by those literally unable to support themselves— but they were not far above. Nevertheless, Toshié's family was long-established in Kosugi; indeed, her ancestors had for generations lived in the very spot where she was now coming into the world.

The house in which Tsugino gave birth to Toshié was also the house in which Tsugino had been born. This was unusual in Japan, where a woman normally went to live with her husband's family upon marriage. The Sakaue name, too, belonged to Tsugino. Tsugino had been born in

1887, the third child in a family that at one point included three sons. Two of Tsugino's brothers died before reaching their fourth birthdays. Her surviving brother, Niichirō, was by nature irresponsible, shirking obligations and wanting nothing more than to be left to his own devices. He quarreled frequently with his father, and finally he demanded a share of the family property and left. Meanwhile, Tsugino's elder sister, Michi, had been married into a farming family in the nearby village of Ishiyama. So it fell to Tsugino to inherit the family home and farm. Following established Japanese custom, her father arranged a marriage for Tsugino, and then adopted the man that she married. Tsugino's husband Kurakichi was therefore a *muko,* an adopted son-in-law: a slave, according to some, at the mercy of his wife and her family and the butt of many jokes. Ironically, Tsugino's father was himself a *muko,* and, by extraordinary chance, both Toshié and Toshié's daughter were also to marry *muko.* Tsugino's father, whose name was Rinokichi, gave up the family headship soon after his daughter's marriage, but he continued to live with his daughter and adopted son at the time of Toshié's birth.

Kosugi is one of seven hamlets that make up the village (since 1995, it has officially become a town) of Yokogoshi, a dozen miles from the Japan Sea in Niigata prefecture. Nowadays, one can get from Tokyo to Yokogoshi in less than three hours—by bullet train through the mountains to Niigata, and then on one of the hourly "express" minibuses.

Today, the route from Niigata to Kosugi is distinctly urban. The bus travels for a short distance on a busy expressway, exits onto a congested four-lane road that runs through the outskirts of Niigata into the town of Kameda, and finally turns off onto a wide two-lane for the short run into the town center of Yokogoshi. The scene has been urban right up to the last mile or so, when it is finally possible to glimpse rice fields behind the suburban stores lining the side of the road. If one is visiting the *kōminkan* (a village meeting hall that now houses the town's historical archive), one exits the bus at the agricultural cooperative, and plunges past a giant video store that seems to be doing a brisk business for eleven in the morning, into the maze of asphalt lanes that make up the center of Yokogoshi. If one is to visit the town center, one stays on the bus for one more stop, exiting beside a largish supermarket. Just after the bus stop, the road winds sharply, and abruptly climbs the levee onto a large bridge, which spans the width of the Agano River.

So far, it has been distinctly hard to tell where urban Japan ends and rural Japan begins. Downtown Yokogoshi is hardly a bustling place, but it appears to be striving mightily to establish the typical urban landscape of Japan: convenience stores, automatic vending machines, parking lots, even a *pachinko* parlor or two. Kosugi, though, even today is a different story.

To get to Kosugi from downtown Yokogoshi, one pedals (on a bicycle borrowed from the *kōminkan*) down a wide asphalt path, past the town's middle school on the left, and then out into the rice fields. The path runs in a straight line beside a swift-running, concrete-lined irrigation channel. On the right is the giant levee containing the Agano River; on the left are rice fields stretched in an orderly patchwork into the middle distance. In the further distance, on a clear day one can see the great mountain range that divides the Echigo plain—in which Yokogoshi is situated—from the Kanto plain and the nation's capital. Skylarks are singing overhead. The rice, which grows out of flooded paddy fields in stalks of perfect regularity, is a brilliant green. Finally, one can believe one is in the countryside.

Kosugi is the first hamlet to the north of Yokogoshi's central district, at a distance of one and a half miles. Like central Yokogoshi, Kosugi sits beside the levee protecting the village from the Agano River. The main street of Kosugi winds past mostly older houses, many of which are clearly used for agriculture. Most are in small compounds that also contain well-tended gardens and agricultural buildings of various ages and purposes. Many contain agricultural equipment of some kind: tractors; compact, Japanese-style combine harvesters; and pick-up trucks. The larger compounds are enclosed with elegant stuccoed walls, in some cases capped with smooth gray tiles. On the walls of a number of houses are advertisements for various agricultural or medicinal products. Most of the ads appear to be at least thirty years old, some much older still. There are few cars on the street, hardly a soul about. The road runs past a shrine, and then an imposing temple, shrouded under the leaves of giant oak trees. There is a tiny and ancient-looking general store on the right, and a slightly newer-looking store further up on the left. Both are closed for lunch. The appearance of Kosugi has clearly not changed so greatly since the time of Toshié's birth.

The ease of access, though, is very much a phenomenon of the postwar era. Although Kosugi was never truly isolated in the way that many mountain villages were, it was not nearly such an easy matter in the 1920s to get in and out of the hamlet. In those days, Yokogoshi and Kosugi were connected by a network of footpaths that wound their way tortuously among the irregularly shaped fields (it was only with the major land improvement works from the 1940s to the 1960s that the rice fields became the uniform rectangles that one sees today). Yokogoshi was connected then, as now, by a bus service, but in the 1920s the charcoal-powered buses were much less frequent, and the bus fare was enough to make villagers hesitate to go into Niigata on frivolous errands. As an alternative, many Kosugi residents walked to the nearby town of Kameda, where they could catch a steam train into Niigata, or they walked the ten miles to Niigata. Even the walk to either Yokogoshi or Kameda took the best part of an hour. While contact with Yokogoshi and the surrounding communities was fairly frequent in the warmer months, in midwinter Kosugi was virtually isolated. This region of Japan is noted for its very heavy snowfall. When the deep snows came, residents of Kosugi had their hands full just keeping the main paths open in the hamlet. A trip to Niigata became a major expedition.

The farmers of Kosugi have in many ways been fortunate. The Agano is one of two great rivers that water the Echigo plain. The river provides ample irrigation, and the soil of the plain is rich from the silt of previous floods. The plain grows some of the best rice in Japan. This is *koshi-hikari* country: a variety of rice similar to a French wine appellation, for which Japanese consumers are willing to pay extra on top of the already exorbitant price they must pay for what remains their staple food. The farmers of Kosugi are for the most part rice growers, and, for the most part, the land has been good to them. Kosugi, protected by its position on a bend in the river, has even been spared the scourge that has accompanied access to the ample irrigation waters of the Agano: the devastating floods that have frequently followed the annual melting of the snows in the high mountains.

Kosugi is a relatively new village. Although humans have lived in the area of Yokogoshi for more than four thousand years, much of the land remained unsuitable for agriculture until early modern times. The uncontrolled flooding of the Agano and Shinano Rivers turned the Echigo plain into a morass of hundreds of lakes surrounding waterlogged marshes. Only the higher ground was settled, its villages virtual islands besieged by the bodies of water that dominated the land. Gradually, though, the hand of man made itself felt; a marsh adjoining a village was drained, a barrier was erected against the roaming waters; and a cluster of fields was added, the green shoots tilting against the muddy immensity of the waters. Kosugi was the product of such an initiative. Reputedly, it was established in the middle of the sixteenth century by a samurai named Suzuki Kan'uemon. Suzuki was probably on the losing side in one of the wars that raged across Japan throughout the sixteenth cen-

tury. The winners appropriated existing land, while losers were often
given a chance to redeem themselves by reclaiming new land. Suzuki
brought manpower—his band of feudal retainers—and energy to the
task of draining the wetlands, laying out rice fields, and building de-
fenses against the ever threatening river.

After the Tokugawa family won control of Japan following the great
battle of Sekigahara in 1600, Kosugi was assigned, together with a large
cluster of settlements known collectively as "Yokogoshi Island," to one
of Tokugawa Ieyasu's faithful retainers, Mizoguchi Hidekatsu. Mizoguchi set up his headquarters in the castle town of Shibata, and Kosugi
came under the administration of the Shibata domain. Subsequently,
Kosugi changed hands a number of times. Hidekatsu created a subdomain as a gift for his second son. The new subdomain was based in the
town of Sōmi, which is now a hamlet of Yokogoshi on the other side of
the town center from Kosugi. For three generations, Kosugi was ruled
peacefully, if strictly, by the samurai of Sōmi domain. However, the
fourth lord was notoriously dissolute, so much so that his excesses
brought ruin down on the domain. After a senior retainer committed
hara-kiri in protest at his lord's wicked ways, and another group of retainers staged a revolt in which they murdered the lord's favorite, the
shogun finally intervened and dissolved the domain, returning its lands
to the direct control of the shogun and his representatives.[2] Thus, from
the early eighteenth to the mid-nineteenth centuries, Kosugi was governed by the shogun's representative (known as a *daikan*) who lived in
the town of Suibara. Then when Japan plunged into civil war as the
southern domains rebelled against the shogunate, Kosugi passed briefly
into the hands of the Aizu domain, one of the loyalist strongholds of the
beleaguered shogunal camp. Finally, after the downfall of the shogunate
in 1868, Kosugi was consolidated, together with the eleven domains
that made up the province of Echigo, into the newly created Niigata
prefecture.

From its creation in the sixteenth century until the end of the nineteenth century, Kosugi was a village in its own right. But with the amalgamation of Japan's seventy thousand villages beginning in 1890, Kosugi lost its administrative autonomy. Concerned at the deficits many
villages were running from the expense of village schools and administration—and perhaps also with the goal of increasing central government control—the government cajoled villages throughout Japan into
groups of from five to twenty. Each group was now known officially as
a "village" *(mura)*, while the former villages were reduced to the status

of *buraku* or *aza* (both words are best translated as hamlet). Kosugi in 1901 became a part of the village of Yokogoshi, together with Sōmi (home of the former domain and now of the great landlord family of Itō), Yokogoshi proper, and four other hamlets.

There is no such thing as a "typical" Japanese village, and Kosugi has its unique characteristics, as does every other rural community in Japan. Using the very broadest brush, one can distinguish four major types of village community in early twentieth-century Japan. On the plains were the rice-growing villages that provided the bulk of Japan's relatively abundant staple diet. Kosugi fits most closely with this group. In the mountains (which comprise more than 80 percent of Japan's land area) were the mountain villages that eked a much more precarious living using whatever resources the land provided—small rice fields on steep terraces; wheat, millet, and barley; wood and charcoal; and wild game—in addition to silkworm rearing and other cash-producing enterprises. In northern Japan were the tenuous agricultural lands of the Tōhoku region, with their short growing season and vulnerability to weather disasters. The mountain villages of Tōhoku typified rural poverty and distress— so much so that they appeared to belong to a different country from the rest of the Japanese nation (they were sometimes referred to in the press as "Japan's Tibet.") And all around the coast of Japan were fishing villages, where villagers mixed small-scale farming with commercial and subsistence fishing. Within each major type, there were of course countless greater and lesser variations. Even in the plains, not all villages could grow rice. Where the land was elevated or where water resources were unavailable, villages were forced to grow alternate crops on dry fields. Villagers in the region surrounding the commercial center of Osaka had for some generations focused on growing cash crops—cotton, indigo, tobacco, and hemp—which they sold to Osaka merchants, using the money to buy the rice they preferred not to grow. Other villages specialized in tea (suitable for low-lying mountain regions), apples (suited to the northern climate), tangerines (in the warm areas of western Japan), sugar (in the far south) and salt.

The society and agriculture of Kosugi were influenced to a great extent by the hamlet's position on the banks of the Agano River. The river was a source of abundant irrigation, giving the region its particular character as a rice-growing district. It was also a source of destruction, as its frequent floods caused losses that small peasant farmers were often unable to recoup. As a result, much of the land in the area had fallen into the hands of money lenders. By the early twentieth century, a few very

large-scale landlords owned a significant portion of the Echigo plain—
a rare phenomenon in Japan, where most landlords were small in scale.

Until modern times, the river had also been a major transportation
route, from the mountainous regions of Aizu down to the coastal plain.
However, in the two generations prior to Toshié's birth the river transportation had for the most part been replaced by road and rail, making
Kosugi probably more of a backwater than it had been a hundred years
earlier. Kosugi was also relatively close to a major commercial center,
the port city of Niigata. This created some opportunities for more specialized agricultural work; for example, farmers with land unsuitable
for rice paddies grew vegetables for the Niigata market.

The availability of irrigation water brought a relative prosperity to
Kosugi, as it did to many other communities on the Echigo plain. But
in the 1920s, the area was far from wealthy. On the contrary, for most
farmers life was a daily struggle to bring forth enough produce or paid
labor to put three square meals on the table. There were a number of
reasons for this, each of which in the 1920s presented a hard and intractable obstacle to improving the farmers' standard of living.

One of the most fundamental issues was the high population relative
to land area. The hamlet of Kosugi had a population in 1925 of about
two hundred families, with an average of close to seven family members.
A land area of 150 hectares had to feed a population of fourteen hundred.
In Kosugi in the 1920s, average productivity was said to be twenty-five
hundred kilograms of rice per hectare.[3] Thus, assuming the land was
fully planted in rice, the average family grew some 270 kilograms of rice
per family member. Although this was enough if used entirely for consumption, rice was also the major cash crop for the community; on average, the farmers of Kosugi sold half of their rice for the cash they needed
for other necessities. Of course, not all of the land would support rice
growing; much of it was sown in less productive crops.

The other major issue was tenancy. The majority of families in Yokogoshi either did not own any land or owned such a small amount of land
that they had to rent as much or more again to make ends meet. Of a total of 1,082 farming households in the administrative village of Yokogoshi, 517 had to rent all of the land that they farmed, while another
312 rented at least some land. A total of 775 out of 1,398 hectares in the
village were rented (55 percent). Much of that land belonged to the seventeen landlord families who did little or no farming themselves.[4] The
rent, paid either in cash or (more commonly) in kind, amounted to any-
where from 30 percent to 60 percent of the crop. Thus, while some land-

lord families had a considerable surplus that they could sell in order to provide themselves with the comforts of modern life, other families were forced to live on only a fraction of the produce of the land.

Most farmers augmented their incomes with some form of commercial activity, most notably the rearing and sale of silk cocoons. Silk had been a boon to Kosugi's farmers in many ways, but the vagaries of silk prices highlighted another important issue affecting farmers' livelihood: their increased commercial activities made them vulnerable to market movements over which they had no control. In years when the price of rice or silk was high (as in the final years of World War I) farmers benefited from windfalls that they could use to pay down debt or rebuild their homes. But when prices fell, farmers were often caught with high fixed expenses that in the worst cases exceeded their income. For example, fertilizer had to be paid for far in advance of the crop, often using borrowed money. Prices were in steady decline throughout the decade of the 1920s, culminating in the violent price collapses of 1930. Moreover, while the cash incomes of many farmers were unstable and at best comprised a portion of their family economy, farmers needed cash to buy many of the essentials of daily life. Mulberry planting had indeed in many cases displaced the staple crops farmers had previously grown for subsistence—making them that much more dependent on cash for survival. Gone were the days when farmers could aim for self-sufficiency in food, clothing, and housing. Rising standards of living as well as the need for fertilizer, schoolbooks, and other necessities—not to mention payment of taxes—created an inflexible need for cash that farmers struggled to provide.

Finally, even with the blessing of abundant water, farmers could only produce food from the land through severe and unremitting toil. Given the high population relative to available land, it was necessary to squeeze every last grain of rice from the soil. Families poured inordinate labor into preparing a rich, smooth soil; into building and maintaining the earthen banks around their rice fields; and into planting, weeding, harvesting, and threshing. The vast majority of the work was done by hand. Even the heaviest tasks, such as plowing or hauling, were commonly carried out with only human labor. Only the wealthiest families in the hamlet could afford draft animals such as oxen or horses. And only the simplest mechanical aids were available to the majority of farmers; for example, the most commonly owned piece of mechanical equipment was a hand-operated thresher. Motorized equipment was almost unknown. Decades earlier, there had been extensive debates among the Japanese elite about whether Japan should adopt Western-style farm machinery in a bid to increase productivity. But most Western machinery was quite unsuited to the Japanese growing conditions of tiny patchwork fields that were flooded for four months of the year. So long as Japan remained a nation of small-scale family farmers, it seemed that there was no hope for increased productivity and reduced labor through mechanization.

The world into which Toshié was born, then, was by no means a gentle one. From her earliest days, her parents were struggling to find ways to bring in enough cash to make a bare living. Their small allotment of rented land was not enough to feed and clothe the family. They had to supplement their farming with any kind of work they could get: day labor on nearby farms, day labor on construction projects, and various kinds of piecework. They suffered from constant anxiety about money and debts, and the harshness of their daily lives to some extent soured the environment of Toshié's childhood.

Tsugino, in particular, was stern and bitter. She had spent her entire life in conditions of poverty and hardship. As a child, she lost two younger brothers to sickness. One of those brothers, Buntarō, was two years younger than Tsugino, and lived into his fourth year—long enough for sister and brother to form close bonds. Then, two months after the death of her youngest brother, their mother also died. Tsugino was ten at the time. In spite of the law requiring six years of elementary education, Tsugino never went to school. Instead, after the death of her mother, her father sent her away from home to work as an apprentice weaver in a small factory in Niigata. Tsugino was skilled with the handloom, but now that factory-produced textiles had become cheap and abundant, she could no longer find work as a weaver. Instead, she took in piecework making baskets, knitting, or whatever else promised to make a little extra money. When it was available, she did not shirk from going out to work on construction or public works projects. And she was constantly busy working in the fields, either those she and her husband rented or those of neighbors who would pay her a small wage for a day's labor. Thin and wiry, her hair untidily bunched, she burned with the fuel of anger and impatience. Toshié lived in terror of her frequent scoldings. "You're nothing but a deadweight here!" Tsugino would scream at her. "Hurry up and grow—you'll be out of this house as soon as we can get rid of you." But until that day, Toshié had nowhere to hide from her mother's anger.

Her father, Kurakichi, was a much gentler soul. He, too, had lived a harsh life. Born into a landless family, he had been sent out as a child for adoption only to be returned when his adoptive parents had a child of their own. Then he had lost the sight of one eye in a fight with another boy. Kurakichi had only four years of elementary schooling, but he loved books and storytelling. He would immerse himself in historical tales whenever he could get his hands on them, and he enjoyed regaling his family and neighbors with dramatic stories of heroic deeds of the past. He was a gentle man, and in spite of the hard work and insecurities of his life, he always had a kind word. He lived in terror of his wife, whose position was all the stronger because Kurakichi was a *muko* and had come into her family with nothing.

In spite of the poverty, in spite of the anxieties, the menial work, and the debts, Toshié never went hungry. In many ways, she was protected from the want and suffering that forever lay just beyond their doorstep. In spite of her mother's rages, her family was on the whole a close and caring one. Her greatest comforts were her grandfather Rinokichi and her brother Takeharu.

Rinokichi was Tsugino's father. He had been widowed as a comparatively young man. He was seventy-six at the time of Toshié's birth, and he no longer worked in the fields. Instead, he was put in charge of the children of the house: Toshié and, after his return from school in the early afternoon, Takeharu. Rinokichi was happy to carry Toshié on his back, change her rag diapers, play games and tell her stories. Born in 1849, Rinokichi often talked about the extraordinary events of his youth—the coming of the foreigners, the economic troubles, the revolution and civil war that brought desperate fighting to within a few miles of Kosugi, the fearful flood of the same year, the collapse of the loyalist domains, and the chaotic changes of administration and laws that followed. Rinokichi was the fourth son in a poor family, but he had attended the temple school (the typical village school before the introduction of a national school system) and learned to write with a beautiful, flowing hand. He, too, loved the old tales of love and war and would retell them for Toshié again and again.

Takeharu was Toshié's closest sibling. The five years that separated them were enough to make him a heroic figure in his sister's eyes. Takeharu took his responsibilities as an elder brother very seriously. Thoughtful and sincere, he was a model for all that his sister wanted to become.

Toshié did not know her two other siblings as well. Her eldest brother, Rikichi, was sent out to work as a hired hand on a nearby farm shortly after Toshié's birth. Although he was working in Kosugi, part of his contract was that he would live with the family that employed him, and they would feed him. Rikichi was twelve years older than Toshié, and he was a remote figure compared to her other brother.

Toshié's sister, Kiyomi, was sent out to work at the age of ten, as a child minder and maid in Niigata. Her employers agreed to send her to a local school for her final two years of compulsory education, and then she would stay with them until she was old enough to be married. If ten seems a cruelly young age to be sent to work, it was nevertheless the custom of the time. Toshié's father benefited not only from the modest advance that the employment agent paid directly into his hands, but also from having one less mouth to feed.

The house in which Toshié grew up was simple and a little decrepit, but it was neither a hovel nor a hut. Rinokichi had built the house, much of it with his own hands. It was built of a few supporting beams of home-hewn wood, filled in with a good deal of bamboo twigs, mud, and straw. From the outside, the dried mud walls presented a stucco appearance, except where the mud had crumbled to reveal the uneven filling underneath. The house was roofed with tiles made of a drab concrete paste. Rinokichi did not have enough land to produce the straw for a thatch roof.

The house contained seven small rooms: a concrete-floored kitchen, two dark rooms in the back of the house used for sleeping, a formal reception room known as the *chanoma*, and two general-purpose rooms as well as an attic room. The rooms were partitioned by sliding doors covered with grimy *shōji* paper. The floors were of plain wood, covered in the *chanoma* by loose mats of straw. Although families in wealthier villages in western Japan were already flooring their houses with tatami, in Niigata prefecture the practice was still a luxury reserved for the landlord class. Against one wall of the *chanoma* was the family altar. Here was the reliquary containing votives to the Sakaue ancestors. It was dominated particularly by the memory of Ito, Toshié's grandmother, who had died of pneumonia while still in her thirties. The family sat together for meals in the *kotatsuba*, a room containing a low table under which was a charcoal brazier to warm the feet on winter evenings. In the summer months the family ate from small, individual trays.

Together with rice mixed with barley, the typical meal also included two or three side dishes of home-grown vegetables, often pickled; soup made from vegetables and homemade miso (a paste made from soy beans, molded into balls and hung out to dry under the eaves)[5]; pickled plums, also homemade; root vegetables from the garden, such as daikon radish, boiled in soy sauce; and, at least two or three times a week, fish bought from the itinerant fishwives who came from the coast on bicycles. After the meal, the family members poured hot water into their dishes and drank them clean. Dishes were thoroughly washed only on special occasions, before a feast or during the summer house-cleaning.

The quantities of both fish and vegetables were small: they were for flavoring and to fill out the rice meal. An outsider might find it hard to accept the sameness of every meal, and the reliance on bulk over substance. Particularly notable was the almost complete lack of oil or fat in the diet. But with the variety provided by the various vegetables grown by the family, it was not a bad diet. In the busy season, farmers ate an especially large amount to keep them going through all their labors. It was not unusual for men to eat as much as three pounds of rice in a day, and the women also provided snacks throughout the day, such as potatoes, beans, and dumplings.

Most days, breakfast and dinner were cooked meals served with hot rice, while lunch consisted of leftovers. Morning and evening, Tsugino also made a small offering to the household shrine before the family began its meal. Once or twice a week the family ate *katé-meshi,* a dish consisting of rice, millet, and barley cooked up with chopped radish. In the autumn when radishes were plentiful, the dish contained more radish than rice. Even before the radish harvest, Tsugino often made *ha-gaté,* the same dish made with radish leaves instead of roots. After the harvest, Tsugino covered the radishes in snow and stored them so that the family could eat them during the long winter months. She tied the leaves in bundles and hung them out to dry, awaiting the time when the roots were all eaten. Toshié hated this dish so much that her mother often scooped out the white rice that had collected at the bottom *(hagé-meshi)* to give to her youngest child. Only on rare occasions did the family eat pure white rice, a dish that everyone knew as "pure boil" *(ippon-ni):* it was an occasion for boasting to one's schoolmates. *Katé-meshi* was universally unpopular, and the ratio of rice to radish and other undesirable additives was a common source of friction between employers and servants, who usually had to eat *katé-meshi* while watching their masters eat pure white rice. There was a bridge in Yokogoshi where dissatisfied employees sometimes displayed the name of their employer and their complaint about the quality of the *katé-meshi.* Tsugino squeezed the sticky leftovers into balls, and hung them out under the south-facing eaves. They could then be eaten as a quick lunch or snack any time, either roasted or mixed with hot tea. On special occasions, Tsugino also used some of this leftover rice to make tea-flavored dumplings *(cha-dango).*

Figure 1. Rural kitchen, 1940s (Photo by Sonobe Kiyoshi, courtesy Gyōsei publishing company)

For variety, Tsugino occasionally ground wheat and barley into flour on a mortar and pestle, using the flour for dumplings or to make noodles. The latter was time-consuming so she only made them on rare occasions. She also made *kōsen*, a mixture of roasted barley and sugar that children ate with wet fingers.

In the summer months, the children gathered in the grounds of the temple and played games such as marbles, catch, and a Japanese version of grandmother's footsteps. In the fall, when the gingko trees shed their hard nuts, the children played elaborate games with the nuts. On rainy days, Toshié and her brother played card games at home, or, when they had any available, read magazines. Until his death in 1934, Toshié's grandfather Rinokichi was always at home to sit with her and tell her stories about Japan in the olden days.

In winter, the snow fell over the village like a shroud, piling up against the houses until it reached the eaves. During the snowiest months of January and February, accumulations of ten or fifteen feet were not unusual. The snow covered the paths between the hamlets, the fallow rice fields, and the barnyards of the farmers, so that it became next to impossible to travel outside the village or to do outdoor agricultural work. Even the paths within the hamlet became blocked up with knee-high snow until the straw-shod feet of enough villagers had trampled them down. In

winter, the farmers retreated to their work sheds, where they did maintenance chores for the coming year: making a supply of straw sandals,
weaving cloth for new clothes, mending tools, and weaving mats for the
inside of the house. Much of their work centered on the sheaves of rice
straw accumulated from the harvest. The straw was a valuable commodity, and none of it was wasted. Toshié, her father, and her brothers used
the straw to make rope for sale for a little extra income; sitting on the
cold concrete floor, they grasped two or three strands of straw and rolled
them together, gripping the lengthening rope with the underside of their
foot for tension. In February, the villagers all turned out in wide homemade straw snowshoes to trample down the fallen snow in the streets,
throwing soybean husks onto the snow for traction.

The snow meant months of isolation during which it was barely possible to travel outside the hamlet. But for Toshié, this was the best time
of year. As soon as her chores were done, she would race out of the
house clutching the bamboo sled that her father used for winter hauling.
Other children were already out on the levee, bundled up in thick padded
cotton jackets, their faces pink and eyes sparkling, as they ran up to the
top and sledded down. Some of the boys made skis by splitting bamboo
poles in half and clumsily skied down the levee and over the snow-clogged
lanes. Sledding, snowball fights, building snowmen, there was no end to
the games the children played until the gathering dark brought their
mothers out calling for them.

Once a week in the cold months, Toshié's mother carried water from
the well and slowly filled the wooden tub sitting in a corner of the
concrete-floored kitchen area. Once it was full, she brought rice-straw,
dried bean-husks, and a little firewood from the stack at the side of the
workshop, and set them in the firebox attached to the side of the tub. Although the firebox had a zinc flue leading out through a hole in the wall,
both firebox and flue were leaky and the kitchen soon filled up with
thick wood smoke, abetted by the smoke from the cooking stove, which
had no chimney. Eyes smarting, Tsugino watched the water slowly heating while the members of the family ate their dinner. Dinner was always
quick on bath nights. The family raced to finish their meal so that they
could enjoy a quick bath before the inevitable guests arrived. The water
was steaming hot, and the sensation of putting cold feet into the hot water was almost unbearable. But once inside the tub, Toshié felt the pene-
trating heat warm her through and through—it was the only time that
she really felt warm in the winter months.

When Tsugino's turn came to get in the bath, she carried the family's dirty clothes with her, and put them in the wash tub next to the bath to soak while she sat in the bath. Then she got out of the bath, washed the clothes with soap, and rinsed them with cold water drawn from the well. After wringing them dry, she climbed back into the bath to get warm again. Once the family members had all had their baths, they put on clean, thick underwear and then their "everyday" gowns *(fudangi)*, and began getting ready to receive guests.

Soon, the kitchen door started opening, and figures appeared wrapped in their winter clothes, calling out apologies for intruding. Tsugino (or Toshié as her deputy) had politely called on them earlier in the day and told them that she would be heating a bath that night. These were friends and neighbors who worked together on communal tasks, and who were always willing to perform small chores to help one another. They carried little bundles wrapped in a cloth that contained a little towel and a change of underwear. "Gomen kudasai!" they called: "Please excuse me!" Toshié's father hastened to welcome them, and they cast off their clogs and took up seats in the reception room, where Tsugino served them tea and a simple snack of corn or boiled beans in their shells. Their faces were dark and wrinkled from the sun, the hair of the women piled simply on top of their heads, with stray wisps falling over their faces. Their hands were hard and callused, their fingernails black with dirt. By eight o'clock there were a dozen adult guests crowded into the reception rooms—the men sitting together in the *chanoma,* the women in the next-door *kotatsuba.* There were also ten or fifteen children, who sat with the women chattering and laughing, playing games, and being scolded by their half-serious mothers.

The guests took their baths one at a time, in the order that they came to the house. Fathers took their small children in with them. The guests stepped down from the raised dais of the *chanoma* onto a wooden platform in the middle of the concrete-floored kitchen. There, they took off their clothes and left them on a stool. The air in the kitchen was dank and cold enough to bring goose bumps to their skin. Hurriedly, the guests washed their bodies in the wooden tub that Tsugino had just used for the clothes (which were piled in a heap on a wooden stand, waiting to be hung out the next morning), before gratefully climbing into the bathtub. The bath area was only dimly lit by a lightbulb snaking out from an adapter in the living room. Sometimes Tsugino stepped into the kitchen to pick up some more beans or to add a little water to the tub. The guests modestly covered themselves if they were outside the bathtub. Nudity was not something to be excessively shy about, but Tsugino and the others respected their guests' privacy as well as they could in the cramped quarters.

By the time the last guests climbed into the tub, it was late in the evening, and the bath water had turned lukewarm and oily from all the bodies that had soaked in it. Finally, the family could go to sleep. Toshié slept with her parents and brother in the room she was born in, while her grandfather slept in the small, single room upstairs. In place of blankets, they slept in fat gowns of cotton stuffed with old cloth, on mattresses made of rice-husk-filled hemp known locally as *kuzubuton*.

The next morning, when Tsugino drained out the bath water into the snow outside, the water was the color of vegetable soup. At the bottom of the tub was a thick scum of human detritus—skin, hair, and drowned lice.

When spring came, new visitors arrived to stay in the house. They came in a box, fetched by Toshié's father and placed with delicate tenderness in one of the bedrooms. The box was covered with gauze. When Toshié's father removed it, they saw a mass of white foam. Like other small-time silkworm rearers, twice a year—in March and September—the Sakaue family "bought" silkworm eggs from a local agent of a silk manufacturing company. No money changed hands, as the price was deducted from the proceeds paid by the same agent when he returned to pick up the spun cocoons.

The agent handed over a single box of tiny eggs—as many as twenty thousand of them spread thinly over the wooden surface—and the family deposited them in one of their two small bedrooms. For the next forty days, the worms usurped the family's sleeping space. The room was equipped with racks, on which wooden trays were arrayed. For now, they were empty. But when the eggs hatched—generally all on the same day—Toshié's father, using a feather, gently brushed the mass of tiny wriggling larvae onto two of the rearing trays, on which was spread a thin layer of chopped mulberry leaves. Before use, the rearing trays were immersed in water, and on the bottom were spread rice husks soaked in water: the worms liked a high level of humidity.

For three days, the larvae ate finely chopped, young mulberry leaves fed tenderly to them by the members of the household. On the fourth day they stopped eating, and went into apparent hibernation. Within twenty-four hours, their skins dropped off to reveal a bright new layer of skin with distinctive striped markings. At first, the worms were almost too small to see with the naked eye, but by the fifth day, they were large enough to distinguish individually, as they hurriedly munched their

way through fresh piles of leaves. Soon some of them had be transferred
to another rearing tray to make space; eventually the worms from that
single tray of eggs would occupy all the rearing trays in the room. From
that point, their growth was extraordinary. Every day, they doubled in
size or more. By the time they began spinning their cocoons, they weighed
ten thousand times their original weight at hatching.

The worms ate busily for twelve-minute stretches, then rested a few
minutes before beginning again. Every three or four days, they stopped
eating for a day or so, and once again molted. They did this a total of
four times. After the fourth molt, they ate for six days. Now they were
ready to begin spinning their cocoons. By this time, they were each more
than a centimeter long, with eight sets of legs and a horn near their tails;
their bright brown heads and the black rings encircling their bodies were
clearly visible. Even their sex was ascertainable: the female has two small,
milk-white spots on each side of her belly, while the male has a single spot.

As the worms grew, so did their appetites. For the young worms,
Toshié and her siblings fed them the tenderest shoots from the top of the
mulberry bush. But once the worms got to the fifth stage, it was all that
the family could do to harvest enough leaves to feed the voracious creatures. During their short time of growth, the worms devoured some thirteen hundred pounds of leaves; more than 80 percent of which was
consumed during the fifth stage. What with cutting and transporting the
leaves from field to home, chopping and feeding the leaves to the worms,
and cleaning out the increasing amount of feces and waste, the family
was kept busy day and night during this last hectic phase. Their single
mulberry field was not enough to meet the appetites of the mature
worms, so Toshié's father had to buy a portion of mulberry leaves, again
on credit against the proceeds of the cocoons. The elementary school
allowed Toshié and other children of silk-rearing families to stay home
during this busiest week to help the family.

The last stage was also the trickiest. Silkworms are notoriously delicate creatures, vulnerable to sudden temperature changes, swings in humidity, and a wide variety of infections. A sudden drop in temperature
or a stray infection could wipe out an entire colony in a matter of a day—
leaving the family with a heavy loss to bear instead of the anticipated
profit. The boxes were kept supplied with damp husks to maintain humidity, and a charcoal brazier was kept on hand in case the temperature
should fall. But for the most part, the Sakaue family had to trust their
luck, which did not always hold out. At least one out of six rearings
ended in disaster.

Figure 2. Silk cocoon rearing, 1950s (Photo by Sonobe Kiyoshi, courtesy Gyōsei publishing company)

Finally, the worms were ready to begin spinning. For this final step, Toshié's father made special frames, using rope made of rice straw. The rope was fashioned into waves, and at the trough of each wave the members of the family, working all together, placed the worms. The worms must be mounted quickly and at exactly the right time. If they were mounted too early, some of them would continue excreting and soil the cocoons that others were spinning. If too late, they would spin double cocoons.

The worms used the rope as a pivot for their spinning. Over the next four days, the worms span translucent white cocoons using a sticky white thread—silk—that they excreted from a special gland. Once they were finished, they began to molt one final time inside the cocoon. If they were allowed to, they would emerge from the cocoon in another eight days as full-grown moths. But they were much too precious for that. On the sixth day after mounting, Toshié's father and Rikichi carefully packed the cocoons and carried them down to the agent's office. Their harvest averaged some eighty kilograms. For that, they received anything from one hundred to two hundred yen, depending on prices. From that income must be deducted the cost of the eggs, fertilizer for the mulberries, and the mulberry leaves that Kurakichi purchased. Most years, Tsugino would boil up the discarded cocoons that were too poor in quality to sell and make a little silk thread. More frequently, Kurakichi used them as fertilizer—those that he did not give away to young boys who wanted them for fish bait. Some families ate the swollen pupa—they were an excellent source of protein, but by no means delicious—while other communities made individually or communally owned fishponds, and fed the pupa to the fish.[6]

In spite of its small holdings and the need to pay rent, Toshié's family continued to rely on farming for its everyday sustenance. The family grew, first and foremost and as much as possible, its own food—rice, vegetables, and beans. However, some edible items had, by the 1930s, come to be seen as necessary purchases. These included soy sauce (some families made their own, but most, including Toshié's, purchased it), tofu (again, some families, including the Sakaue, occasionally made their own), salt, sugar, cooking oil, occasional sweets, and—the most frequent purchase—fresh or salted fish. Most of these items were things that a family fifty years earlier would have made or done without—this itself is an indication how much the cash economy had already permeated village life, generally accompanied by a higher standard of living.

Even with these purchases, Tsugino stayed very busy preserving her own crops to turn them into constant sources of food throughout the year. Tsugino pickled a wide variety of vegetables, from cucumbers that she lightly pickled in rice vinegar and the family ate within a few days, to the notorious *takuan*—an extremely pungent pickle of daikon radish, that keeps for months. Pickled plums *(umeboshi)* are actually held to improve with age, and families often proudly produced vintages of ten or more years past. Other preserved staples included miso, and *nattō*, an evil-smelling preserve of fomented beans.

Self-sufficiency extended well beyond food alone. In most years, Tsugino held back some of the inferior-grade cocoons to spin and weave a little silk thread. She also purchased cotton thread, which she wove into cloth on her foot-powered loom. Naturally, the finished clothes were also made at home. Straw sandals and sedge hats were also homemade.

However, for all the items that they made for themselves, there were others that her parents had made but Tsugino now purchased. In the Tokugawa period (1600–1868), farmers grew hemp or flax and made cloth and clothes from these crops. With the arrival of inexpensive cotton, a place was rapidly made in the fields for alternative crops (Tsugino grew a very small amount of hemp, but most of her thread was purchased). In earlier days, too, farmers would have prepared some of their own dyes using vegetables from the farm. Now, Tsugino bought chemical dyes, or she bought colored thread or cloth. And although Tsugino might weave the cloth to make the family's everyday clothes, she purchased finer materials for special clothes such as kimono or Western-style outfits. For the children, Tsugino bought oiled, cloth capes at the Kameda market.

The family had numerous other cash expenses, which reveal the extent to which farm families were integrated into the national cash economy. Toshié's parents bought matches, tobacco, writing paper (such as notebooks), books and magazines, children's toys, wooden clogs, medicines, sake, and some items of clothing or accessories (such as buttons and combs). Other cash expenses included payments to the hairdresser, doctor, and temple, as well as village taxes. As early as 1900, a survey of a village in Kanagawa prefecture found virtually all households purchasing their basic household furnishings for cash. Some of these, such as pots, rice bowls, trays, and kettles would have been cash items long before the Meiji period (1868–1912). Others were clearly indicative of a slow spread of manufactured goods. The average family, for example, owned two kerosene lamps and three Western-style umbrellas. One family in two owned a metal bucket; one in five owned a Japanese flag, a wall clock, or a pocket watch.[7] All of these added up to substantial cash outlays; Toshié's family was mostly unable to cover them with farm income, since they had insufficient surplus to sell.

The farmwork was truly hard. The family had no farm animals, so everything had to be done by hand. Rice is a demanding crop. The soil of the field in which it is planted must be as smooth as cake, deep, and richly fertilized. To get the soil to that condition, Kurakichi and Tsugino had to spend the early spring months working at it with fork, plow, and, finally, feet. First they dug the field with fork and spade. They followed this up using a single-bladed iron plow, which was pulled by Kurakichi and pushed by Tsugino. The initial digging was necessary because the plow could not otherwise furrow the earth deeply enough.

Next, they scoured the riverbanks and the sides of the levee for grasses, which they cut and strewed over the field for mulch. They followed this with applications of fertilizer. The principle source was compost and human excrement, which Kurakichi carefully collected in a wooden tub under the privy. In other parts of Japan, farmers purchased commercial fertilizers in the form of dried fishcake, soybean cake, or the new chemical fertilizers. But Kurakichi and Tsugino did not have enough cash to purchase fertilizers, and they were luckier than some in that the riverbanks still offered a source of vegetable fertilizer.

Next came one of the hardest and most painstaking parts of the whole process. After the fertilizer was applied, Kurakichi and Tsugino once again dug carefully over the whole extent of the field, turning the soil up into loose crumbly clumps. Kurakichi excavated from the work area of his house all the soil that had been softened up by the use of water in the house, and carried it to the field where he added it to the surface. Finally, husband and wife beat the field with mallets and bare feet to soften the earth and make it of a uniform, smooth consistency. Finally, the field was ready for flooding.

Kurakichi flooded the field by tapping one of the village-maintained irrigation channels that flowed nearby. Once the field began to flood, he and Tsugino worked to build up a bank around the field to hold in the water. They continued flooding the field until the earth was under nine inches of water. Once the field was flooded, they once again waded into the cold and leech-ridden water in bare feet and attacked it with hoes for a final breakup. Next, Kurakichi pushed the plow himself or rented a horse for the final tilling, which left the soil smooth and glutinous and of a uniform height. The field was now ready for planting.

The rice planting—or transplanting, since the seeds had already been germinated in communal seed beds in a warm part of the village—took place in early June, just at the onset of the rainy season. In many villages this was a communal affair, the labor typically shared by the members of the neighborhood group. Wives from each household in the neighborhood group would come to help carry the tender rice shoots from the seed bed to the field in baskets slung on poles from their shoulders and then slowly work their way in a line down the field, planting one shoot at a time. It was backbreaking work, as they were constantly bending over, and their feet were numb from the cold water. But still the line of women would sing as they worked their way slowly down the line. During the day, the farm wife would bring snacks of rice cakes and dumplings to keep up the workers' strength, and at the end of the day she rewarded the helpers and their families with a large meal at which sake flowed. Perhaps in Kosugi the work had been communal in earlier times. But during Toshié's childhood, each family was responsible for its own fields, and only the wealthier families hired help in exchange for a money wage.

Once the rice was safely planted, the great enemies were weeds, insects, and the lack of water. Kosugi was blessed with an abundant supply of water throughout the year, so as his field dried out Kurakichi was able to replenish it periodically from the irrigation channel. In other villages with less reliable supplies, or in fields that were further from a source of irrigation, farmers (or their children) had to spend much of their day carrying or pumping water using a primitive wooden treadle. Seven days after the transplanting, Kurakichi and Tsugino once again took to the field for another digging over, this time to loosen up the soil around the roots of the plants, allowing them to take a firmer hold. At least two or thee times during the season, Kurakichi and Tsugino thoroughly went over the field, pulling up weeds that also took to the moist and fertile conditions, leaving the deracinated remains in the fields to work as mulch. They also added fertilizer periodically from the family latrine.

All this care and attention made foreign visitors to Japan comment on how the countryside appeared to be one big garden. The tended rice shoots grew strong and brilliant green in the glistening wet fields, until the fierce summer heat slowly dried them out and turned them yellow-green. By the end of the summer, the shoots were heavy with the weight of the swollen grains growing at their tops. Finally, in early October, it was time to harvest. The family took their sickles to the bottom of the plants, cutting and tying them into bunches that they then hung from specially constructed trellises where they dried out until they were ready for threshing, winnowing, and hulling.[8] Even then, the heavy work was not over. Other than plowing, the heaviest chore for farmers was carrying. Everything—seeds, crops, straw, firewood (usually driftwood from the river)—had to be carried in baskets or bundles on the backs of family members, often from far away from the home. Some villagers had fields on the other side of the river, and they hauled everything first by boat, and then on their backs. The river was crowded with heavily laden boats going back and forth. Kurakichi owned a bicycle and a hand-pulled trailer, both major investments and very useful for hauling. But from the mid-1930s, much of his land was across the levee, on the riverside, making these tools all but useless.

Government statistics reveal something about average levels of income and expenditure in the year of Toshié's birth. In 1925, the Ministry of Agriculture reported that the average farm family had a net agricultural income of 1,163 yen (590 dollars at the then-current exchange rate). About one-quarter came from silk-cocoon rearing. In addition, the average family earned a net nonfarm income of 270 yen, bringing the total income up to 1,433 yen (715 dollars). The family had debts totaling 807 yen.[9] A tenant farmer and day laborer like Kurakichi would have been lucky to pull in more than eight hundred or nine hundred yen in a year.[10] In the poorest regions of Japan, annual incomes might not rise above one hundred yen.[11]

Food consumption varied greatly depending on geographic location as well as economic position within the village. Very few villagers in pre-war rural Japan ate pure rice. For the vast majority, rice was either non-existent, or it was too precious a cash-producing commodity to consume in the family. But there is a good deal of difference between eating 60 percent rice and 40 percent barley (as was common in the wealthier rice-growing villages of the plains) and 90 percent millet to 10 percent rice (as was reported by families in one village in mountainous Iwate prefecture).[12] Food consumption also varied depending on the time of year. Tenant farmers in particular were liable to run out of rice by the summer, with the rice harvest not due until October. During these months, they must either buy rice or do without. A study of Kamikitadani, a mountain village in Niigata prefecture, reported that tenant farmers on holdings below the middle level must buy rice from August onward. Yet this group was the least equipped to earn cash incomes to pay for extra food; on average, they earned only a little over one hundred yen cash per year. Cash expenditures accounted for only 11 percent of their total consumption, and their Engel coefficient (the percentage of income they spent on food) was 79 percent.[13] In spite of its poor economic circumstances, Toshié's family was able to eat rice all year (her father bought it when he ran out in the summer months). Although Toshié hated the adulterated *katé-meshi*, most meals that she ate contained at least 50 percent rice.

Conditions of health and hygiene depended on the availability of clean water, housing conditions, access to medical services, income levels, and education, and they varied widely depending on circumstances. Once again, the villages of northern Japan were the most unfortunate. A British traveler in the 1870s, Isabella Bird, observed conditions in a mountain village at which she stayed overnight:

> The houses were all poor, and the people dirty both in their clothing and persons. Some of the younger women might possibly have been comely, if soap and water had been plentifully applied to their faces; but soap is not used, and such washing as the garments get is only the rubbing them a little with sand in a running stream. . . . The persons, clothing, and houses were alive with vermin, and if the word *squalor* can be applied to independent and industrious people, they were squalid.

Bird added, "The married women look as though they had never known youth, and their skin is apt to be like tanned leather." Asking one woman whom she took to be about fifty years old, she was astonished to hear that the woman was only twenty-two.[14] Conditions had evidently not changed much by the 1930s, when a study group commented that villagers' "hands were like elephant skin and caked with dirt, their children's heads were covered with lice, their clothes stank, there were fleas jumping around the room."[15] Their clothes "were like old mops, too patched and old even to wash." Many of them did not even own a mattress, sleeping instead on straw.[16] A 1934 survey in Aomori (northeastern Japan) found that out of forty-four thousand households surveyed, 17,500 bathed only once or twice a year, and 13,300 bathed less than once a year. The same study found that 43 percent of conscription-age men suffered from trachoma, and that in 1933, 654 people had died because they were unable to procure a doctor.

By contrast with this extreme case, Toshié's conditions of housing, clothing, and personal hygiene were relatively good. While not large, the house she was born in was by no means a hut; it was solidly constructed using appropriate building techniques. Although it contained no luxuries such as *tatami* or fine woods, it was a place where the family could entertain friends and neighbors without feeling shame. Although it was not warm, the family had plenty of fuel to heat the *kotatsu,* where they could gather together in cozy companionship. The house was electrically lit—albeit dimly—and the family owned a number of purchased goods, such as pots and pans, umbrellas, books, utensils, braziers, a bicycle, paraffin lamps, and a sewing machine. Each member of the family had at least one set of clothes to wear at formal occasions. The family bathed regularly and washed clothes with at least a minimum of regularity. Toshié's family's greatest hygiene worry was water. Their well water was very metallic, and they had to filter it using a homemade filter of charcoal and sand. In the summer, the well often dried up altogether. From spring to autumn, the irrigation channel that ran next to the house was full, and the family used its water freely for washing clothes and dishes and bathing. But there was always the worry that the water might be dirty and cause them to become unwell. Dysentery was endemic in Yokogoshi, claiming between twenty and thirty lives a year, and there were occasional outbreaks of typhus; dirty water was usually blamed as the cause.

Lice and fleas, too, were a normal part of everyday life. At school, before class children would customarily pick lice out of the hair of the child sitting in the desk in front of them. In Sué Mura in the southern island of Kyūshū, anthropologist Ella Wiswell was so upset by the poor hygiene and the ubiquity of lice that she sent her three-year-old son to Tokyo to be taken care of in the city.[17] Perhaps Wiswell was also alarmed by the extremely high death rate of children, either from birthing trauma, sickness, or accident. During her stay in Sué, one child died by drowning in an irrigation canal. This was also a common accident in Yokogoshi, where at least one or two children were said to drown each year. Overall in Japan, rural statistics consistently show a death rate of 20 percent for babies from birth through infancy. This statistic did not markedly improve until the 1950s. A report from Yumada village in Niigata prefecture states that of 1,048 children born between 1905 and 1909, 110 were stillborn, and a further 278 died before their fourth birthdays (a total death rate before age four of 37 percent). Prewar Yokogoshi was roughly on par with the national average: in 1928, seventy-six infants died compared with 379 born (20 percent); in 1930, forty-nine out of 388 died (13 percent), and in 1932, it was sixty-six out of 392 (17 percent).[18]

Access to medical care was a constant worry for most rural families. Those in mountain villages, in particular, had to travel long distances on often-dangerous mountain paths in order to find a doctor. As a result, villagers would usually set out for the doctor only in extreme circumstances—at which time the patient was often unable to cope with the journey.[19] A woman in a Tohoku (northern Japan) village commented on her personal circumstances:

> There's no doctor in this village, so we have to get him to come from the neighboring town, which costs five yen. We can only call him in an extreme emergency, and even if we call him we can't pay him without borrowing. For a short illness we're taking [traditional] Toyama medicine and sweating it out. But that medicine too costs seven or eight yen [per year]. The other day the medicine seller came to collect her money, but all I could pay her was ten *sen* [0.10 yen]. I hated to do it to her, but there was nothing else I could do.[20]

By contrast, Toshié appears to have used medical services quite freely. Although there was no doctor in Kosugi, she would either walk to the doctor in Kameda or, if seriously ill, be carried on her father's hand-pulled trailer. She recalls that the doctor's fee was not excessive, and her frequent illnesses sent her to the doctor often. Nevertheless, a village report published by Yokogoshi laments that "there are at present no doctors in the central or northern parts of the village, and overall, given the large population of the village, the number of doctors [two] in the village is inadequate. This is one of the greatest worries of the villagers."[21] Yokogoshi was also afflicted by its own particular health and environmental problems. One of these was the constant danger of flooding, which was liable to afflict one part or another of the village at least once in a decade, bringing with it not only economic loss, but also water contamination and the threat of epidemic disease. Parts of the village were flooded in 1924, 1926, 1941, and 1947. Another problem was the presence of a deadly insect, the *tsutsugamushi,* which lurked in the rushes near the riverside. This nearly invisible mite harbored a disease known as Japanese river fever, or scrub typhus. After a bite, a small red welt would be all the victim would see of his or her affliction, until serious and often fatal fever set in after two weeks. On average, the disease caused six or seven deaths a year in Yokogoshi, and it was a source of great fear and anxiety for those who worked near the river.

In spite of the relative physical isolation of Kosugi, the community was very much a part of the industrialized imperial enterprise that was Japan in the 1920s. Already by the second decade of the twentieth century, regional and national corporations were striving to integrate rural communities into their sales networks as they created brands for soy sauce, beer, cosmetics, and bicycles. Such activities in turn stimulated the spread of urban commerce into the countryside, with the opening of shops and the expansion of sales and advertising in the villages. The rising importance of money also made it more and more likely that at least some members of every rural family would participate in wage labor: the first example being the mass enlistment of young rural girls in the new industrial silk filatures.

The greatest symbol of the increasing integration of village and nation was the railway. By 1925 Japan's railway network extended to twelve thousand kilometers, and a railway line passed within five miles of Kosugi.[22] As a result, a journey to Tokyo that would have taken days of arduous mountain hiking in the nineteenth century could now be accomplished in sixteen hours. The impact of the railway clearly varied greatly depending on how close a village was to the railway, and where that railway line went. Most affected were villages within a short distance of major cities. In the 1870s, the western parts of Tokyo were farming villages, but by 1910 the city had grown along the main railway lines, turning the villages into residential suburbs. Even where the village was not overrun by the city, the ability to transport produce to the cities transformed the economies of peripheral villages (although rice was already integrated into a national transport system centered mainly on water transport). Observers commented—often with disapproval—that after the coming of the railway, nearby villagers rapidly adopted urban fashions and habits of life.[23] The railway also affected daily life to a lesser extent in more remote villages that were close to a main line. A 1934 study of a poor village in Iwate prefecture notes that since the coming of the railway to within a few miles of the village, villagers' diets had expanded to the year-round consumption of cheap dried fish imported from Hokkaido. Nagatsuka Takashi's novel of rural life, *The Soil,* also refers to the steep drop in the price of eggs due to the availability of imports from Shanghai.[24] And Kären Wigen has documented in detail how villages in the Shimoina district of Nagano prefecture became dependent on food and fertilizer imported by railroad as they increasingly devoted their land resources to mulberry for sericulture.[25]

The case of Kosugi illustrates some of the complexities of assessing the impact of railways. Compared to many remoter villages, Kosugi was well integrated with the national transport network long before the coming of railways. Situated only ten miles from Niigata, the residents of Kosugi have always had relatively easy contact with a provincial center. Throughout the Tokugawa and into the Meiji eras, the Agano River was a major communications route connecting the mountain areas of central Japan to the coast. For those living in the plain, the river allowed ready transportation and delivery of goods between the cities and villages along its banks. At any time in the nineteenth century, the river must have presented a lively prospect of countless vessels, large and small, carrying produce and people up and down. Indeed, in the 1890s a steamboat service opened up, promising to increase river commerce still further. But the road and rail systems superceded the river, leaving Yokogoshi somewhat less centrally positioned in terms of transportation than before. Nevertheless, the bus and train clearly brought Niigata closer to the residents of Kosugi. The railway also enabled the residents of Kosugi to travel further afield to work, as is evidenced by the departure of Kosugi villagers to Tokyo to take up apprenticeships.

The railway enabled the spread of urban culture in ways that had not been possible before. Printed materials—newspapers, magazines, standardized educational supplies, and textbooks—could now be distributed throughout the country. Urban lecturers, teachers, exhibits, and commercial goods also traveled from the capital to the provinces in search of new audiences. Influential villagers, including landlords and school principals, also had the opportunity—even the obligation— to visit the major cities for the purpose of instruction or study. By the second decade of the twentieth century, group travel by villagers was becoming increasingly common. By 1915, some four million people a year (urban and rural) were traveling on group visits to shrines, temples, provincial cities, or the capital.[26]

Commentators were not slow to point out the influence of railways and commerce in changing village life. The narrator of the novel *Cotton (Men)* comments:

> When I think about it, things had certainly changed a lot since my childhood. The coastal railway line runs three *ri* [about twelve kilometers] from the village, and several years ago the trains had started running on it. If you climbed the mountain above the school, you could just see the white plume of the passing trains. The year before, the valley over the mountain had been developed into the Y mine. And in our own village, a pottery factory and a textile factory had been built three years earlier, and many men and women now worked there. The village now had a dry goods store, a hairdresser, a general store, and a sweet shop. The homemade "tengu" tobacco disappeared, and it was replaced by "Okami" tobacco. Paper-covered lanterns became paraffin lamps; indigo kimonos became striped and patterned bought cloth. Instead of the spindle and loom, cocoon trays took over the houses, and mulberry fields replaced the cotton. The village roads were widened, and the bridge was rebuilt. Certainly "civilization" was entering into this cold winter village.[27]

In villages close to towns or cities, improved transportation fed the natural ardor of villagers for new experience and for travel. Naturally, this desire was by no means new. *Before the Dawn,* a novel of village life before the Meiji restoration, eloquently portrays the life of constant travel (on foot, and usually between nearby villages and towns) that the more leisured villagers participated in during the late Tokugawa era.[28] But when Yokoi Kenshirō in 1924 walked six hours to the nearest town from his isolated mountain village, he was able to gaze into shop windows selling industrial produce, get his watch repaired, and observe electricity at first hand. Igarashi Hirasaburō, a young farmer from Ōsaki village in Niigata prefecture, wrote in his diary in June 1916 after a day trip to town with a friend: "Today was very interesting and pleasant. Ah, sightseeing is the mother of progress, travel is the father of pleasure."[29]

The railway also made it easier for villagers to travel to cities in search of work. There had always been a symbiosis between cities and the villagers who provided their labor force, but railways brought the two closer together, while industrialization greatly increased the opportunities for employment. The railways also allowed villagers working in the city to pay more frequent visits to their families—each time bringing back goods and ideas from the city to the village. Indeed, the relative ease of travel between village and city increasingly fed a "city fever" among village youths, which caused great concern to the authorities who wished to preserve the traditions of village life. Villagers moving to the city could "bathe themselves in the marvels of the new age, and enjoy civilization," while in the village they came to believe that "there is neither civilization nor culture." This led village loyalists to retort back in a local publication:

> Why do village youths have such a yearning for the city? Are they not driven by a superficial, man-made beauty, and by what seems to them to be a brilliant lifestyle? And do they not believe that the city is the land of success, and are they not filled with envy at the sight of one or two successful people? But is the city really such a pleasant place as it appears in the dreams of village men? Look, please, at the poisonous hand of vanity that is in the city, and are there not tens of thousands of failures struggling in a dark abyss behind every success? Wake up, village youths![30]

The yearning for the city also tied in with the education fever that gripped village youth from the early part of the twentieth century. A 1915 report by the Tokyo employment exchange commented that "Out of 100 young men coming to Tokyo from the provinces, 95 of them are driven by the desire for education. On the other hand, only four or five of them are from the outset coming with the aim of working or gaining some other practical experience."[31]

Nevertheless, it is important to stress that for the majority of villages, the direct impact of the railway was very limited, at least until the middle of the twentieth century. Until the second decade of the century, the railway was essentially a system of trunk routes connecting the major cities. Since these cities were already connected by a well-established road and river transport network, the main effect of the railway even here was to speed up the process of transportation rather than to create new links. Moreover, even if a railway line was close at hand, most villagers who were not expressly planning emigration to the city had neither the motivation nor the means to make major trips by rail. In theory, it was possible for a Kosugi villager to walk five miles to Niitsu station and board a train to Tokyo. But few actually made the journey. In the mid-1920s, a third-class roundtrip ticket from Niigata to Tokyo cost some six yen—by no means an insignificant sum for Japanese farmers. Rather, it is more realistic to say that the social and economic effects of railways profoundly influenced provincial cities such as Niigata, and that villages were influenced mainly as a corollary of changes in their provincial capitals.

Improved transportation and communications also brought villagers into a more direct relationship with their national government. Standardized school textbooks were distributed nationally, so that children in every part of Japan studied the same homilies on the greatness and goodness of the emperor, on respect and obedience, and on the glories of Japan's military achievements. The national post-office network offered savings accounts in most villages in Japan by the end of the nineteenth century. By 1910, Japan's five million farm families held some 3.6 million postal savings accounts, with average savings of thirteen yen.[32] And village administrations responded to increasing exhortations from the Home and Agriculture Ministries to standardize holidays, promote punctuality, and encourage thrift and saving. For example, in the first decade of the twentieth century, the village of Kawahigashi in Niigata prefecture campaigned vigorously to convert all its hamlets to a standardized system of holidays. Previously, each hamlet had had its own rest days and holidays, many of them based on the old lunar calendar. Kawahigashi aggressively promoted use of the Western calendar (officially adopted in Japan in 1872), urging the standardization of rest days and the reduction of their overall number (the village wished to reduce the number to eighty-five per year). In particular, Kawahigashi strove to promote enthusiastic observance of the major national festivals: the New Year based on the Western calendar; the National Foundation Day on February 11; the emperor's birthday; and three agricultural holidays on which the emperor performed ceremonial agricultural functions. Still, in 1916 a village report could write: "There are still people who are so lacking in national spirit that they are unaware of national holidays".[33]

Military service, compulsory for the 30 percent or so of male villagers who both passed the physical examination and were selected by lottery, also brought village men into contact with national systems of transportation, industry, and urban life; for many, it was the first time that they used running water and flush toilets, traveled on trains and in trucks, wore boots or even trousers, slept in beds or ate meat. Although the basic diet of the soldiers differed little from that of humble Japanese urbanites, even this probably contained more variety and higher quality than most farmers had eaten at home. In addition, field provisions included canned food, bread, and biscuits—all undoubted novelties for village men. From their (frequently urban) barracks, conscripted soldiers also participated in urban entertainments, including dining in inexpensive restaurants, visiting brothels, and theater.[34] Military service also tied village men to the developing national mission of imperial expansion. Top-level bureaucrats led by Tanaka Giichi worked in the first decade of the twentieth century to create a national network of reservists and veterans' associations, creating permanent ties between village men and the central military authorities. The village reserve association became an important institution in village life, reflecting and reinforcing for the most part the existing hierarchy, but also instilling and maintaining patriotic and military values for the village as a whole. For example, members of the reserve association were almost always chosen for leadership roles in the village youth association, and reservists contributed increasingly to military-style drill instruction and physical education for village youths.[35]

Toshié's parents were well aware of their place in, and obligations to, a modern nation. Their consumption and labor activities reflected to some extent their participation in a national market, as they worked on government-financed projects and purchased simple, mass-produced goods such as cloth, kitchen utensils, and tools. But their case also illustrates the limits of the penetration of national consciousness and obligation by the mid-1920s. Presumably due to the loss of sight in one eye, Kurakichi never served in the military. He paid no direct taxes other than to the village. Until the 1930s Tsugino's brother Niichirō was the only family member who had traveled beyond the confines of Niigata prefecture. The family subscribed to no newspapers or magazines. And trips by rail were strictly limited to visits to the local capital. It was not until the mid-1930s that the family was to be exposed to the increasing pull of the modern industrial nation, as its members were pulled into the national mission of imperial expansion and, ultimately, "total" war.

Toshié's parents were also aware of their place in the village. In spite of the veneer of civility and harmonious relations that characterized most day-to-day contacts between villagers, class was a fact of life. Although it enjoyed some prestige from its long presence in Kosugi, Toshié's family was close to the bottom of a social ladder that was defined mainly by quantity of land owned. In the decades prior to Toshié's birth, the political and social hierarchy had been affected to some extent by the amalgamation of hamlets into larger village units at the end of the nineteenth century. With its amalgamation into Yokogoshi (completed in 1901), Kosugi had lost its legal autonomy as a political entity. Yokogoshi was governed by a mayor, who was elected by a village council that included representatives from all of the hamlets in the village. The village council was in turn elected by villagers who met minimum income qualifications: in effect, the independent landowning class. The mayor of Yokogoshi was answerable to the county authorities (until the abolition of the counties in 1923), who were in turn appointed by the prefectural governor. There is no doubt that this political regime meant a loss of power for the families that had for generations governed Kosugi; but the new village system by no means spelled the end of hierarchy in Kosugi.

The leading family in Kosugi was the Nakagawa. The Nakagawa were landlords with holdings in and around Kosugi exceeding twenty hectares. They had been leaders of the Kosugi community for generations. During the Tokugawa period, the Nakagawa were hereditary *shōya* (village headmen), and after the collapse of the Tokugawa regime, they continued as mayors of Kosugi. Such was the status of the Nakagawa that in the latter years of the Tokugawa era they had been permitted to use their own family name—a privilege normally reserved for the warrior class. The Tokugawa-era office of village headman brought with it a wide range of powers, which served to consolidate the Nakagawa family in its position of privilege. For example, they were custodians of the village tax registers and thus able to manipulate the tax liabilities of village families, while the Nakagawa themselves remained exempt from tax. Although the Nakagawa, as hereditary headmen, were first in the village, they were also members of a village elite that consisted, roughly, of those families that had both long standing in the village, and above-average wealth. During the Tokugawa era, the members of this elite had been given official status as group heads *(kumigashira,* heads of the neighborhood associations to which all villagers belonged) and farmers' representatives *(hyakushōdai).* All were hereditary. Collectively, this group had been known as the *osabyakushō,* or chief peasants. The rest of the village was composed of "little" peasants *(komaebyakushō),* and landless "water drinkers" *(mizunomi).* Following the Meiji restoration, official classifications were abolished, to be replaced by a semblance of representative village government. But the reality of the village class system did not change greatly. In 1925, the head of the wealthiest branch of the Nakagawa family, Nakagawa Sakichi, still represented the hamlet on the Yokogoshi village council; and he had served as mayor of Yokogoshi from 1913 to 1919.[36] The handful of resident landlords in Kosugi (excluding several small-scale farmers who, for convenience, rented out small plots of land) lived in large houses on spacious walled compounds. They employed the villagers of Kosugi as hired labor or as domestic servants. They spoke to villagers of inferior status using familiar speech, while the villagers must respond using formal speech. And the subservient families of the hamlet continued paying various forms of ceremonial and actual tribute. Most entrenched of all was the economic relationship between landlords and tenants. The Japanese Civil Code gave landlords extensive rights to dictate the terms of tenancy agreements, while tenants in turn received few protections.

Family relationships within the village were as stratified as the status groups. Families attempted as much as possible to pass along their property in its entirety to the eldest son. Tokugawa law, indeed, forbade the splitting up of property, while the Meiji Civil Code formalized the principle of primogeniture. But in cases where the family had created new land through reclamation, or if the number of families in the village was decreasing, families sometimes gave grants of land to a younger son, who then formed his own "branch" family *(bunke)*, which remained perpetually subservient to the main family *(honke)*. The relationships between main and branch families were governed by strict protocols. Branch families would perform work for the main family, and visit to pay their respects at the New Year and the summer festival of o-Bon. Usually, branch families did not have enough land to be fully independent, so their relationship with the main family was often an economically dependent one, something like a master-servant relationship. In addition, there was another kind of patron-client relationship within the village, one that was formed voluntarily. The "client" in the relationship *(kokata)* was usually a needy peasant, who attached himself to a better-off villager to provide security. In return, the "patron" in the relationship *(oyakata)* could call on the "client" for services. This relationship often became hereditary, paralleling the main-branch family relations.[37]

Even within the family, status and power were clearly apportioned. The family head was (usually) the oldest able-bodied male. Within the family, his word was law. This was not a meaningless authority, since families were held collectively responsible for the deeds of their members. Since most families included three generations, and families with eight or ten children were not unusual, the head of the family could be a remote and forbidding figure to the junior members. Junior most of all was the eldest son's wife, who entered the household on her marriage, and had to live in submissive obedience as she worked under the often-harsh direction of her mother-in-law.

CHAPTER 2

The Making of
a Japanese Citizen

The years of Toshié's early childhood were marked by challenges to the
established village order, and conflict such as had not been seen since the
days of the Meiji restoration. The conflict came in the form of organized
action by tenants to improve their bargaining power and economic position vis-à-vis the landlords. The move to unionize tenants gained mo-
mentum at much the same time as the industrial labor movement; both
reached their peak of activity and hopefulness in the mid-1920s. Tenant
unions were organized throughout Japan, sometimes independently, but
often with the involvement of Tokyo-based organizers working on a national scale.

   The farmers most active in tenant disputes were not the poorest or
most desperate group, but rather those who farmed in relatively prosperous, commercialized areas. Thus, the poorest rural region of Japan—
the northern provinces—saw few disputes (at least until the famine of
the early 1930s) in spite of the fact that the region included some of Japan's largest landlords. However, the rural hinterland of the great cities
of western Japan saw frequent disputes. The tenant leaders of the disputes were generally small businessmen as much as they were farmers—
cash crops or cottage industries provided an important share of their income—and the disputes reflected frustration with a variety of causes:
the unfavorable economic structure of landlord-tenant relations; the
effects of economic blows from the boom and subsequent bust in rice
prices; frustration at the "stalling-out" of productivity improvement;

specific grievances such as the tightening of quality requirements; but also a distinctively working-class political consciousness.[1]

This consciousness was in large part the consequence of rising literacy. Japanese Marxist theorists and labor leaders assumed from an early stage that the village poor—tenant farmers and landless laborers—were part of an emerging proletariat, and a number of city-based labor leaders attempted to include tenant farmers in their organizing activities. Much of the spread of radical ideas was through the medium of the printed word. Moreover, many rural youths were swept up in education fever because they saw education as a passport out of the stultifying society of their villages. For example Satō Watōji, a youth from Kizaki village in Niigata prefecture, spent hours every day digging up wild arrowroot in order to earn the money for a correspondence course that would lead to a middle school equivalency. Satō later became a union leader, convinced that education was necessary in order for workers to fully understand the inequalities to which they were subjected.[2]

Conscription also helped undermine the village hierarchy. The meritocracy of military service might well elevate the son of a poor tenant farmer over the landlord's son. When the two went back to their village after completing their service, they would find it difficult to return to their old relationship of servility and benevolent paternalism. A 1921 report by the Gifu prefectural police on "conditions for the rise of tenant problems" stated: "Military education does not distinguish between landlord and tenant, and makes no distinction based on assets, status, or class, but only on academic or other results. Promotion is based on ability. Since tenants work harder and are usually stronger, they have become much prouder of themselves."[3]

But ideology was by no means the only motivation for tenant unrest. Better educated and relatively prosperous tenants were quick to grasp that through organized action they could get a better deal for themselves. The report continued:

> During the China [1895] war they were eating barley, then after the Russian war [1905] barley mixed with rice, but now they are eating rice alone. Many tenants now have *tatami* on their floors, and many now have scroll pictures in their *tokonoma* [an area for the display of art in elegant living rooms]. In particular, silk-rearing families have become very extravagant. Moreover, many people are now reading newspapers and magazines. In these circumstances, the economic awareness of tenant farmers is increasing together with their standard of living. They have reached the point where they are thinking about whether they are receiving a sufficient share of the profits from their farming activities.[4]

Economically, Kosugi and its surrounding communities fell somewhere in between the feudal, poverty-ridden regime of the north, and the commercial, relatively prosperous society of the west. Landlord-tenant relations in Niigata tended to be more "feudal" than in other parts of Japan, and, for special reasons (namely, the frequent flood disasters that afflicted the region), Niigata had many large-scale landlords. But the abundant rice crops in the Echigo plain, combined with the proximity of many rice-growing villages to the cities of Niigata, Shibata, and Nagaoka, gave the region some of the same commercial makeup as the western villages. Niigata was, in fact, a relative hotbed of tenant unrest, in both the 1920s and the 1930s. Tenants throughout the region (including many tenant farmers of Kosugi, though not Toshié's father) formed or joined tenant unions that acted with various degrees of aggression to combat the dominant position of the landlords. In milder cases, tenant unions demanded and were granted one-time reductions in rent or more favorable terms in their contracts. In more extreme cases, tenants virtually went to war against the landlords. In either case, tenants were successful in gaining reductions in the burden of rent. In the rice-growing plain surrounding Niigata, the percentage of rent to produce fell from 56 percent in 1912 to 35 percent in the mid-1920s.[5] This decline was in part the result of increasing productivity. But it was also the result of very frequent tenant disputes, which were usually resolved by compromise. In Yokogoshi, tenants in 1917 were reported as paying on average one *koku* (150 kilograms) per *tan* (about 0.1 hectare) of rice field. The same report lists the average yield per *tan* as 1.71 *koku*, bringing the percentage paid as rent to 58.5 percent. By 1935, the yield per *tan* was 2.7 *koku*, and the average rent paid was 0.9 *koku*, or 33.3 percent. It is also noteworthy that the 1935 report listed two separate numbers for "contractual rent" and "rent actually paid." The difference was some 20 percent.[6]

Yokogoshi was noteworthy in one respect in particular. It was home to one of the greatest landowning families of Japan: the Itō of Sōmi. In the 1920s, when their fortunes were close to their peak, the Itō's total landholdings approached two thousand hectares. Three thousand farmers in the district worked the Itō lands in exchange for a cash payment or a share of the crop. Their tribute enabled the Itō family to live a magnificent lifestyle, in their vast and elegant house in the family compound at Sōmi, or in their other grand homes in Niigata, Karuizawa, Zushi, and Tokyo. The head of the family, Itō Bunkichi (he was the seventh generation to hold that name) was a graduate of Pennsylvania State

University, and had lived in the United States for eight years. Bunkichi was a splendid example of the urbane, civilized landlord who did so much to influence Western opinion on the side of the landowners in the "tenant question" of the 1920s.

The Itō mansion in Sōmi is still standing. Since the end of the war, it has been reincarnated as the Northern Culture Museum, a repository of family treasures and mementos of the landlord era, and a monument to the splendors of the great landlord's way of life. The immense house (reputed to be the largest wooden residence in Japan) is built entirely of age-darkened, unpainted wood, with a roof of gray curved tiles. The house is understated by the standards of European country chateaux, but it has a muted elegance and comfort that suggest all that is best in the life of a Japanese landlord. Two immense rooms, each capable of seating easily one hundred people, dominate the high-ceilinged main floor. The rooms are floored with smooth white tatami mats, each edged in rich, embroidered silk. On the walls are delicate brush paintings mounted on silk, and imposing calligraphic scrolls. In the summer, the sliding doors are pulled aside and the entire length of the room opens onto a polished wood veranda overlooking an exquisite garden. From a hill decked with miniature maple and crooked pine trees to suggest a mountainside, a waterfall trickles down into a pond, in which carp of orange, bright yellow, red, black, and white are lazily swimming. At a narrow point, a bridge made of a single bow-shaped stone straddles the pond. Two ancient stone lanterns stand sentinel, one on either side. Other rocks are covered with a smooth coat of rich green moss. On the far side of the pond, on the low slopes of the "mountain," a small wooden hut is hidden amidst the trees—a teahouse, where the museum director and current head of the Itō family (Itō Bunkichi VIII) continues to perform the ritual of the tea ceremony.

The house was built at the turn of the twentieth century, on the site of a much smaller and humbler residence, to celebrate the breathtaking increase in prosperity of the family since the Meiji restoration. The Itō entered the modern era wealthy: their five generations of indigo dyeing, followed by money lending and land ownership, ensured that. But the favorable conditions for landlordism propagated by the aristocratically inclined new regime helped consolidate their position, and the crises of the small-farm economy pushed dozens of smallholders over the edge into tenancy during the last decades of the nineteenth century. The Itō landholdings quadrupled in the course of fifty years, and the rice pouring into the family's great warehouse every October was, by the 1920s, worth upwards of four hundred thousand yen (two hundred thousand dollars)—an enormous sum in a land where farmers scraped by on twenty or thirty yen per month.

Itō lived with his newlywed wife and a staff of fifty. His home was a place of business and constant activity. Agents *(sahainin)* from around the countryside visited in a constant flow, to report on their area of responsibility or to seek advice or instruction. Much of the day-to-day business was carried out by a staff of ten *bantō,* or managers, who sat cross-legged at low tables covered with ledgers. During the rent-collecting season—shortly after the harvest in October—there might be tens of agents staying in the house. For most of them, an overnight stay was a necessity, as their holdings were too distant to return to within the day. At lunch and again in the evening, vast cauldrons that a man could climb into cooked thirty-five pounds of rice at a time, to feed the large numbers of people in the house.

The agents were the lifeblood of the management system of great landlords like the Itō. The agents were onsite residents of the many communities to which the Itō holdings extended (the furthest were some two days' journey from Sōmi). Most of them were members of local landlord families themselves, though they might not be in line for the family headship. As the Itō's agents, they would be responsible for collecting and delivering rent and adjudicating minor disputes. For most tenants, the agents were the face of landlordism.

Once a year, however, shortly before the harvest, the Itō's professional managers *(bantō)* would visit every district in the Itō family domain, and interview tenants pleading for rent reductions. Such reductions would normally be granted if poor weather or disease had affected crops: but the managers were trained to sniff out fraud in such claims. "They would take a couple of rice stalks in one hand, and squeeze them through their fingers. If two fingers of ripe grain emerged, they would estimate a crop of five bales per *tan;* if three fingers emerged, then it would be six bales," recalls the current Itō family head, who occasionally accompanied the managers. The managers would always travel in pairs, and when negotiating with tenants, one would adopt a hard line and the other would act the tenants' friend; psychologically, the ultimate compromise would feel more acceptable to the tenants. "One time I went with a manager to a nearby rice field. I was amazed when he scooped up some mud and licked it. 'Mm, not bad' he said. He was testing how well the [human] manure was working."[7]

The Itō were known as benign landlords. A good deal of noblesse oblige accompanied their position as the principal family of the region. Their rents were usually lower than average, they supported the communities in which they owned land with money for festivals, and they were often responsive to tenant distress. In addition, their distance (socially and geographically) from the communities in which they owned land prevented much of the personal hostility that arose between petty landlords and their tenants. Indeed, the bulk of disputes in 1920s Japan were not between tenants and great landlords like the Itō, but between tenants and middle-scale or minor landlords. It was the latter who suffered the most from the changing climate of tenant-landlord relations. One landlord wrote to the governor of his prefecture:

> In our village the tenants demand rent reductions every year, and this year being no exception, the dispute ended with my conceding two thirds of their demand. This may be fine for a big landlord or a wealthy family, but I am a small landlord and I am burdened by debts. It is not a question whether or not I can pay my taxes, I do not even have enough to eat. On the other hand, are the tenants not at year end making rice flour for the whole year? Landlords like myself who have no land to cultivate themselves are not able to eat, and are suffering.[8]

Indeed, large landlords like the Itō were able to diversify their income by investing in corporate stocks, while smaller landlords suffered from declining rental income.

In the 1910s, the village of Yokogoshi contemplated with pride the harmonious relations prevailing between landlords and tenants. A document from 1917 proclaimed, "Relations between tenants and landlords in this village are exceedingly smooth. We have heard of no disputes, and in general, tenants place their trust in landlords with simple warmth, while . . . landlords believe in following the beautiful custom of loving and protecting their tenants."[9] This concept of 'beautiful customs' (*bifū*) was indeed central to the ideology propounded by landlords, who did not hesitate to use their sway over channels of communication at the village level to spread its virtues. However, by the 1920s it was clear that tenants of Yokogoshi, like those in most other communities in the Niigata area, were resistant to these messages. Yokogoshi's position as host to one of the region's great landlords indeed made involvement in the conflicts inevitable.

The disputes took place on Itō-owned land both within and outside the boundaries of Yokogoshi. Within the village, tenants in the hamlet of Kitsu organized in 1927 into a "farming promotion society," demanding rent reductions, the retraction of a recent new requirement to pack

rent rice in bales of double thickness, and the abolition of penalties for
rent rice that failed to pass the strict new standard. As the Kitsu tenants
put it: "In recent years the soil has become exhausted, and production
can not be increased except through additional fertilizer and labor. If we
wish to produce rice of quality we cannot also increase production, and
if we increase production then the quality of the rice suffers. Thus, the
quality of rice is becoming a vexing problem threatening the livelihoods
of us tenants." [10]

The most serious trouble was between the Itō and tenants in the village of Ogikawa, at some distance from Yokogoshi. As early as 1921,
tenants in this village had formed a union to press for rent reductions
and other concessions. When the Itō family refused to grant these, the
tenants threatened to return their land en masse, and turn instead to day
labor at which, they claimed, they could make a better living. The disputes in this village continued throughout the 1920s, with the Itō in
1924 persuading the tenants to form a joint landlord-tenant union for
the peaceful resolution of disputes. In 1932, with the farm depression in
full swing, the Ogikawa tenants' union called for the Itō to reduce rents
as a concession to the financial crisis in the countryside. Bunkichi refused the tenants' demands, and demanded instead the return of the
tenanted lands. The dispute flared into a major confrontation. On August 5, 1933, three hundred Ogikawa tenants marched on Sōmi carrying staves, and surrounded the Itō family mansion. Setting up a headquarters across the street from the Itō mansion, they threatened the
landlord's family and made vocal demands for rent concessions and the
reversal of the eviction orders. The police declared the site of the dispute
headquarters to be illegal, so the tenants regrouped their headquarters
on a boat on the river just behind the Itō mansion. With the tenants still
in Sōmi, the Itō on August 12 ordered their managers to seize the lands
in Ogikawa. At least one hundred of the Ogikawa tenants then threatened the Itō home brandishing scythes. The police arrested dozens of
tenant protesters over the next three days and ordered the destruction of
a shelter that the tenants had built for themselves. Still, the tenants continued their daily demonstrations in front of the Itō house. The confrontation continued for another month, with incidents of increasing violence. Finally, in mid-September, a violent clash occurred between
police and tenants, resulting in serious injuries on the tenant side, and
bringing the full force of the police down on the heads of the tenants. [11]

The Ogikawa dispute illustrates the increasing militancy and violence
of tenant disputes as the relatively calm bargaining of the 1920s gave

way to bitter confrontations in the more desperate atmosphere of the depression-hit 1930s. The conventional scholarly wisdom is that tenant disputes during the 1920s were well organized, large in scale, and prosecuted by businesslike farmers eager to achieve a more equitable distribution of the proceeds of farming, while those in the 1930s were smaller in scale and more likely to be the work of desperate farmers suffering the ravages of the depression. Niigata prefecture was somewhat unusual in that a number of major disputes spanned both the 1920s and 1930s. Yet in the Ogikawa dispute and other well-known cases such as the famous Wada dispute of 1928 to 1937, the 1930s clearly witnessed an increasing breakdown of the social order, as both tenants and landlords resorted to violence, class hatred, and the politics of confrontation.

The increasing bitterness of landlord-tenant disputes was only one aspect of an explosive crisis in the countryside that was to affect the shape and direction of Japanese politics in the crucial decade of the 1930s. The crisis was triggered by the dire economic events of the early 1930s, which began with a far-off and utterly remote event: the collapse of the New York stock market in October 1929. That collapse, and the sudden end that it brought to the prosperity of the 1920s, precipitated a devastating plunge in the price of raw silk. Even at the height of the American economic boom, silk prices had been threatened by the steady encroachment of cheaper alternatives. With the stock market collapse and the end of the long party, the luxury market support for silk vanished. Middle-class consumers who had been willing to pay for silk during the good times now settled for nylon.

Most of the two million Japanese farm families cultivating their twice-annual colonies of "house-guests" probably had little appreciation of how dependent they were on market forces operating in distant lands. Indeed for the past seventy years increases in silk cocoon production had consistently been met with increased demand and stable—or even rising—prices. But in a world linked by international business, the electric telegraph, and rapid transportation, the effects of the convulsion in New York were instant. Within days, quotations at the warehouses of the Yokohama merchants plummeted, falling from thirteen hundred yen per sixty-kilogram bale to a low of less than six hundred yen.[12] The contagion next spread to the silk factories, concentrated in the Suwa valley in the lowlands of Nagano prefecture. Many—particularly those that had extended themselves through loans or prepayments—were engulfed in a matter of weeks. And finally, the collapse intruded on the no-longer sheltered world of village Japan.

Of course, the degree of dependence on silk cocoon income varied greatly from household to household. The most vulnerable were those in the mountainous regions of central Japan, who had limited access to arable land, and for many of whom silk was a major source of income.[13] Farmers who had received an average ¥7.49 per box of cocoons in the spring of 1929 got only ¥3.93 in the spring of 1930. For the late summer crop, the price fell to as low as ¥1.50.[14] The blow was exacerbated by the very short timeframe in which all cocoon-producers brought their product to market—because they sold the cocoons with the pupa alive inside, the sale had to take place within a week of completion of the cocoon, before the moths hatched. With farmers all rearing their silkworms within the same two-week window in spring and late summer, the market was flooded by a torrent of silk cocoons. Moreover, farmers had no bargaining power against the consortia of silk mills that bought their cocoons. This meant not only a decline in income; for many, it meant an absolute loss, since they bore a variety of fixed expenses for the cultivation of the mulberry plants that fed the silkworms. Through the 1920s, the average family in Niigata prefecture had been earning from ¥150 to ¥250 per year from cocoon production, but in the 1930s the income declined steeply, bottoming out at ¥41 in 1935. Many continued rearing silkworms because they hoped prices would recover, or because they already had mature mulberry plants they were reluctant to destroy, or because they had no better prospects. In Niigata, the number of cultivating families actually continued to rise in the first three years of the recession to a peak of sixty-five thousand, and even after that it only slowly declined, dropping below fifty thousand only in the final years of World War II. The quantity of silk thread produced increased from 120 tons in 1917 to more than seven hundred tons in the peak year of 1935, before going into a steep decline. Cocoon production did not begin to decline decisively until 1940.[15]

For cocoon-producing farmers in mountainous central Japan, there was another blow to come from the silk price collapse: in the winter of 1930, their daughters came tramping back over the mountains from silk mills that had closed their doors. The income brought home by these employed daughters had been a mainstay of many farm families, and its loss contributed to the dire poverty into which many fell.

The collapse of silk was only the first of three successive blows that were to strike rural Japan in the early 1930s, combining to drag the entire farming sector into economic disarray, and the countryside into the center of the public consciousness. The second came in late 1930. This time, it was a disaster brought on by abundance. On October 2, word spread that the government was about to issue a report predicting a bumper rice harvest. Since Japan's imperial policy committed the government to guarantee the free importation of Korean rice, the report concluded that almost 20 percent of the crop would be surplus to Japan's needs. Immediately a panic set in on the market. Prices, which had been slowly falling throughout the decade, suddenly crashed from twenty-nine yen to as low as sixteen yen per 150 kilograms. For the next three days, the Tokyo, Nagoya, and Osaka markets remained closed, unable to cope with the flood of sell orders. Other crops suffered similar declines, with soybeans falling 45 percent, and potatoes falling 69 percent.

The collapse in rice prices was a consequence of well-intentioned but ultimately destructive government policies. The severe rioting that accompanied high rice prices in 1918 (at the peak of the World War I boom in Japan) had been a sobering lesson for the government: the urban working classes must be supplied with basic food commodities at a low price, or the government might face widespread civil unrest. In an era of international revolution, the prospect of such unrest was sufficient to make experienced bureaucrats shudder.

Rice was the staple of the Japanese diet and the single biggest expense in most family budgets. As a result, the Japanese government took strong steps to bring down the price of rice. The government adopted a long-term policy of liberalizing the import of Japanese-style rice from Korea and Taiwan (both colonies of Japan) to the mainland. The timing was fortuitous, since two decades of efforts to establish the cultivation of Japanese-style rice were just now coming to fruition. Rice imports grew from between fifty and one hundred thousand tons per year in the second decade of the century to a high of almost eight hundred thousand tons in the mid-1920s.[16] By the end of the 1920s, with imports from the colonies still high and per capita rice consumption stable (it was soon to start declining as the Japanese began increasing consumption of wheat, meat, and other alternative foods), there was a chronic oversupply in the Japanese market, which put a constant pressure on rice prices. Although the government had passed a bill in 1921 allowing government intervention to force rice prices down, administrators found themselves torn between their desire for low rice prices, and their concern about the effects on the Japanese farm economy. In practice, the new law was used mainly to support rice prices, but such intervention was generally weak and ineffective.

The 1930 price collapse came just as the harvest was about to begin.

Typically, rice farmers borrowed money for seed, fertilizer, and ot
penses, repaying the money after the rice harvest. Although f
prices showed some decline during the course of the year, it was nothing like the steep decline in the price of rice. The government estimated
that the average cost to grow 150 kilos of rice was between twenty-seven
and twenty-eight yen (in fertilizers and other expenses). With rice fetching as little as sixteen yen, the majority of farm families were plunged
into a deep deficit. A research organization conducted an income survey
in the years 1929 to 1934, and found that the net income (farm and nonfarm) of the average tenant farmer fell from ¥901 in 1929 to ¥601 in
1930. Household expenses did not fall nearly so quickly: the total decline was from ¥867 in 1929 to ¥654 in 1930. As a result, 76.4 percent
of the surveyed farmers experienced a net deficit in 1930.[17]

In order to finance the deficit, farmers had no choice but to borrow, often against the security of their land. A Gunma prefecture survey found
that within the prefecture, the average debt per farm family was eight
hundred yen, or ¥604 after deducting savings balances. This was equivalent to about one year's income for most farmers during the depression
era. As one delegation of farmers from Saitama prefecture put it:

> The truth is that we farmers are on the border between life and death;
> truly, the era we are living in is so hard that it makes one weep. The cab-
> bages that we expended such efforts to grow will only buy one [pack of]
> Shikishima [cigarettes] in exchange for fifty cabbages. It takes one hundred
> bunches of turnips to buy a single pack of Bat cigarettes. We get no more
> than ¥10 for 5 kilograms of silk cocoons or 3 bales of barley, and when
> we deduct from that the costs of fertilizer, then what do we have left?[18]

To compound the problems of the farmers, the depression brought an
influx of unemployed into the countryside—in some cases, apparently,
with money provided for their train fares by city governments.[19] In Niigata prefecture alone, some 180,000 returnees and migrants took up temporary residence in the prefecture in 1930. The influx of unemployed
from the towns, and the rise in unemployment in general, meant a sharp
drop in wages for casual labor, by which many farmers eked out their
livelihood between growing seasons. Wages fell by almost 40 percent between 1929 and 1933. But in a counterbalancing move, far more villagers left their villages to try their luck in the cities or overseas. In 1930,
some 530,000 people left their villages in Niigata prefecture to take
up temporary residence elsewhere, many of them in cities. A survey of
Ōomo, a mountain village in Niigata prefecture, indicated that from
1929 to 1934, at least twenty-six entire families out of a total of 813

abandoned the village altogether, to seek their fortunes elsewhere. Some of those who left disappeared in the night, to evade debts. Of those who could be traced, several had gone to Hokkaido, some to Tokyo, and some to the nearest city, Sanjō.[20]

If farmers were suffering from the economic disruptions of the 1929 crash, so was most of the rest of the country. Certainly, farmers had a smaller cushion of security than the more affluent urban classes, but farmers, with their relative self-sufficiency in the essentials of life, were perhaps better able to weather the economic storm than urban laborers, who were being thrown out of their jobs in unprecedented numbers. If the price collapses of farmers' two main cash crops had been the only disaster afflicting farmers at the turn of the 1930s, it is possible that they would not have become the focus of a growing sense of national crisis.

The final blow that brought the farming community squarely into the center of the national consciousness was a one of nature. First 1931 brought a poor harvest, which, on top of the losses of the previous year, compounded the hardships of farmers throughout Japan. Then the growing season in 1934 was among the worst ever recorded. That year brought extraordinary weather throughout Japan, with a drought in southern Japan, a major typhoon in western Japan, extremely heavy snow and cold in the Niigata area, and, above all, severe cold weather and snow in the Tōhoku region of northern Japan. Tōhoku experienced its worst harvest since 1905. In many areas, the 1934 crops of rice, barley, potatoes, and silkworms totaled only 25 percent of normal.

Above all, this new crisis affected the mountain villages of weather-vulnerable northeastern Japan—the communities living closest to the subsistence level, and hence the most vulnerable to such a blow. As always in crises, it was the most marginal families that were hit the hardest. Even in a single village, the most protected areas might achieve a moderate or even normal crop, while those in the poorest soil, or in the area most prone to flooding, might lose almost their entire crop. For these families, the economic disaster meant hunger and even the threat of starvation.

Northeastern Japan was no stranger to hardship. Famine was endemic in the marginal areas and among the poorest classes in the region. In the 1930s, however, newspapers and magazines competed furiously for fast-growing readerships. Stories of life in the mountain areas of Tōhoku made excellent copy for the mass urban readerships. Were these horrors of hunger, squalor, and the sale of daughters taking place in the same proud nation that boasted its modernization and military prowess?

It was not only the ongoing crisis and threatening famine that fixed attention on the blighted northeast. The journalists traveling to these benighted parts were equally shocked by the deep-rooted endemic poverty and the primitive cultural state of the regions they visited. When journalist Yamakawa Kin visited a small village in the mountains, he found that

> there is hardly a single house that has futons. In the best houses, there might be straw futons wrapped in cloth, but even those homes have no over-mattresses. Most homes do not even have straw futons. Instead, a pile of straw is just thrown in a corner on the bare floorboards. Or else, the bedding is just composed of assorted rubbish, like a rat's nest, in which the family burrows down to sleep. I did not see a single house that contained *shōji* (paper window panes) or *fusuma* (room dividers).[21]

A 1935 newspaper interview of a villager from Kasé in Aomori prefecture dwelt at length on the conditions of one family:

"How are you getting by these days?"

"We are renting two *tan* of rice fields, and we normally get six bales [about 360 kilograms] of rice per *tan*. Then we pay two bales [120 kilograms] per *tan* as rent, and five *tō* five *shō* [about thirty kilograms] for the fifty *tsubo* [165 square meters] our house is on. The rest we can eat. Then my husband does a little bit of day laboring, or helps with roof thatching, so up to now we have had just about enough to eat. But last year with the cold we only got three bales per *tan*, and this year with the floods we got nothing at all. So we don't have a grain of rice in the house, and if we don't get some help from the authorities there'll be nothing for it but to die of starvation."

"If you only got three bales last year how have you been eating until now?"

"The landlord reduced our rent, and so somehow or other we had rice to eat until March, and from then on we've been borrowing here and there, and eating pumpkin and potato and radish from our dry field, and my husband has been working five days a month or so for ¥0.70 per day, so we've just about been able to eat."

"What about loans?"

"Five or six years ago my husband was sick, so we borrowed money. Adding that to the money we've had to borrow to buy rice, the total comes to about one hundred yen."

"What kind of people have you borrowed from, and what interest do you pay?"

"We borrowed about seventy yen from some of the better-off people in this village. We also borrowed some money from a money-lender, and we're paying 15 percent interest per year. When my husband was sick we borrowed about fifty yen, but since we couldn't pay the interest the amount of the debt has grown, until now it's up to seventy yen. If things go on like this we'll never be able to pay even the interest let alone the principal, and our debt will just keep growing."

"What are you eating these days?"

"Look for yourself."

And she took the lid off the pot hanging from the ceiling and showed us. On examination, I saw that it was a soup of barley with chopped radish leaves. The woman continued:

"Right now I don't have a single grain of rice, so with the money my husband earned I'm buying the cheapest barley and making this kind of thing, and we're eating at least something, but when the snow comes there'll be no work for him, and even if he wants to do thatching, this year there was no straw, and even if we want to borrow more money, we can't pay back what we owe now so no one will lend it to us, so I just don't know what we'll do this winter."

And with that, she stopped talking and wiped the tears from her face. I felt myself close to despair, and hardly dared ask her more questions.[22]

In addition to the primitive living conditions of northeastern peasants, journalists focused on one issue above all others, which has come to be synonymous with the Tōhoku famine: the sale of daughters into the brothels and entertainment houses of the cities. The government estimated that throughout the country, sixteen thousand girls were sold to urban brothels in the first six months of 1931, for an average price of a little more than one hundred yen per girl (fifty dollars at then-prevailing exchange rates). As the Tokyo Asahi reported, "Kamihei County has had its crop completely wiped out, and it is said that there is no sign of young girls in this area because the normal way for poor farmers just to survive is to exchange their daughters for rice."[23] A local paper in Akita commented:

[A village called Naoné] has 100 families farming some 80 hectares. Due to the cold, their crop has been virtually destroyed. In the schoolhouse, 90 children from first to sixth grade are all gathered together, many of them carrying babies in filthy, worn kimonos on their backs. When one starts crying it spreads to the next one, and indeed the minders themselves, unable to support their burdens, often end up in tears. In this situation, it is impossible to have satisfactory classes. And once this compulsory education, which is education only in name, is over, then the fifteen- or sixteen-year-olds will be sold as apprentices or waitresses for a pathetically small up-front loan.[24]

The sale of human beings was illegal in Japan. The girls (or, rather, their parents) entered into legitimate labor contracts with the institutions of employment. But effectively, the conditions into which the girls were contracted were close to slavery. Prostitution itself was legal, and the police assisted brothel owners in rounding up escapees, while those who were unable or unwilling to earn enough to repay the up-front loans were subject to the full sanctions of the debtors' laws.[25] A report from the mid-1920s detailed a typical contract, between a prostitute, her parents, and a brothel owner. The contract advanced to the parents the sum of twenty-four hundred yen (an unusually large sum, apparently) at an interest rate of 10 percent per annum. The daughter was required to repay this loan over the course of a six-year contract. The price of each sexual encounter was set at two yen (about one dollar), of which the brothel's commission was ¥1.20 and the girl's share was ¥0.80. Of this, ¥0.50 was to go to repaying the loan, and the remaining ¥0.30 was for her own use. Out of this "pocket money," she was to pay for all of her own clothes, although the brothel provided food. Any personal possessions that she bought were considered the joint property of the brothel until her loan was repaid. Including interest, the girl would have to have sex more than sixty-four hundred times, or an average of at least four times per day for the entire six years of her contract (allowing for holidays and menstruation times).[26] The report found that other than those born in Tokyo itself, the greatest number of girls working in Tokyo brothels came from Yamagata (11.1 percent), Akita (8.3 percent), Ibaragi (7.4 percent) and Fukushima (6.7 percent)—in short, the poor northern prefectures.[27] The average up-front payment (in the form of a loan, usually to the parents) was ¥1,018 for a median term of six years. The cheapest girls could charge ¥1.50 per hour (four yen for four hours), while the highest class charged eight yen for four hours. In general, the brothel kept 60 percent of the fee and credited 40 percent to the prostitute. Of the 5,152 girls in the survey, 818 (16 percent) had received no schooling at all, and only 42 percent had completed their (supposedly compulsory) elementary education. The report listed the primary reasons for becoming a prostitute as "to help their parents out of poverty" (42 percent) or "to help their parents repay debt" (54 percent).[28]

Linked both to the crop failures and to the sale of daughters was the issue of debt. A 1932 study by Aomori prefecture indicated that 93 percent of surveyed farm families had debts, averaging ¥913 per family. One family of eight had total cash income of ¥63.40, mainly from carting with their horse. In addition, they kept a net twenty-one bales (1,260 kilograms) of rice from their 0.7 hectares of rented land, after paying an equal amount to the landlord. Their total cash expenses were thirty-one yen: fifteen yen for fertilizer, six for fish, ¥5.40 for tobacco, ¥3.60 for school supplies, and two yen for medical expenses. However, they consumed twenty-five bales of rice, so they had to buy four bales at twelve yen per bale to make up the deficiency in food. As a result, they were some seventeen yen short for the year. They made this up by borrowing, which brought their total debt up to ¥830, at an average interest rate of 24 percent. The family had fallen into debt after the failure of an expansion plan in 1925. The husband had planned to rent 1.2 hectares of land, and he had borrowed ¥250 for a horse and fertilizer. However, the harvest had failed and he had ended up owing the entire amount, plus rent for the land. The farmer's wife had subsequently become sick.[29]

Another family of six had cash income of ¥133, forty-eight yen from making straw bags in the winter months, and eighty-five yen from seasonal labor as a fisherman in Sakhalin. The family also grew 24.5 bales (1,470 kilograms) of rice, for which it paid land rent of twelve bales, leaving 12.5 bales for food. The family ate eighteen bales, thus had to purchase five bales during the year for a total expense of sixty yen. Other expenses totaled ¥109.40, comprised of ¥12.60 straw for basket making, ¥20 for fertilizer, ¥10 for horse rental, ¥36 for fish, ¥7.20 for soy sauce and miso, ¥10 for clothes, ¥3.60 for school supplies, and ¥10 for "luxuries." The total deficit for the year was therefore ¥42.60. Rather than borrow, this family chose to make ends meet by selling its eighteen-year-old daughter to a geisha house in Toyama prefecture. The family received ¥650 for a three-year contract, leaving them with ¥200 after repayment of existing debts. The family claimed that their daughter was "very happy" to become a geisha.[30]

The intensity of media coverage and popular consciousness of the crisis in the countryside brought forth reactions from both the government and from all levels of civilian and military society. The sense of crisis in the government came to a head in August 1932, with the convening of an extraordinary session of the diet to deal specifically with rural problems. This session, the so-called village relief diet, set in motion a number of major initiatives funneling government money as well as bureaucratic ingenuity into solving the problems of rural Japan. The "village relief diet" voted a special budget providing loans, grants, and prefectural contributions totaling ¥1.6 billion over a three-year period. But even this large amount was insufficient to provide more than minimal relief—particularly after unscrupulous contractors had siphoned off sizeable sums.[31] By contrast, another major initiative, the Rural Economic Rehabilitation Campaign, aimed at a more fundamental solution to the intractable problems of rural Japan. The campaign provided methodologies and a limited amount of funding for villages all over Japan to develop and implement "rehabilitation plans." The emphasis was on self-help: farmers and other village residents set goals to reduce spending, increase efficiency, and nurture profitability in order to work their own way out of debt and deficits.

At the most extreme, the crisis was used as justification for the assassination of business leaders and politicians, including Prime Minister Inukai Tsuyoshi, whose murderer stated at his trial: "It is extremely dangerous that . . . soldiers should be worried about their starving families when they are at the front exposing themselves to death. . . . I thought that to let a day go by without doing anything was to endanger the Army for one day longer." [32]

Yokogoshi was protected from the worst of the depression by its abundance of high-quality rice land and its relatively favored location. Nevertheless, the village was severely affected by the price collapses of rice and silk. This is evident in the village accounts, which show a sharp drop in income between 1928 and 1931, from ¥81,148 to ¥45,731. As a result, expenditures had to be curtailed across the board (the biggest reduction was in maintenance, which declined by twenty-one thousand yen).

Toshié knew nothing about the financial problems of her village, or of the events taking place in the world outside her home. She was protected because her parents avoided the worst of the crisis. As a marginal farmer and day laborer at the lowest end of the social scale, Kurakichi might have been gravely hit; but as luck would have it, he had regular work on a river management project that continued through the recession. The first Toshié knew that anything was amiss in her little world was the arrival in October 1931—her seventh year—of a bedraggled group who one day stood forlornly in front of the Sakaue house: a mother, a father, and two children, faces drawn with exhaustion and hunger, carrying a few poor possessions on their backs. The mother's belly was swollen beneath the stained cloth of her gown. The father, his face prematurely lined from hard labor and failure, still mustered a look of easy familiarity as he greeted Toshié's mother. He was, after all, her elder brother.

Niichirō should have been by rights the one living in the family home in Kosugi. But he had renounced his rights fifteen years earlier when he had left the family to make his way in the world. Since leaving, Niichirō had been all over Japan working at odd jobs and never settling down. In the Chiba plain east of Tokyo, he had met and married a local girl who was five years older than him; but the marriage had not worked out and the couple had divorced two years later. Then Niichirō had married Kisé, thirteen years his junior (Niichirō was thirty-six and Kisé just twenty-three), and two months later they had had their first child. In the nine years since then they had had three more children, but two had died before reaching their second year. In the meantime they had moved to the mountain city of Aizu, and then back to Niigata city, where Niichirō had been working as a casual laborer. With the sudden depression, though, he had been thrown out of work, and now they had been evicted from their lodgings. They stood on Toshié's doorstep with their firstborn and only surviving son, Riichirō, and a five-year-old daughter. Even under the travel stains and in spite of her thin face and shadowy eyes, it was possible to see that Kimié was a girl of unusual beauty.

Niichirō had nowhere else to go, and so his sister Tsugino and her husband Kurakichi took him in. The family of four crowded somehow into the already crowded house with the three adults and two resident children of Toshié's family. Taking care of the newcomers was a major challenge to the hospitality and generosity of Toshié's parents. The family's poor allotment of rice and vegetable fields yielded nothing close to the food needed for nine people—and there was next to nothing that could be sold. The fall crop of silk cocoons had already been sent out, though the money had barely covered the cost of the eggs and mulberry leaves. There was no prospect of more silk money until the following spring. Only work on the great river management project on the Agano was keeping Kurakichi and his family in food.

And then there was Kisé's pregnancy. She was already at eight months when she came to Kosugi, and at the end of November, as the evenings drew in and the heavy rains of early winter presaged snow to come, Kisé went into labor and bore a son. Mother and child rested in the little back room while the rest of the family crowded into two other rooms and did their best to sleep through the fitful wailing of the baby boy. Only Toshié and her pretty cousin Kimié were oblivious of the hardship around them. Kimié helped Toshié with her chores, and in their free time the two played on the slopes and in the temple grounds amidst the accumulating snow. They were soon fast friends.

Soon the snowdrifts banked up around the houses, plunging the village into its winter shroud of silence and immobility. Work on the river also came to a halt, and there was nothing to do at home but the regular winter chores of weaving sandals, baskets, and snowshoes out of rice straw. The money had dried up, and there was no longer enough to feed the ten people living in the house. The logic was plain for all to see: although the family could offer shelter, they could not support their guests through the winter. Niichirō had no choice but to try one more time to find work in Niigata. This must have been a formidable challenge in the midst of the worst industrial depression in Japanese history. But in January, Niichirō was able to move his family out of the Sakaue home and back to Niigata. Still, their misfortunes were not at an end. The entire family was weakened by homelessness, malnutrition, and poverty. The new baby, born in the midst of this adversity, never had a chance to flourish. Early in the New Year he sickened and died.

This visit by Toshié's reprobate uncle and his beautiful daughter who was to be her lifelong friend is one of Toshié's earliest vivid memories. At six, Toshié was now about to embark on the journey that would take her through school and service to adulthood. What sort of a person was developing in this unremarkable home in an ordinary village on the verge of an extraordinary era? There was nothing to mark Toshié as exceptional. Quite the opposite: What was notable about her was her complete acceptance of, and by, the hamlet and society that surrounded her. She was already making the friendships that would stay with her for the rest of her life. Her best friend was Tanabe Emi, a girl of the same age who was to share many of Toshié's experiences in life. Toshié seems to have acquired very early a complete sense of identity with her hamlet community. If her memories of home are mixed because of the frequent scolding by her mother, Toshié's memories of her friends are bright. She was most herself when laughing and playing in their midst. Undoubtedly her friends valued her for her loyalty and her stolidity. There was a streak of stubbornness in Toshié's personality; she loathed being ordered around, both at home and at school. Most of the time, she avoided confrontation by behaving well. But there were times when she cried from frustration at her inability to change the basic circumstances of her life: a demanding mother, and, later, the necessity to go out to work in jobs that she detested.

Toshié began her very first job at the age of five. Apart from her mother, Toshié was now the only female in the family. Since Kiyomi's departure, Tsugino had been doing the best she could with the women's chores. Now she welcomed having a helping hand, and she made her daughter help with making dinner and preparing the bath, washing pots, cleaning, and sweeping. Toshié helped reluctantly. Her mind was usually elsewhere, on the games she would like to be playing with her friends. But when Toshié heard that the family across the street was looking for a babysitter for its baby boy, she jumped at the chance to take care of him. For a

Figure 3. Children carrying rice straw, early 1940s (Courtesy, Yōtokusha publishing)

girl with few toys or dolls of her own, the thought of a real baby to take care of appealed to her. So during the year before school, and then for an hour or two a day during the school term, Toshié began looking after the baby, Ma-chan. He was to be her friend and neighbor for the next seventy years. Toshié enlisted her grandfather Rinokichi, now in his eighty-second year and in failing health, to help take care of the little boy. Sometimes Toshié slipped off to play with friends, leaving Ma-chan in the hands of her grandfather. She did not receive any money for her work. But in August at the Bon festival, and again in the New Year, Toshié received a gift of clothes, which was more than enough to delight her.

In April 1932, Toshié entered her first year at elementary school. Schooling had been compulsory in Japan since 1872, when the new Meiji government announced that "henceforth . . . there shall be no house without learning and in no house an individual without learning."[33] Kosugi's school had been established in 1872 on a plot of land just across the street from the Sakaue home. Rebuilt in 1913 and expanded in 1920, it was an imposing wooden hall of two stories, bigger even than the village temple, and in the Western style with large sash windows and desks and chairs over plank floors. In front of the school was a wide, dusty yard where the children exercised in the mornings and played later in the day. In front of the school doors was a stone statue of a young man with a satchel on his back: Ninomiya Sontoku, patron saint of Japanese education.

Toshié must have resembled countless other village schoolchildren as she began her six years of schooling: hair crudely cut high on her forehead and straight at the sides in the style known as *kappa* (river goblin); dressed in a brightly patterned cotton kimono (there was no standard uniform at the school until after Word War II: a uniform would have imposed too heavy an economic burden on village families); feet clad in wooden *geta* clogs while outside, bare feet inside; face and hands smudged with dirt; skin and hair infested with fleas and lice.

The seventy children in the first grade studied Japanese language, arithmetic, singing and gymnastics, and morals. Of the twenty-one hours a week that the first-year students spent in school, almost half were devoted to learning to read.[34] Starting with the simple syllabic *kana* scripts, the students began in their second year to learn the pictographic *kanji:* all the same, they would achieve only a bare minimum of literacy within their six years of schooling. The textbooks (which their parents had to buy) were illustrated with simple phrases and pictures: "saita, saita, sakura ga saita" (it has blossomed, it has blossomed, the cherry tree has blossomed) or "heitai san, susume, susume" (Mr. Soldier, advance, advance). On page two was a large picture of the Japanese flag with the caption "hinomaru no hata, banzai, banzai" (rising sun flag, banzai, banzai).

Indeed, for all the children, school brought the outside world of soldiers, war, national expansion, and the emperor much closer to home. The government's goal in educating the children was not only to give them a chance to better their lot in life; it was also to make them obedient members of the national community. Soldiers and the military featured prominently in textbooks from the very beginning. The first-year morals textbook featured under the heading "loyalty" the story of Private Kikuchi, who "was hit by an enemy bullet, but even in death did not take the trumpet from his mouth."[35] In later years, the content expanded to include exemplary tales of many of the great heroes of Japan's martial past (Toshié does not, however, have any recollection of the Japanese takeover of Manchuria in September 1931, or its aftermath). By the time that she reached her third year, Toshié was able to read the following homily on how to be a "good Japanese":

> In order to become a good Japanese, you must always pay reverence to the emperor and empress, revere the imperial shrines, and display a spirit of devoted loyalty and patriotism. You must show filial loyalty to your parents, reverence for your teachers, kindness to your friends, and consideration for your neighbors. Behave with honesty and generosity, as well as deep sincerity. You must not forget the debts of gratitude you owe others, and you must help others by working together with them, following rules, observing the distinction between your own possessions and those of others. You must work for the public good.[36]

In addition to support for the military as well as the traditional virtues of loyalty, respect, and unselfishness, children were taught at school to love and revere the emperor, a distant and glowing figure whom the children were encouraged to believe was like a second father to them. In spite of his diminutive physique and pronounced shyness, the young emperor cut a dashing figure in full military uniform sitting astride a pure white horse, and this is how he was normally portrayed in images released for general consumption. In the textbooks, he was a kind, benevolent figure. At his enthronement, "the emperor kindly said that he would make us happy and make our country prosperous."[37]

In the classroom of the sixth-grade students was a wooden cabinet, the doors of which were firmly closed and fastened with ornate brass fittings. Inside the cabinet was a precious document, a hand-written copy of the Imperial Rescript on Education. The rescript, which was issued in 1890 in the name of the Meiji emperor, was an exhortation to Confucian virtue:

> Know ye, Our subjects:
> Our Imperial Ancestors have founded Our Empire on a basis broad and everlasting, and have deeply and firmly implanted virtue; Our subjects ever united in loyalty and filial piety have from generation to generation illustrated the beauty thereof. This is the glory of the fundamental character of Our Empire, and herein also lies the source of Our education.[38]

On special occasions—on national holidays, and at graduation and commencement ceremonies—the head teacher would reverently remove the rescript from the cabinet, where it sat on a velvet cushion flanked by

Figure 4. Kosugi elementary school, 1937. Toshié is on the far left, second row from the back (Courtesy, Sakaue Toshié)

photographs of the emperor and his consort, and ceremoniously read it to the assembled school. For most of the year, the doors of the cabinet remained closed. But because of what it contained, the cabinet itself was an object of reverence. Anyone walking past the sixth-grade classroom had to turn in the direction of the cabinet and make a brief bow as they passed. Students must never turn their backs on the cabinet; that would be a mark of disrespect.

Toshié's education was clearly designed to turn her into a loyal, patriotic and obedient citizen. But for Toshié, school was by no means all about patriotism and emperor worship. Much of the time, these were the last things on her mind. More significant for her was the friendship of her fellow students, many of them destined to be her companions for life. Although she enjoyed her classes, much more enjoyable were the games that she played with her friends after school—many of them in the grounds of the temple, where the children were allowed to run wild.

As a six-year-old, Toshié was old enough to understand more about her place in the village. Her family was poor: it did not take long for Toshié to learn this lesson. At school, the children of wealthier parents were distinguished by their clothes. While the sons of poorer families wore sometimes-ragged cotton gowns, the sons of wealthier families wore shorts. Western clothes were the mark of affluence. Girls, too, came to school in pretty one-piece dresses, setting them apart from the others. The distinction was less obvious during the winter, when even the wealthy must wear Japanese-style clothes to accommodate the warm Japanese-style wrap-around underwear. But in winter, the wealthier children had something else that was an object of envy: rubber boots to keep out the rain and snow. Toshié was still trudging around the village in her straw snowshoes.

In Toshié's third year at school, her grandfather died. Although at eighty-four he was well advanced in years, he had been Toshié's most constant companion since her birth. It was the first of the losses that were to empty her world over the coming years. At the end of the school year, her brother, Takeharu, graduated from the higher elementary school in Yokogoshi at the age of fourteen. He was the only member of the family to go beyond the basic six years of elementary school. Takeharu was able to use his higher educational experience to land an urban job, arranged by a local broker. While his brother Rikichi continued to labor as a hired farm hand, Takeharu took the train to Tokyo, where he went to work as an apprentice in a clothes shop owned by a Yokogoshi native. At this point, three out of four of Tsugino's children were out at work. The oldest, Rikichi, was twenty-two, and now he would in the normal course of events come home, take a bride, and before long take over the headship of the family. Kiyomi was eighteen, and she had already been away from home for eight years. A quiet, sensitive girl, she saw her family only three or four times a year, when she was released for an occasional holiday. Now with Takeharu gone, Toshié was the only nonproductive member of the family.

CHAPTER 3

The Village Goes to War

In July 1937, a skirmish took place over a bridge on the outskirts of Beijing. Japanese soldiers, who were guarding the Marco Polo bridge as
nominal protectors of the foreign community in Beijing, either confronted or were confronted by a contingent of Chinese, and an exchange
of small arms fire ensued. It was the sort of incident that could be forgotten in a matter of days, if the will was there. But the local Japanese
military leaders were spoiling for a fight: flushed with the success of their
takeover of Manchuria and its outlying provinces, and worried at the
chaotic internal situation of the rest of China, they believed that extend-
ing Japanese control was the only path to stability in the area. The Japanese army sent reinforcements, and the Chinese government of Chiang
Kai-Shek, unable to bear another round of humiliation at Japanese hands,
brought in counterreinforcements. The two sides dug in, and, in spite of
initial conciliatory pronouncements by the Japanese government, within
a week Japan and China were at war. The war was to continue for eight
years, and, via the route of Pearl Harbor and Potsdam, it was to lead to
Japan's defeat and occupation by a foreign army.

Although, until the late 1930s, issues of global geopolitics might have
appeared remote from the perspective of Kosugi's sleepy main street, the
military and political events of these years were intensely relevant to the
people of Kosugi. Toshié shared in the struggle, defeat, and painful rebuilding of Japan as much as any other citizen in the nation. To what extent she also shares the responsibility for Japan's war of aggression is an

important, but very difficult question. But whether her participation was willing or not, the period from 1937 to 1952 saw an unprecedented level of mutual involvement between the state and the daily lives of ordinary villagers. This involvement was not only in the form of authoritarian dictates by the government to the villagers—although there were plenty of those. The government of Japan during this period used every technological resource at its disposal to enlist the full cooperation of villagers; and villagers appear to have responded with considerable fervor.

The year 1937 opened with an ominous development for Toshié's family. In February, Toshié's twenty-year-old sister Kiyomi quite unexpectedly showed up at home. She had taken the train from Niigata and walked to Kosugi from the station at Kameda. She carried no belongings. Poised and neat as ever, she told a surprised Tsugino that she had not been feeling well, and her employer had told her to go home and rest. When Toshié came home from school, she was delighted to find her sister helping their mother in the kitchen. Glad to see her sister, Toshié was also happy to be relieved of household chores for an evening.

At dinner, Kiyomi was quiet (as always), but she gave no indication that anything was seriously wrong with her. The family went to bed at ten o'clock as usual, and Toshié fell into a deep sleep. She was aroused in the middle of the night by a commotion. Kurakichi and Tsugino were up and dressed. "Kiyomi's disappeared," said Toshié's father. Soon afterward there was a knock at the door. A neighbor stood at the door. Kiyomi, he told them, was in his house. She had walked in, taken off her clothes, and climbed into the bath, where she was singing at the top of her voice. Indeed, stepping outside, Toshié could hear her sister's voice from the neighboring house.

The next morning, Kurakichi and Tsugino discussed what to do. It was clear that something had gone wrong with Kiyomi. They had never heard of a cold leading to such strange behavior. Kurakichi decided to take her to the doctor—a general practitioner in neighboring Kameda town. The doctor could find little wrong with her, but he prescribed a calming medicine. The medicine did no good. A few days later, Kiyomi once again tore off her clothes, this time trying to jump into the irrigation channel in front of the house. It took several weeks for the family to understand that something in Kiyomi's mind had snapped, and that the damage might be irreparable.

The sickness in Toshié's home was matched by developing international events. In July 1937, just as the family was busy turning an allotment of land into new fields, word arrived in Kosugi of the fighting that had broken out in China. Kurakichi did not take a daily newspaper, but the gist of the word spreading around the hamlet was clear. This was serious. Japan was going to go to war. The September edition of the farmers' magazine *Ie no Hikari* confirmed the seriousness of the events in China. The magazine made it clear that this was a severe crisis that would bring unprecedented demands on villagers—for manpower, for horses and equipment, and for food to supply the military and the nation.

With the coming of war against China, the involvement of ordinary village people in the military affairs of their nation became inescapable. Not only did the war effort demand mobilization of most of the village's young men; it also demanded a wide variety of other contributions from noncombatant villagers. These included higher taxes; the purchase of war bonds; the provision of personal possessions to be melted down and used in the war; increased food production to feed the army, even while manpower was taken away from the village; the provision of horses to the military; air defense and air raid preparedness; voluntary labor on airfields and other military projects; and the provision of support and encouragement for the more than two million young men under arms. In short, as military planners had foreseen ever since World War I, the entire population was mobilized in support of the war effort.

In retrospect, unsurprisingly, few Japanese remember supporting the war with any great fervor. On the contrary, most remember the coercion that they experienced, as well as the deprivation. And many—including Toshié—recall their sense of betrayal when Japan lost a war that their government had assured them they would win. However, virtually any document surviving from the period, including those from the villages, overflows with loyalty to the emperor and with burning ardor for the war effort. Of course these sources, too, can scarcely be relied on as windows into the rural soul. Almost any published document had at least some official provenance. Village newspapers, for example, were often published by the village office under supervision of the mayor. Published pronouncements were strictly controlled. While a few farmers' diaries have survived from the wartime era, these concentrate almost exclusively on local matters. Still, hints filter through as to what villagers must have been thinking. The mayor of Ishiyama, a village in Niigata prefecture, commented in the village newspaper on his reaction to the declaration of war against the United States and Britain in December 1941: "When I heard the announcement on the radio of the declaration of war on the morning of the 8th, I felt a chill throughout my body and the flow of my blood reversed its course. The recognition that a great affliction was facing our empire was carved in my heart" (however, the mayor goes on to say that he subsequently came to have faith in the country's glorious military).[1]

The government went about mobilizing its population through a mixture of emotive propaganda and economic and political controls. The institutions charged with implementing policy at the grassroots level were the neighborhood associations, the farm cooperatives, and the town or hamlet councils.

These institutions were not new. Neighborhood groups *(tonari-gumi)* had been in existence in various forms since earliest historical times. Through much of Chinese history the principle of mutual responsibility within the *pao chia,* or neighborhood group, was a key instrument of government. The Chinese system, which grouped families into blocks of one hundred *(chia),* and *chia* into blocks of ten *(pao),* reached its most complete form during the Qing dynasty (1644–1911). The system was paralleled in Tokugawa Japan (1600–1868) by the "five-family groups" *(goningumi),* which imposed controls and responsibilities on family groups in Japanese villages. By the time of Toshié's birth, the neighborhood group was less an instrument of government control than an organic part of hamlet life, a part of the mutual assistance network that was characteristic of Japanese village society. For Toshié (or her mother), the *tonari-gumi* (she was in "group number four," a group of ten households living in close proximity) were the families whom she would invite over for a bath; who would help out in the event of a family crisis— a birth, a death, or a shortage of manpower at harvest time; to whom she would make gifts of a surplus crop or a homemade delicacy, in the knowledge that they would do the same for her when the time came. It was part of the very fabric of hamlet life.

The hamlet council *(buraku-kai)* also had an ancient history. When Kosugi was still an independent village, this council was one of the governing institutions of the village—though not to be confused with the elected village council. Every household was represented on the hamlet council. Although the council had no executive powers, its assent was important in the management of the hamlet's internal affairs. With the amalgamation of Kosugi into Yokogoshi, the role of the hamlet council became even more circumscribed, but it remained in existence nevertheless.

Farm cooperatives were formed from the turn of the twentieth century, principally to assist farmers with credit for buying fertilizer or for investing in improvement projects. For the most part, the cooperatives were at the administrative village level, but hamlet farmers continued to meet in smaller groups, known as "small groups" *(kokumiai)* or "implementation groups" *(jikkō kumiai)*.

The government initiatives of the 1930s breathed new life into these institutions, at the same time as bringing them once again into the sphere of government control. By giving them new powers, and also new responsibilities, the government raised the importance of all three institutions in the everyday life of villagers. The process of co-opting these institutions did not begin suddenly with the declaration of war against China and the launch of the "spiritual mobilization campaign." Some bureaucrats had been campaigning for an increased role for them long before. In particular, the Economic Rehabilitation Movement of the mid-1930s raised the profile of the implementation groups, which were charged with developing important parts of the rehabilitation plans at the hamlet level.

The first major salvo in the government campaign to involve ordinary citizens fully in the war effort was the National Spiritual Mobilization campaign, launched by Prime Minister Konoe Fumimaro in August 1937. One of the primary goals of the campaign was to co-opt and incorporate the large number of independent and semi-independent groups and associations in Japan into full cooperation with the prosecutors of the war effort. As such, the campaign became a kind of umbrella organization for all the semipublic activities that had hitherto been carried out by independent women's groups, youth groups, farmers' groups, and patriotic societies—as well as hamlet councils and neighborhood groups. The government created a National Spiritual Mobilization Central Committee in October 1937. Seventy-four national organizations immediately joined: they included the Patriotic Women's Association, the Women's Defense Association, the Committee of Patriotic Farmers' Organizations, the National Farmers' Union, and the Patriotic Labor-Farmers' Association. Thus, virtually any organization that a rural resident was likely to belong to was now officially allied to the spiritual mobilization campaign. In 1941, the entire umbrella organization was folded into another government invention for the mobilization of daily life, the Imperial Rule Assistance Association.

A September 1940 regulation strengthened the organization of the spiritual mobilization campaign, codifying the activities of ward and hamlet councils, and making membership compulsory in both town and hamlet councils, and in ten-family neighborhood associations. By the end of the year, there were some nineteen thousand town and hamlet councils in place, and 1.2 million neighborhood associations.[2] By the time of the outbreak of war with the United States and Britain, the Orwellian aspects of "spiritual mobilization" had come to the fore. The Home Ministry began regulating the activities of regular meetings *(jōkai)* held by town and hamlet councils. Each month, the Home Ministry would issue a series of "thoroughgoing points for regular meetings" to the prefectural authorities. The prefecture would in turn pass the "thoroughgoing points" down to the village level, which would pass them on to the hamlets. The agendas typically included various observances to mark respect for the imperial family, armed forces, and war dead. For example, the June 1942 meeting of the hamlet of Kamimito in Ishiyama village, Niigata prefecture, included on its agenda:

1. Opening worship of the sun goddess Amaterasu.

2. Prayers for the military success of the hamlet's serving men and those of the country; silent prayers of thanks to the war dead.

3. Report from the agricultural affairs union.

4. Discussion of extension of hours of communal day care.

5. Discussion and critique of previous month's communal activities.

6. Concluding worship of the sun goddess Amaterasu.[3]

One of the key barriers to the mobilization of civilians in places like Kosugi was the lack of access to channels of communication. With no television and few radio sets, and only partial access to newspapers, the residents of Kosugi inevitably were somewhat isolated from the war. At the outbreak of war with China, Toshié's family's only regular reading was the farmers' magazine *Ie no Hikari*—and even this had only achieved significant circulation in the past five years. The government fully recognized the barriers to the dissemination of mobilizing propaganda, and it made every effort to increase the consumption of information by villagers. These efforts took a number of forms. Army officers, even those of high rank, spent a surprising amount of time traveling personally around the villages of Japan, explaining the war situation and the obligations it placed on villagers. At the same time, the Home and Communications Ministries joined forces with the Army and Navy Ministries to encourage the purchase and use of radio. Radio ownership in 1937 was approaching 40 percent in the cities, but had yet to reach the 10 percent mark in rural Japan. The consortium put out posters under their combined names, exhorting people to "[pull] together for the defense of the nation; [listen] together to the radio."[4] Japanese bureaucrats were influenced by the success of the Nazi Party in Germany, which placed a heavy emphasis on technology as a means of mobilizing the mind. Germany implemented a highly successful "one household, one radio" campaign from 1934, which resulted in three-quarters of German families owning radios by the end of the decade. After 1937, Japanese bureaucrats recognized the importance of radio for "the total mobilization of the people's spirit, as well as . . . the arousal of domestic opinion and of correct thinking." [5]

The government campaign to promote radio ownership included public lectures on the importance of radio in the "spiritual" mobilization of the people, advertising campaigns, and, most significantly for the villagers of Kosugi, successive reductions of the license fee and complete exemption for the families of active service men. Meanwhile the national broadcasting company Nihon Hōsōkai (NHK) helped keep the costs of radio sets down by building transmitters at close intervals around Japan. Still, Toshié's father was among the pioneers when in 1942 he put down his scarce and hard-earned money to buy his own radio set. This was no small investment. The cheapest radio cost ten yen in 1942.

In 1937 Toshié's eldest brother, Rikichi, was twenty-four. He had so far avoided military service, since his physical exam (like all Japanese males, he took this at the age of twenty) had found him unfit for front-line service. He had been designated in the second category of physical fitness *(otsu)*, which meant that (after a brief training) he would be held in reserve for support work in the event of a crisis. Now the crisis had arrived.

For the villages of Japan, the consequences of Japan's sudden plunge into warfare followed swiftly and implacably. In order to prosecute the rapidly expanding war, the military had immediate need of resources from the countryside. The Manchurian campaign of 1931 had been fought by a force of some three hundred thousand well-trained conscripts under the orders of a permanent expeditionary force based in southern Manchuria. But in 1937, the new war covered a vast sphere of operations. A push south from Beijing took direct aim at the Nationalist capital of Nanjing. At the same time, a heavy Japanese contingent landed in the international city of Shanghai, and a fierce struggle quickly erupted for the surrounding countryside. Hundreds of thousands of troop reinforcements were needed, and the military authorities in Japan responded with a call-up of eligible conscripts and reservists. A flood of "red letters" *(akagami)*—call-up letters written on pale red paper—arrived in villages around the nation. By the middle of August, five hundred thou-

sand men—mainly reservists and those who had completed one round
of military service—had been mobilized. Rikichi was one of them.

And so the time had come for Toshié's eldest brother to follow the
time-honored ritual of going off to be a soldier. First, a gathering at the
Sakaue home, attended by the notables of the hamlet, and at which sake
flowed. Then, a visit to the hamlet shrine for prayers and more sake. At
the shrine, a family photograph: Rikichi and his family in their best
clothes, holding onto banners attached to bamboo poles, on which Rikichi's name and resolution to fight for his country were emblazoned under images of the rising sun flag; the next day, the send-off. In the hamlet, the entire elementary school turned out along the main street, the
children carrying tiny flags and waving Rikichi on. At Kameda station,
the volunteer women of the Patriotic Women's Association, white sashes
draped over their aprons, served refreshments and shouted greetings to
the handful of soldiers off to join their units. Several of Rikichi's comrades from the hamlet youth association were there, some as conscripts
themselves, others to see off their fellow villagers. On the train, more
sake as Rikichi's father and brother accompanied him to the barracks at
Shibata where he was to serve. Had he been conscripted at the normal
time—starting his service on January 10 in the year following his physical exam—then his family members would have listened to an address
by the company commander, who would have told them that "the regi-
mental commander will be as a father to them, while their company officers and NCOs [noncommissioned officers] will treat them as younger
brothers."[6] But this was an emergency call-up, and Kurakichi and Takeharu returned to Kosugi without further ceremony, while Rikichi was
immediately put into a brief training course before being sent to China.

Rikichi was to serve in China for the next two years. What sort of a
person was this young man who was sent off by his flag-waving family
and youth association comrades at Kameda station in the summer of
1937? There is a photograph of Rikichi, taken in the new photographic
studio in Yokogoshi shortly before his departure. He is standing with
four fellow conscripts, ready to take up their marching order. Three of
them are in uniform, the fourth dressed in Japanese clothes, with the addition of a watch and a soft-brimmed hat. Even the uniforms, though,
look like romantic make-believe. The smooth-skinned, clear-eyed young
men look untouched by hardship or horror. One could almost believe
that they are playing a romantic game, make-believe in which hard labor, poverty, war, and death have no true place. It was the job of photographic studios to create such a romantic ambience, but the full lips,

Figure 5. Rikichi (second from left) prior to joining his regiment, 1937
(Courtesy, Sakaue Toshié)

the smooth skin, the clear lines of the young men's faces depict a youth
and innocence that could not be manufactured.

During and after World War II, there was a school of thought that the
brutality of Japan's military on overseas campaign was explained by its
peasant origins. Many of the private soldiers in the army, according to
this view, were uneducated farmers who had grown up living brutish
lives in an environment of harshness and repression. Some Japanese
scholars theorized after the war that Japanese brutality had been the result of a "transfer of oppression" in which peasants and workers, having been subjected to an oppressive political regime at home, inevitably
resorted to oppressive acts once they themselves became the direct representatives of the emperor in subject nations.

> Given the nature of Japanese society, it is no wonder that the masses, who
> in ordinary civilian or military life have no object to which they can trans-
> fer oppression, should, when they find themselves in this position, be driven
> by an explosive impulse to free themselves at a stroke from the pressure
> that has been hanging over them. Their acts of brutality are a sad testi-
> mony to the Japanese system of psychological compensation.[7]

But this description does not seem to me to fit the Rikichi who stares
so naively out of that studio photograph in 1937. Rikichi had without a

doubt known hard labor of a kind that few of us today would want to
be exposed to. He had also been subjected to a fairly strict discipline, at
school and, undoubtedly, within the family for which he worked as a
hired hand. He had perhaps also felt a hatred for the rural class system
that seemed to condemn him to a life of poverty while forcing him to pay
obeisance to the wealthier families in the village. But Rikichi had an established place in a village society that, although in some ways rigid,
nevertheless afforded a large measure of dignity and sense of belonging
to those who accepted its structure. Radicals (such as union leaders)
who fought the village hierarchy and the landlord system might well
have become alienated from this society—and, as we have seen in the
stories of tenant disputes, the society did not hesitate to resort to oppressive measures against such people. But they were a minority, and
there is no evidence that Rikichi was one of them. For the majority, the
village was a place where they belonged, and they ensured their position
there by fostering peaceful relations with their fellow villagers.

Nor was Rikichi uneducated, at least compared with peasant soldiers
from Europe, the United States, or the Soviet Union. His six years of
schooling had made him literate, and, if he was like many of his peers,
they had left him with a love of learning and a desire to further improve
himself as his circumstances allowed. Indeed, at least within the context
of Japanese society, there is every reason to believe that Rikichi's education and upbringing instilled in him an appreciation for human dignity
and an aspiration for a better and more refined life. Young rural men
and women appear to have had a high regard for the trappings of urban
middle-class life—as is evidenced by the careful hiding of rough peasant
edges in the photographs taken by the Yokogoshi studio. Even poor
members of the village community often took part in cultural activities
such as poetry circles, Japanese chess contests, and drama perfor-
mances. None of these activities and aspirations indicates a people who
have been beaten into such a state of oppression that they have lost their
essential humanity. Indeed, Japanese politicians and intellectuals frequently pointed to villagers and village culture as the essence of what
was best in Japanese civilization. Toshié's brother Takeharu appears to
have written more letters to his teacher than to his own family while
serving in the military; many of these are couched in language of high
and fervent idealism. A compilation of letters by fallen soldiers from rural Iwate prefecture includes many moving testimonials to the sensitiv-
ity and idealism of these young men. One man, Hatayama Kikuji, wrote
to his parents:

Can there be any existence without one's beloved home in one's heart? . . .
How many times has my heart pounded with gratitude for my parents'
thoughtfulness? So long as you are living, mother and father, it doesn't matter where I am, I can live with pride . . . So far I have been of no use to any-
body—I feel there is no excuse. I am waiting urgently for the day when I
will become a man and show some filial piety to you.[8]

These words are surely not those of a brute, at least in relation to those
whom the writer loved. And yet, these were the same men who perpe-
trated the notorious rape of Nanking. They were the same men who could
write home to their parents:

At ——— we captured a family of four. We played with the daughter as
we would with a harlot. As the parents kept insisting that their daughter
should be returned to them, we killed the father and mother. We then
played with the daughter again as before, until our unit marched on,
when we killed her.[9]

The participation of peasant soldiers in atrocities is undeniable. Rikichi himself never gave any indication of having participated in such
acts. But there is a photograph of Rikichi, taken after a year on campaign, that speaks volumes for the changes that had taken place in the
naive young man. In this photograph, taken against a crumbling wall
somewhere in China, Rikichi's uniform is rumpled and stained. On his
feet and those of his comrades are faded boots that show every sign of
having done hard walking. Rikichi stands in a swaggering position, one
leg placed forward as he stares coolly into the camera. In his hand is a
cigarette. His face sports a moustache, and the expression in his eyes
appears to be one of arrogance, even cruelty. Two of his comrades are
sitting, legs wide apart, holding onto long curved swords that look as
though they have seen real action. Of the three comrades, two have their
eyes closed as though they have little patience for the ritual of the photograph. The third, an older man with a hard, experienced face and a
thick moustache, looks at the camera with tough, shrewd eyes. These are
the faces of men who have killed.

If I to were point to any factor that might help account for the willing participation of peasants in wartime atrocities, it would perhaps be
the excessive naiveté of these young men who for the most part had been
persuaded of the sanctity of their nation and military, and who often
believed wholeheartedly in the infallibility of their superiors. The over-
whelming evidence from war crimes trials was that atrocities were sanc-
tioned and frequently commanded by senior Japanese officers, acting in

Figure 6. Rikichi (standing on the right) somewhere in China, c. 1938 (Courtesy, Sakaue
Toshié)

the name of the emperor.[10] That said, there will always be individuals
who, as the result of brutal treatment in childhood or just from innate
cruelty, willingly participate in acts of bestial cruelty. Such acts were encouraged during World War II not only by the orders and example of superiors, but also by the explicitly racial nature of the war, in which all
sides were taught to believe that their opponents were racially inferior
and of less value as human beings. The Chinese, in particular, were the
subject of merciless racial stereotyping by Japanese publicists. Seeing the
chaos and difficulties experienced by the crumbling Chinese imperial regime and its warring successors, influential Japanese found it easy to
portray the Chinese as bumbling, corrupt, and inferior. The very real
cultural gap between the Chinese and the Japanese (who, as Japanese
leaders had often commented, had cut themselves off from Asia in order
to pursue equality with the West) allowed Japanese leaders to portray
the Chinese masses as less than human, their lives unworthy of respect.

In addition, the cruel traditions of army life might well have had a brutalizing effect to a greater or lesser degree. Many writers have commented on the brutalities of barracks life in prewar and wartime Japan, of the hazing to which new recruits were subjected by their elder comrades-in-arms, and of the merciless discipline of military training, which in extreme cases resulted in the deaths of dozens of men from exhaustion or exposure. Itō Keiichi, in his semireminiscent account of army life, stresses not so much the "official" treatment of recruits by NCOs and officers, but the private system of hazing and punishments that operated within the barracks. He recalls that when the second year conscripts completed their service and were discharged from the military, "it is impossible to describe the relief and the sense of release. . . . The sound of the bugle rang out with a joyfully musical peal." Itō interprets the hazing as a part of the toughening process necessary to train soldiers capable of withstanding the much more severe cruelties of war.[11] But it may also have contributed to a brutalizing of impressionable young recruits.

Rikichi was called up and sent away at a busy time for the Sakaue family. For the past twenty years, the prefectural and national governments had been sponsoring a major improvement project on the Agano River. The project began in 1915 and was completed in 1934 at a total cost of thirteen million yen—a very large project for the time—and of eighteen lives. This project was important for the Sakaue family in a number of ways, not least because it provided employment for Kurakichi over a long period, including during the difficult years of the depression. The project encompassed some twenty-five miles of the river's length, and was intended to shore up pressure points where the river tended to burst through the levee and flood the surrounding area—often changing its course in the process. One of the worst of these was in Sōmi, some three miles upstream from Kosugi, where a wide bend in the river was the source of repeated flooding. The improvement project completely removed this bend, straightening the river and, in the process, placing a part of the village of Yokogoshi on the far side of the river. Just below this spot, the workers on the project constructed a large lock, allowing the authorities to control runoff into a branch stream in the event of flooding. The improvement project also strengthened the banks of the river along its length, and this was to have important consequences for the Sakaue family. As a result of the works, the river ran fast and deep, with much narrower banks than before. Consequently, a wide area on either side of the river between the newly confined banks and the levee became more or less dry land—more or less, because when the river was in spate this would be the first area to flood.

The prefecture, which owned this new land, decided to make it available to local farmers for a nominal rent. The renters were responsible for improving the land into fields, and the prefecture offered no protection in the event of flooding. Kurakichi applied for, and was granted, 0.8 hectares of the land—more than double his existing area of cultivation.

The Sakaue took possession of their new land in the early months of 1937, and throughout that year they worked on turning the boggy, reed-strewn ground into rice fields. The work was extremely difficult. Virtually everything had to be done by hand and with human muscle—only on one or two occasions could Kurakichi afford to rent a horse to help with the heaviest tasks. It was in the middle of this heavy work that Rikichi—who was helping his own family in addition to working on a neighbor's fields—was called up and sent away from Kosugi. Takeharu was in Tokyo. Toshié, at twelve, had just graduated from elementary school and was helping her parents in the heavy work. Kurakichi and Tsugino managed to complete the new fields and put them into production in 1938. The land was very sandy and difficult to irrigate, producing only three bales of rice per *tan*—about half the produce of the hamlet's best paddies. Ironically, Kurakichi gained this major increase in the family's assets just as his family embarked on an inexorable process of hollowing out.

The Sakaue household was shortly to lose yet one more member. The next to go was Toshié herself. There was nothing that she wanted more than to go on to the two-year higher elementary school program in Yo-kogoshi. A higher elementary education would ensure her a clerical job in Niigata and a life removed from dirt and physical labor. Toshié longed for such a life, but she knew that it was a hopeless cause. The combined power of custom and economic necessity assured her of the fate reserved for the daughters of tenant families; domestic service, followed, if she was lucky, by marriage to the eldest son of another tenant family. Her father immediately began looking for a domestic position for her, and in the new year she was apprenticed to the Yamazaki family in Nishiyama, a hamlet three miles to the east of Kosugi.

Mr. Yamazaki senior was a small-scale landlord. His son was a school-master. He belonged to that minority of villagers who owned a surplus of land, which in turn enabled them to receive an education, and to apply themselves to pursuits beyond the hard-muscle drudge of farming. The Yamazaki family lived in a sprawling house in an enclosed compound. In addition to the elder Yamazaki and his wife, the eldest son and his wife, and six children, there was also a maid and a pair of young men hired to do farm work. The twelve-year-old Toshié took up the humblest position in this family.

Toshié's job was to look after the baby of the family, whose name was Masaki. Although the younger Mrs. Yamazaki (whom Toshié was told to call "older sister") did not work, she had a maid to cook for her and Toshié to look after her baby. Toshié had never seen such a leisured lifestyle. The family had a radio, and Mr. Yamazaki took a daily newspaper, so that their lives were much like those of an urban family. Indeed, it was while she worked with the Yamazaki family that Toshié first tasted bread, first ate curry, and first saw a permanent wave hairstyle.

Toshié's day began at four in the morning, when she was roused from bed by Riyo, the maid, who needed help in the kitchen preparing breakfast. Together they would fire up the smoky *kamado* stove and put a cauldron of rice on to steam. Then they would chop vegetables, prepare miso soup, and arrange the breakfast in the living room for the master's family before eating their own breakfast hastily in the kitchen. For the rest of the day, Toshié was in charge of baby Masaki. Strapping him on her back in a cloth pouch, she carried him about while she ran errands for Mrs. Yamazaki or met with other child-minders in the temple grounds. The work was not especially arduous, but the hours were long, and Toshié was homesick much of the time.

She was entitled to a salary for her work in the Yamazaki home. The salary had been agreed upon in advance with the broker who had arranged the position: forty yen in the first year, sixty in the second, and one hundred yen in the third. One hundred yen (about forty dollars at the then-prevailing exchange rate) was a respectable salary; a day laborer like her father would have to work two or three months to earn that much. In addition, Toshié received all her meals from the Yamazaki household, a calculable saving for the Sakaue family (the common word for sending a child out to work was *kuchi-berashi*—mouth reduction). Toshié herself never saw any of her salary. The money was paid directly to her father, who added it to the family budget. Most of the time, Toshié had no money at all. But sometimes Mrs. Yamazaki gave her a few *sen* in pocket money, and occasionally she received tips from visitors to the Yamazaki household or from her own brothers. Rikichi wrote to her once or twice enclosing a generous gift of money. And Takeharu wrote her frequently from Tokyo, although more often than money, he would enclose magazines and picture books.

These magazines were Toshié's greatest pleasure. She waited avidly for the latest adventures of the dog-soldier Norakuro. Norakuro, by the cartoonist Tagawa Suihō, appeared in *Children's Club (Shōnen kurabu)*, a magazine that featured true stories, folk tales from around the world, fiction, poetry, and cartoons. Norakuro was the craze of young Japanese in the 1930s. Norakuro was a dog whose life reflected the times. He started out in 1931 as an army conscript, "Private (second class) Nora-kuro." Over the years, and as his popularity grew, Norakuro was re-peatedly promoted, becoming a second lieutenant in 1937, during which year Norakuro's "Wild Dog Brigade" went to war against the "Pig Army." At the time that Toshié was reading, Norakuro had devel-oped from a humorous character who was notable mainly for getting into trouble with his bulldog captain into a professional officer fighting an inept and cowardly army led by "General Pork Chop" *(tonkatsu shō-gun)*. Much of the humor was now in the antics of the enemy rather than of Norakuro himself. The "Pig Army" spoke Japanese with the same grammatical errors usually attributed to Chinese, and even young read-ers would have been in no doubt whom they were intended to represent.[12]

Toshié's parents needed all their time and energy to take care of the fields and assure a harvest. With their new plot of land ready for culti-vation, they badly needed the labor of their sons, both of whom were now far away (Rikichi in China, and Takeharu working in Tokyo). Ku-rakichi and his wife had to work diligently to bring their enlarged hold-ings in. They gave up the silkworm business; they no longer had the manpower for it. Also, their small patch of mulberry was about to be torn up and amalgamated into one of the large new rice paddies that the hamlet was building. Now that the river management project was com-plete, communities up and down the river were installing pumping sta-tions to pull water out into new irrigation channels. Over the next eight years, and after extensive negotiations between owners regarding the amalgamation of farmland, Kosugi was to convert fifty-six hectares of land into regular-shaped, large, well-irrigated paddy fields, changing the irregular patchwork outline of the village forever.[13] With the American depression the income from silk had sunk to a point where even those who were desperate for cash would hesitate to undertake silkworm cultivation.

Much of the time, Kurakichi and Tsugino left Kiyomi to her own de-vices, but she was a constant worry. One day they came home and found that she had cut her best kimono—a prized possession, bought for her before she became ill in recognition of her labor contribution to the family—into tiny shreds. Frequently, they arrived home to find that she had disappeared. Sometimes they would find her wandering about the village. Other times, she was farther afield. Several times the police brought her home, filthy and bedraggled after hitchhiking half way across the province.

The treatment options available to the family were limited in the extreme. Since the doctor in Kameda was their only resource, they took Kiyomi to see him. But there was little he could do to help. For the sake of appearance he prescribed medicine—but it is very hard to imagine what he had in his arsenal that might have helped.

Even if Toshié's family had the financial resources and knowledge to seek appropriate treatment, they would have faced grim options. Hospitalization, the most obvious choice, would certainly have helped the parents; indeed, the most common goal of hospitalization for mental illness was simply to rid the family of an impossible burden. There were a total of approximately 150 mental hospitals in Japan, providing beds for eleven thousand of the estimated ninety thousand mental patients in the country. But these were hardly benevolent institutions. Many of them had been constructed under a government-sponsored program to rid the streets of those who were considered a menace to society. A significant part of the hospital population consisted of criminals who had been declared insane. Incarceration in mental hospitals was often by order of the prefectural authorities. Families did not want to send their loved ones to such places. Moreover, the family was expected to pay the costs of hospitalization (even in the case of involuntary incarceration), amounting to an average two yen per day. This in itself was far beyond the means of Kiyomi's family.

As in other societies, a major part of the problem was the stigma of mental illness. In the early decades of the twentieth century, the complex internal causes of mental illness (and its profuse manifestations) were not well understood. The common understanding, even among psychiatrists, was that mental illness had an external cause, such as financial worry, grief, family strife, or problems in love. There was thus a strong measure of blame attached to the mentally ill. Kiyomi's sickness cast a deep shadow over the family. In a small community like Kosugi, the shame of such an affliction was impossible to run away from. Indeed, Kiyomi's actions frequently drew the attention of the whole village down on the Sakaue family. Although she had a quiet and introspective personality, her sickness drove her to take highly public and visible actions. On more than one occasion, she stripped off all her clothes and wandered round the neighborhood singing at the top of her lungs. One time she stole some petty change and ran off in the middle of the night, hitching rides on carts pulled by traveling vendors and finally getting on the train without a ticket and traveling as far as Aomori in the far north of Japan. On this occasion, Kiyomi managed to find her way back as far as the nearby town of Niitsu, where the police picked her up and contacted their counterparts in Yokogoshi. The shame of these public scandals, any one of which threatened to wreak some havoc on other villagers, was a heavy burden for Toshié's parents to bear. In spite of their poverty and their low social status, they had always been able to hold their heads up in the village as long-standing and upright members of the community. But in a Japanese village, nobody wants to cause trouble *(meiwaku)* for other members of the community.

Toshié chafed at her work and longed to be home, where she was needed to help take care of her sister. When her contract expired at the end of 1940, she prevailed on her father to let her come home and work with the family. She came home at the end of the year. Meanwhile, in another happy event, Rikichi came home from the China campaign. He had fallen sick in China and had been sent home and finally discharged. It seemed as though life could begin again.

For the next year, an uneasy stability prevailed in the family. The newspapers remained full of dark accounts of the international situation. The war in China seemed never to draw to a resolution, and the number of dead from Yokogoshi slowly mounted.

Still, Toshié and her family lived their daily round without any great sense of impending doom. Indeed, for the young people in the family, it was a time for making plans and for high hopes. Rikichi, who soon recovered his physical strength, went to work in a paper factory in Niigata. It was regular work, and he received a weekly pay packet. He began thinking about marriage. After looking around and consulting with friends, Kurakichi found his son a bride: a Kosugi girl named Masu.

Masu and Rikichi were married in July of 1941. Their wedding was a major celebration for the family, though it was simple compared to the elaborate festival that a landlord would have staged (Yokogoshi has records of one wedding in 1920 that cost three thousand yen. The more normal range in 1937 was two hundred to seven hundred yen. Rikichi's wedding was on the low end of this scale[14]). On the afternoon of the wedding day, Kurakichi and a small group of relatives wearing their best kimono with the family crest on the sleeves went to the bride's house carrying a pair of "fetching clogs" *(mukaegeta)*. At the bride's house, the party drank a cup of sake, while the bride prepared herself in another room. At about seven in the evening, the whole party, including the bride, said a prayer at the family altar and set off for the groom's house. Along the way, villagers came out to call to the bride. In earlier days, the villagers would play malicious tricks on the bride, such as throwing snowballs at her or tripping her up with a muddy rope. These activities were said to be for the purpose of dissuading her from going away. By the 1930s, though, ceremonies had become much more dignified. The groom's family lit lanterns and burned firewood in the street outside their house to welcome the bride. Once she entered the house, Masu was given "calming rice cakes" *(ochitsuki mochi)* before changing into her wedding kimono and saying a prayer in front of the Sakaue family altar. Then Masu, Rikichi, and the *nakōdo* (middleman or arranger of the marriage) went alone into the *chanoma* where they exchanged cups of sake, formalizing the marriage (the marriage became official when it was recorded in the family register kept in the village office). The wedding party followed, lasting into the early hours of the morning. Each guest brought a bottle of sake, cakes, and a pair of clogs. Trays bore elaborate meals prepared by Tsugino, Toshié, and helpful neighbors. The main door to the house was left open so that villagers could stop by and look at the bride. While Masu sat in a place of honor, Rikichi was not given a place in the circle—according to a Kosugi proverb, "cats and bride-grooms have no place to sit." He was expected to sit in the kitchen, drinking sake to console himself. After the meal was over, the bride re-tired to sleep with her mother. In more elaborate weddings, the festivi-ties went on for two or three days.[15]

Rikichi and Masu returned from their honeymoon (at Yahiko shrine, a popular tourist spot down the coast from Niigata city), and life settled down to a companionable routine for a while. Toshié enjoyed having a new sister-in-law. She and Masu shared the household chores with To-shié's mother. They helped working in the fields. They went out to work when work was available, usually on the fields of other Kosugi farmers. And they helped earn small amounts of extra income by making *ka-masu*—large straw bags used for hauling loads—together with Tsugino, who had invested in a handloom for weaving the bags. Sitting together in the work shed during the daylight hours, Toshié, her mother, and Masu made about twenty of the bags per day. The income was never very good from this work, and in 1943 the use of electric looms became wide-spread in other parts of the country, resulting in the plummeting of prices for the bags.

Meanwhile, Toshié enrolled in the "youth school" *(seinen gakkō),* which met in the elementary school building three afternoons a week and offered classes in agricultural technique, music, and politics. A law of 1939 made it compulsory to attend these schools after graduating from higher elementary school as part of a series of changes aimed at strengthening the national educational system. In April 1941, elementary schools were renamed "National Schools" and they adopted the new mission of "washing their hands of the former Western view of life, and correcting the view that education is an investment or a path to success and happiness." Rather, the schools were to "restore the former spirit of Japanese education, nurture the innate disposition of the Japanese people who are the support of the world and the leaders of the Asian league, return to the imperial way, and wholeheartedly promote the Japanese spirit."[16] The curriculum was substantially revised in accord with the new spirit of education in Japan. In the national schools, the former morals, Japanese language, Japanese history, and geography course components were all amalgamated into a new program called "national studies" *(kokuminka).* Mathematics and physics were combined into one program, as were gymnastics and kendō. Music, calligraphy, drawing, sewing, and crafts were all combined into an "arts" program. Schools stopped giving out prizes based on academic performance, preferring instead to "train and judge the children from a variety of perspectives."[17] The textbooks were also substantially revised under the direct supervision of the army, which placed several supervisors in the textbook division of the Ministry of Education. In addition to making extensive changes to the language and morals programs in order to emphasize their military and patriotic content, the new syllabus also redefined aesthetics, now removing it from the "objective sphere of craft objects" and placing it instead in the "subjective sphere of the actual practice of labor and war." Beauty was to be reinterpreted as "the beauty of death."[18] As a part of the new educational spirit, schools placed a greatly increased emphasis on military-style drill, parades, and national observances. Schoolchildren were also among the biggest contributors of "voluntary labor," for a variety of projects, including helping out with planting and harvest, weeding the village roads and banks, prefectural public works, and cleaning shrine and temple grounds. On the principle that "there are no holidays in wartime," the summer holiday was renamed "summer training period"—and devoted to "voluntary" labor.[19]

An important provision of this 1941 law was the extension of compulsory education from six to eight years. The higher elementary school, which for Toshié had been an object of hopeless longing, was now to be compulsory for all boys and girls. The higher elementary program had a strong vocational element (as did the youth schools) with courses on agriculture, industry and manufacturing, trade, and aquaculture.

Schools tried to inculcate a stern discipline in the children. Frequent military drills were held regardless of the cold, often bare chested and in bare feet. One father asked his son's schoolteacher, "My boy has chapped and bleeding feet: Would you please let him wear something on his feet when he goes outside?" The teacher answered, "Yes, that's fine. But I don't think he'll agree to wear anything. For a child, it's more of a problem being embarrassed because he's not doing what the others are than having chapped feet." [20] A biology teacher remonstrated with his students who felt sick at the sight of a dissection: "What's this? Are you crying over one measly little creature? When you are bigger you'll have to kill a hundred, maybe two hundred Chinks." However, the emphasis on "spirit" over "academic" learning was not always good from a practical educational point of view. One student teacher explained in a geography class that the Inland Sea was created by the subsidence of land that had originally connected the mainland to the island of Shikoku. The teacher was surprised when the schoolchildren corrected him. The sea, he was informed, was created when the gods used the land to build a bridge to the heavens.[21]

Meanwhile, in spite of appeals to restrain extravagance among ordinary people, the schools built increasingly lavish repositories *(hōanden)* for the imperial photographs and education rescript. The cult of the emperor loomed larger and larger in the lives of schoolchildren. The poet Yoshida Rokurō wrote of the prominence of the repository in village life:

It's morning, it's morning!
As the village people hurry past the school
They bow their heads
To the *hōanden*.[22]

The youth school that Toshié attended also included a heavy component of discipline and military-style training. Students drilled out of doors, and they also attended lectures on military spirit, the progress of the war, and the role of villages in the war effort. But the school also included a slightly bizarre mixture of elegant accomplishments—for example, music and singing—and practical courses aimed at producing more effective farmers. For Toshié, the classes were a welcome relief from the busy activities, and the worries, of her daily life.

Then, on a cold morning in December 1941 came fateful news. A special radio announcement at 7:00 A.M. on December 8 announced "Before dawn today, the 8th, the Imperial Army and Navy entered into a state of war in the Western Pacific against the American and British militaries." Later in the morning, the military authorities broadcast reports of Japanese attacks on Hong Kong, Malaya, and Singapore. At noon, after the broadcast of the national anthem, an imperial rescript beginning, "We have the support of heaven . . ." was announced on the radio, followed by a speech by Prime Minister Tōjō Hideki, who assured the Japanese people, "We have never yet lost a war," and "the key to victory is the firm belief that we must win at any cost." The villagers of Kosugi crowded into the school building to listen to the news on the radio there. It was only in the evening that the radio reported the attack on Pearl Harbor as well as the sinking of British and American ships off the coast of Malaya and the attack on the Philippines.[23]

The following day, newspapers published accounts of a glorious victory: the U.S. Pacific fleet had, it seemed, been destroyed without a fight. The Japanese had achieved total surprise and had sustained few casualties. The newspapers, and those who solemnly or excitedly discussed the events, were in no doubt that Japan was embarking on an epochal struggle, one that would change the face of the world and, once Japan's objectives were met, ensure a new peace that would endure for a thousand years. Toshié heard the news in a subdued frame of mind. Certainly, Japan had embarked on a terrifying course. But she was in no doubt as to the outcome. Japan would surely prevail.

The village held a series of rallies to commemorate the declaration of war, starting with special festivals in the hamlet shrines. December 12 was declared national "Declaration of War Commemoration Day," and all work stopped as the entire village offered prayers for victory in a special ceremony. Newspapers reported on the great rallies being held in Tokyo: the "Crush America and Britain" rally on the 10th, the "National Rally on the Propagation of the War Rescript" on the 13th, the "Strengthening Air Defense Spirit" rally on the 16th, and the "Axis Pact Certain Victory Promotion" military rally on the 22nd. With every day of the waning year, the newspapers chronicled glorious victories: Hong Kong, the Philippines, the Malay Peninsula, and shortly into the new year, Singapore itself, the "impregnable fortress" of the British. The newspapers (which most Kosugi families had to beg or borrow to get a look at) carried pictures of Asian peoples welcoming their liberators, celebrating at long last their release from imperial subjugation. Celebrations were held in Kosugi, with extra allowances of sugar provided by the rationing authorities to sweeten the occasion. Suddenly, news that had seemed remote enough not to matter if it came a day or two late became the very top concern of villagers in Kosugi. They needed daily news that was up to the minute. The lack of communication sources was frustrating.

The declaration of war against the United States and Britain was accompanied by an outpouring of prayer, resolution, and statements of support from countless village organizations throughout Japan. Some of these were part of regionally or nationally organized efforts—for example, prefectures throughout Japan held public prayers at village shrines in mid-December. Others were theoretically more spontaneous. An example is the following declaration by the women's association of Ishiyama, a village in Niigata prefecture:

> The imperial announcement has been made of a holy war against America and Britain, which have for four and a half years been obstructing the creation of a Greater East Asian Co-Prosperity Sphere. We women on the home front will, with a resolution as hard as iron or stone, strive to fulfill the imperial will, bearing any kind of hardship or deprivation in our daily lives, protecting and caring for the families of serving troops, and working for the defense of the village.[24]

Now that Japan was involved in an all-out war against the world's great powers, calls for "spiritual mobilization" were no longer sufficient. The government used the provisions of the April 1938 National Mobilization Law to impose strict controls on the economic activities of Japanese people. The government targeted agriculture as an essential defense industry; the nation must rely as never before on self-sufficiency in food production. The mobilization law extended the co-optation of local associations and councils a further step; from the turn of the 1940s, the government began enlisting them as the implementing agents in its system of economic controls. In October 1942, the hamlet councils, and the neighborhood associations under them, became officially responsible for distributing rations, giving them a major role in public life.[25] Neighborhood associations were also charged with selling government bonds to help finance the war efforts. By some accounts, these sales were near compulsory, with the bonds being allocated by the association to all the households in the group.[26]

In addition, the Home and Agriculture Ministries moved to co-opt the agricultural cooperative movement into their system of economic controls. Under the 1942 Food Management Law, the farm cooperatives took full control of the collection and distribution of rice and barley. Farm families were to be allotted a fixed amount of rice necessary for their own consumption; the rest, they would be forced to sell. In 1943, this system was strengthened still further as the home consumption allowance was abandoned, with villages instead becoming responsible for delivering an overall quota of rice to the government (a system very similar to that in effect during the Tokugawa era). In 1944, the system was toughened up yet again, with quotas being fixed in advance of the harvest.[27] In September 1943, following passage of the Agricultural Groups Law *(nōgyō dantaihō)*, the entire cooperative structure was folded into a new Imperial Agricultural Association, with each village hosting a village agricultural association—responsible for collecting the produce of farmers under the compulsory purchase policy—with subunits at the hamlet and neighborhood levels.[28]

In spite of the public professions of support by village and hamlet organizations, there was bitter resentment among farmers at the appropriations policy. A secret police survey of attitudes among farmers found a huge amount of dissatisfaction, including comments such as:

- If we contribute both money and rice, our own bodies won't sustain us.
- If they revise the quotas, I won't have enough to eat so I'll go and hang myself.
- They're telling us to hand over our rice and not eat ourselves, aren't they?
- No matter how much they tell me to hand over I can't hand out something that isn't there.
- For a peasant, there's no pleasure in having the rice that he has sweated to grow taken away compulsorily.
- If we produce extra we'll have it all taken away from us so we'd better do something with our time to earn extra money instead.
- The authorities are really taking us for a ride, making us give away the food that we broke our backs growing without even eating it, so that people who are playing around in the cities can have plenty to eat.[29]

Even the Imperial Agricultural Association commiserated with the farmers' plight, commenting in a 1943 report:

> The nation's 5.6 million farmers [last year] grew sixty-six million *koku* of rice, but delivered forty million *koku* of it (62 percent) to the nation. In previous years, farmers never sold more than half the rice they grew. When you consider the fierce demands for their labor, and the poor clothing and poor food they must accept, it appears that Japan's farmers are being asked for services that amount to suicide.[30]

Toshié's family were worse off than most. Their land was unusually unproductive, so it was hard for them to grow enough rice to meet their quota. But they knew that if they did not provide enough rice, someone else in the neighborhood group would have to provide extra to make up the quota. As a result, they were left with next to nothing for themselves.

It must have been tempting to cheat. Some families hid rice for their own consumption. Villages with a known delinquency problem held inspections, one of the village leaders going from door to door, poking a long stick into the corners of the work shed and the cupboards where futons were kept, making the family open drawers, and looking under the wooden dais of the floor. Villagers had to find clever places to hide their rice; some sneaked out to the family grave plot, or down to the river, and hid a bag or two of rice among the wild bamboo grass. Others slung it underneath the floor in the toilet or stuffed it in a hollowed-out piece of firewood. Those who were caught were labeled "anti-citizens," and were taken to the police station for lengthy questioning and, sometimes, prosecution.[31] But on the whole the villages of Japan met their obligations. For many farmers, including Toshié's father, the pressure not to let his neighbors down overrode the natural instinct to protect his family. Right up to the last year of the war, villages met the quotas for delivery of rice established by the government. Farmers met their commitments even if it meant delivering the food that they needed for their family to live. They did this in response to government promises (not always kept) that those without enough to eat would be allotted rations.

Rations were distributed monthly to representatives of the neighborhood groups. Each group would be responsible for distributing the rations among its members. Only families with insufficient produce to feed themselves qualified for food rations. Families with adequate rice supplies were glad to exchange a portion for sugar, cigarettes, or other supplies they needed. All families received rations of cloth and soap. The soap was made of fish oil, and some complained that its only effect was to feed the lice that inhabited the bodies of most villagers. Still, it was a precious commodity. If soap ran out, the only alternative was to use ash from the cooking hearth. Farm wives complained bitterly that urban families got double the soap ration of farm families, even though the former had access to laundry services, had smaller families, and did not have to get their clothes dirty, as did farmers.[32] Salt was rationed from January 1942, and families that wanted extra to make pickles had to make a written request to the regional monopoly board via the village office. By this time clothes, nails, needles, bandages, shoes, sake, cooking oil, tire tubes, miso, soy sauce, and milk were all rationed (special sake allowances were available for weddings and funerals, however).

Clothing, too, was in short supply almost from the beginning of the war. The government introduced ration coupons in February 1942 (rural residents were distinctly resentful that they were entitled to only eighty coupon points while city folk got one hundred). Even so, clothes became increasingly unavailable to buy even with the coupons. Japan's cotton industry depended on raw material imports that were no longer available, and much of the cloth that was available was requisitioned by the military. As a result, new clothing became almost impossible to find from 1941 onward. *Ie no Hikari* recommended its readers to make cloth out of wild ramie or from weeds.[33] An article entitled "Let's fight to the end with a decisive wartime lifestyle" comments, "In wartime, shortages are inevitable. We must make up for shortages though our efforts." The article offered specific advice on clothing: "If you take old clothes and sew them together in two or three layers, sewing vertically, horizontally and diagonally, you can make a fairly sturdy outfit."[34] However, some farm wives wrote in to complain that they could not even get thread to sew up rags.[35]

With the growing shortage of cloth, the government encouraged families throughout Japan to wear *monpe* trousers, a simple pantaloon made of rough cloth. These trousers were similar to the traditional farm clothes of northern Japan, but in other parts of the country they were very unfamiliar. From the turn of the 1940s, the government first encouraged, then required families to use cloth made of cotton or wool mixed with *sufu,* a factory-produced "staple fiber" made of wood pulp (the word "*sufu*" comes from the abbreviation of the Japanese rendition of *suteepuru fuaibaa* [staple fiber]). *Sufu* was notoriously weak, particularly when exposed to water, and magazine articles exhorted wives to think of ways to strengthen clothes made with this material.

The rations should have been a time for celebration, as at least some of life's essentials were assured for another few days. But their delivery often ended in bad feeling and tears. If an item arrived in insufficient quantity, the families drew lots to see who would get what. For the people who ended up without something they needed, it was a bitter blow. The situation was worst for those landless families who depended entirely on the rations, which were never adequate to feed them. Around dinnertime, as one villager reminisced, there would often be a soft knock on the door and a plaintive request: "Have you got anything that you can share a little of with us?" [36]

Villagers resorted to all sorts of measures to increase the food supply. The villagers of Gotoku in Niigata prefecture erected nets in which during the course of twenty-five days prior to the harvest they caught 11,062 sparrows. The birds had been feeding on the burgeoning rice crop, and the villagers opened up their stomachs to reclaim the rice they had eaten. The average came to twenty-eight grains per bird, for a total of 0.422 *koku* (about sixty-three kilograms). In addition, after eating 1,660 of them, the villagers sold the rest of the birds for ¥0.06 each, earning themselves about five yen per participant. The government and village lifestyle improvement advocates also called for an increase in goat husbandry as a way to improve the nutrition of children. Goats were considered particularly beneficial; unlike with eggs, there was no ready market for goats' milk, so there was little temptation to sell it. [37] Toshié's family fished with nets for mudfish and eels in the irrigation channels. There was a special bamboo basket for catching eels, long and wide at the rim, but gradually tapering to a closed end. Also, in the summer they caught crickets in the rice fields and boiled them with soy sauce. These were all known sources of protein within the village, but the food shortage made them all the more precious.

The government was concerned about the physical well-being of villagers, who bore the heavy burden of feeding the nation through their manual labor. With the outbreak of war and the disappearance of many of the village men, rural health took a sudden and sharp turn for the worse, with increasing rates of tuberculosis and child death and decreasing average heights and weights of children. [38] All of these were caused in large part by malnutrition. The health problems had a direct effect on the war effort, since villages depended for production increasingly on the weaker members—women, children, and the elderly. The quality of conscripts was also affected. Yokogoshi, for example, saw declines in the average height and weight of its young men as they came up for conscription.[39] As one bureaucrat put it,

> The spiritual mobilization movement has been calling for the simplification of lifestyles, including the reduction of consumption, but this is mainly aimed at the urban upper classes, and those in prosperous businesses, while on the other hand for villagers, the basic expenditures on food, clothing and housing should rather be increased. If the consumption of these items were to decline, there would surely be a risk of a decline in production capabilities. [On the other hand, added the commentator, unnecessary expenses such as those for births, weddings, and funerals should be eliminated.].[40]

A 1940 government report concluded:

> Rationalization of agriculture is being implemented to some degree, but the semi-feudal relations between landowners and tenants, as well as other natural limitations, prevent its thorough implementation. We are now endeavoring to develop a plan for the maintenance of agricultural production in the face of the primitive and unscientific conditions that currently require extreme physical labor on the part of farmers. The labor left in the villages is that of the elderly, of children, of the weak, and of women; and this weak labor has to struggle against all sorts of poor conditions in order to maintain the level of food production. It will be very strange if that does not result in an overall reduction in the physical condition of the farm community.[41]

The concern of government and health experts about the possible effect on the war effort led to unprecedented efforts by the government to improve health conditions. For example, the 1938 National Health Insurance Law called for the creation of insurance associations in all rural communities. Premiums were subsidized by the state. However, the insurance system remained underfunded, and it could do little in these early years to provide for the medical needs of villagers who still in many cases lived two or three hours walk from the nearest doctor. From 1938, the newly created Welfare Ministry began offering financial assistance for health care facilities and the creation of health centers, as well as for the prevention of parasitic diseases and tuberculosis in the villages. The scheme relied less on financial subsidies for treatment than on prevention activities.[42] In addition, the farm cooperatives became involved in health activities, with the goal of promoting health insurance, establishing health centers and clinics, distribution of food, promotion of communal cooking and day care centers, and the promotion of school meals.[43] In Yokogoshi, by 1942 free health care was being offered to nineteen needy families under the auspices of a string of new welfare laws, in combination with the Red Cross and other charitable organizations.[44] By 1942, all the hamlets in Yokogoshi were offering temporary day care facilities during the busy farming season, with a total of 368 children receiving day care.[45] The eyes of Japanese villagers remained among the worst medical problems. In many villages, more than 20 percent of the population suffered from trachoma, an eye disease caused by bacteria and aggravated by the constant irritation of wood smoke. However, during the 1940s the government mounted a concerted campaign against trachoma, sending doctors to the villages to perform operations on the worst afflicted.[46]

The war also saw an increase in the communalization of women's activities such as cooking and childcare. Critics had been calling for such communal efforts for years, but the labor shortage of the war finally persuaded villages to take the requisite actions. By 1941 there were more than eighteen thousand cooking groups in Japan's ten thousand villages. Many of them received financial support from the Imperial Agricultural Association or their local farm cooperatives. Food was normally provided by each of the roughly thirty households that made up a typical group, in addition to some purchases made with collected funds. A difficult issue was who to appoint as cook for the group. Different groups handled this issue differently, with some appointing the least busy women on an unpaid basis, others appointing the most skilled cooks and paying them.[47]

Concerned that tenant farmers would not be motivated to put in the extra labor needed to maintain or increase production if they had to give a large share of the proceeds to their landlords as rent, the government in 1939 introduced farm rent control regulations, and, when it introduced a system of compulsory purchase the following year, it created a two-tiered pricing system that paid tenants more for their crops than landlords. By 1945, landlords were getting the "base" price of fifty-five yen per *koku* (150 kilograms) of rice, while tenants got the "bonus" (theoretically an incentive payment) of ¥245 per *koku* (owner-farmers received "base" plus "bonus," or three hundred yen).[48] This discriminatory incentive system did more to undermine the influence of landlords and resolve the "tenancy problem" than any actions of the tenants themselves. By the end of the war, many landlords had come to recognize that their glory days were over.

Toshié's father represented the family in the hamlet council and the neighborhood association. But Toshié, too, was expected to play her part in village activities. Toshié, who was sixteen at the time of Pearl Harbor, became a part of the village's new social fabric, which was woven of communal efforts to make up for the lack of men and organizations placed in the service of the war effort. Since she was under twenty-one, Toshié was expected to join the Kosugi Youth Association *(seinendan)*. With the outbreak of war, she was also enlisted in the *keibōdan*, the air raid wardens. And as an adult woman, she participated in the *Kokubō Fujinkai*, or Women's Defense Association.

Membership in the Women's Defense Association was effectively, if not legally, compulsory. One of the principal responsibilities of this association was to see departing soldiers off to war with appropriate ceremony. Already by September 1937, Yokogoshi had three hundred men in uniform. Taking care of, and sending off, conscripts was a matter for the whole village, led by the Women's Defense Association, but also including the elementary schools and crowds of general well-wishers. Given the likelihood that the recruits would never come back (by 1944, call-up appears to have been associated with near-certain death), it is not surprising that these ceremonies tended to get more emotional and more extravagant. However, the last thing village and national authorities wanted was to encourage extravagant ceremonies at a time of severe shortages. At least one military authority issued instructions strictly limiting the extent of the ceremonies: flags were not to be distributed by anyone but families or designated organizations; gifts were not to be offered the families of departing soldiers, and were to be refused if offered; the drinking of sake at the shrine before departure, on the platform or on the train, or after the conscript's departure was to be strongly discouraged; traveling on the train together with the conscript for one or more stations was to be limited to one or two family members; and platform tickets or railway tickets were not to be purchased for the families of departing conscripts.[49] The authorities also increasingly suppressed ceremonies in the name of military secrecy. When Rikichi went to war for a second time, only his wife and Toshié were allowed to accompany him, and even they were not allowed inside the station.

Women's association members were also called on for a wide variety of local defense activities, which had previously been shouldered by the youth associations or army reservists. These included fire prevention and fire fighting, air raid marshaling, village improvements, and entertainment. In many ways, the absence of men gave village women a much higher profile and greater responsibility in village affairs—a situation they recalled with some nostalgia after the return of the men following defeat.

As the war progressed, the send-offs orchestrated by the Women's Defense Association came gradually to be outnumbered by the funerals. The association was closely involved in these, too. In many cases, family members would travel to a central depot to pick up the wooden box containing the soldier's ashes. The Women's Defense Association would meet them at the station on their return and accompany them back to the village, administering what help they could to the grieving family. The village was responsible for organizing a public funeral ceremony for the dead soldier, which all the village officials would attend, together with much of the remaining population of the village. Parents at these ceremonies were expected to show composure and even to thank the gods for allowing their son to die for emperor and country. But the Women's Defense Association maintained a discreet backup to help the family keep up this appearance.[50]

Toshié and countless other defense association women also spent much of their free time preparing "comfort bags" and supervising "thousand-stitch belts" for the soldiers on the front. The former contained a variety of items that soldiers might find useful or reminiscent of femininity and home: cigarettes, magazines, local newspaper clippings, letters from village friends, candies, soap, razorblades, photos of Japanese film stars, and so on. In the larger cities, many women would purchase these bags in ready-prepared sets available in department stores; the more elaborate ones cost as much as five yen, a week's wages for a village laborer.[51] Village women would make up their own comfort bags, often sending them to people they knew personally, making the village comfort bag a much more intimate (though perhaps less luxurious) affair.

Together with the army reserve association and youth association, Yokogoshi's Women's Defense Association organized a variety of cheerleading efforts including lectures, dramas, and patriotic ceremonies. Once a year, Toshié and her cohorts staged a drama for the benefit of the village. The event was part entertainment, part patriotic cheerleading, and part just plain fun. Since there were virtually no young men in the village, the women took the male parts. Lectures were on topics related to health, hygiene, and village welfare, as well as emigration and the progress of the war. The lecturers were often local notables such as school principals, teachers, local agricultural experts, or doctors. However, the

Figure 7. Toshié (left) acting in a wartime
village entertainment. (Courtesy, Sakaue
Toshié)

village also received visits from eminent national figures, particularly
military leaders, who were apparently ready to make the rounds of small
villages throughout the country in order to spread their message of national solidarity. In all, Toshié was expected to attend at least two or
three of these lectures a month.[52]

Toshié participated in regular ceremonies to celebrate National Foundation Day, Army Day, Navy Day, the anniversaries of various military
victories including the Russo-Japanese War, the Manchurian Incident,
and—after 1941—Pearl Harbor. In some villages, women went on mass
pilgrimages to shrines to pray for the survival of their men: for example,
the women of Kamimito hamlet in Ishiyama village traveled en masse at
hamlet expense to Yahiko shrine in April 1942. Ishiyama also held a
"Crush America and Britain Rally" *(beiei gekimetsu taikai)* in March
1943. The rally, held in the grounds of one of the village schools, included prayers to the imperial palace, singing of patriotic songs, reread-

ing of the imperial rescript declaring war, and prayers for victory and to thank the dead.[53]

The Women's Defense Association was closely involved with the economic life of the village, particularly in supporting the war effort through savings drives, patriotic contributions, and donation of metal goods for recycling into munitions. The often-enthusiastic support for these efforts is one indication of the genuine enthusiasm and support for the war effort by many rural women. In another indicator, occupying U.S. forces conducted a survey in late 1945 of five thousand men, women, and children to determine the level of their will to fight. The survey found the strongest fighting spirit and will to work among women, particularly young women, and schoolchildren.[54] Toshié surely speaks for many when she says that at the time, she sincerely believed that Japan was involved in a just struggle that, with the dedicated efforts of all citizens, it could not lose.

The activities of women like Toshié gained particular importance in wartime villages because of the absence of men. In addition to conscription into the military, the male population had also been depleted by migration of farm laborers to the factories and the mines. From the time of the China Incident, the nation began experiencing a severe shortage of industrial labor, and the government took active measures to ensure enough labor was available to munitions and military supply industries. In 1937 alone, close to 1.8 million members of farm families were said to have left their villages for the munitions factories of the cities.[55] The government recognized that an outflow on this scale—while solving the perennial problem of rural overpopulation and underemployment—would lead to a breakdown in the food production system, so by 1940 the expanding labor needs were being met by enlisting elementary and middle school graduates and by imposing severe restrictions on movement by laborers out of essential industries. In subsequent years, farmers were forbidden to leave their farms for factories. Still, the exodus from the villages continued as younger sons (those who had not been called up) and their families took advantage of the once-in-a-lifetime opportunity to find industrial jobs in the cities. Young men and women over the age of fourteen, moreover, were still required to register with the National Work Guidance Center for potential labor mobilization. As a result, the numbers of those engaged in agriculture declined drastically. Niigata prefecture, for example, witnessed a decline from 620,000 farm workers in 1932, to 450,000 by 1944.[56] Often, it was the most able-bodied who were absent. Villagers, meanwhile, continued to leave the

village for seasonal or day labor, taking advantage of rising wages in essential industries even as farm produce prices were controlled by strict
government regulation.

One immediate consequence of the many absences was that some
families were hard-pressed to plant and get their crops in during the
agricultural "busy seasons." Reservist associations, youth associations,
and the Women's Defense Association were all roped in to provide labor
help to these families. A 1938 survey of forty-four towns and villages indicates that in nine of them, the Women's Defense Association was helping the families of soldiers with farmwork.[57] As the war absorbed more
and more of the village men-folk, women were called on more frequently
to help maintain the productivity of the village as a whole. Indeed,
women and children were called on to provide a wide variety of voluntary and "patriotic" labor services. In winter, families were encouraged
to make and sell rope and donate the proceeds toward the purchase of aircraft. Youth groups sent volunteer contingents to work on airfields, irrigation projects, or other large-scale land improvement projects aimed at
increasing food production.[58] When, in 1943, the government decided
to establish a shrine to the war dead in every prefecture, the prefectures
used volunteer labor to construct the new buildings. In Niigata, the prefecture enlisted a total of 250,000 volunteers to work on its Gokokuji
shrine, which was finally completed in May 1945.[59] In June 1945, Yokogoshi created a "People's Volunteer Corps" charged with "turning all of
[Japan's] one hundred million people into soldiers and preparing for the
decisive battle." The corps was to include all men and women over elementary school age, excluding the sick, weak, and pregnant. The corps
was to be called out by the prefectural governor to assist in air defense,
increase of food production, air raid warnings, help with evacuation of
cities and factories, dispatch of essential resources, assistance with military construction projects, and fire prevention and fighting. The unit
was in fact called out in early August to help with construction work at
Niigata airfield; Yokogoshi sent groups of sixty villagers with shovels to
work for seven-hour shifts on three successive days. Those on the morning shift got up at four to catch a 5:50 A.M. train from Niitsu to Niigata.
On August 14, one day before Japan's surrender, the corps was called
out to prepare for conversion into a fighting unit in anticipation of
an invasion of the Japanese mainland. Assembling in the exercise ground
of the elementary school in nearby Kameda town, the volunteers from
four surrounding villages plus Kameda itself drilled in basic military

Figure 8. Commemorative photograph on the occasion of Takeharu's call-up to the military, taken in front of Kosugi shrine. From left: Kiyomi, cousin with child, Tsugino (Toshié's mother), Takeharu, Kurakichi (Toshié's father), Toshié, Rikichi. (Courtesy, Sakaue Toshié)

maneuvers—in spite of the fact that they had no weapons other than bamboo staves.[60]

With Japan's entry into World War II, red letters once again began flooding the villages. Before too long, Rikichi's second call-up letter came. In early 1942 Takeharu, too, presented himself for military service. He had passed his army physical the previous year, at the regular age of twenty. Toshié now had to live with the worry of two brothers fighting in the war. Rikichi and Takeharu were two atoms in a vast apparatus of military requisition of human beings and matériel. By the bombing of Pearl Harbor in December 1941, the combined army/navy manpower of the Japanese military was close to three million. The coming years were to see combat casualties approaching two million; yet, in spite of the heavy toll, the military build-up continued. By the end of the war in 1945, the combined army and navy had almost seven million men in the field. The total population of Japan was seventy million: the armed forces thus represented some 20 percent of the entire male population. By this time, the army was forcing virtually anyone who was not seriously ill into the military. Recruitment standards were lowered repeatedly, while the upper age limit for conscription was lifted, reaching forty-five by 1944. Voluntary enlistment was also accepted from elementary school graduates who had not yet reached the age of conscription. Since farmers lacked the skills for technical, engineering, or other exempt work, a disproportionate number of the frontline soldiers were from the villages.[61]

In the cold winter evenings, Toshié's family would sit with their feet as close as they dared put them to the charcoal brazier sunk into the floor under the *kotatsu* table and listen on the radio to news of Japanese successes in Malaya and in Burma, and of the great struggle taking place on the strange-sounding island of *Ga-tō*—Guadalcanal. They had only the vaguest idea where their sons were, and could only hope that the good news on the radio meant safety for them.

By the turn of 1943, the telegrams announcing deaths of sons and brothers began arriving at the Yokogoshi village office with alarming frequency. In the Sino-Japanese War (1894–95), Yokogoshi had lost four sons. Although hard, this may have seemed an acceptable price to pay for a great victory. The Russo-Japanese War of 1904–5 was much more costly: Yokogoshi lost thirteen young men, an appreciable sacrifice for the village as a whole. When war with China broke out in 1937, Yokogoshi's casualties started mounting again: twenty-three young men died between 1938 and 1941. But in comparison to any of these casualties, the Pacific War was a holocaust. A total of 252 sons of Yokogoshi lost their lives. These were horrific casualties for a village with fewer than ten thousand inhabitants. On even a conservative assumption of age distribution in the village, they amounted to more than 30 percent of all males between the ages of twenty and thirty.[62]

The war dead included both of Toshié's brothers.

Rikichi was sent to participate in the ill-fated defense of Guadalcanal. Participants on both sides remember this battle with horror. The battle began in August 1942 when an American expeditionary force landed on well-defended beaches. At first, the Americans suffered heavy casualties as they struggled to establish a beachhead. For six weeks, the American forces poured in troops and weaponry, until by the beginning of October they had seized approximately one-third of the island. Meanwhile, the Japanese military began a large-scale reinforcement of the island, which was becoming a focal battle in the war. On October 24, after several delays, the Japanese army launched a massive counterattack, in an all-or-nothing attempt to drive the Americans back. The attack failed. From this point, the Japanese strategy changed from offensive to resistance. The Japanese army in Guadalcanal was virtually cut off from supply or retreat by a powerful American blockade of the harbor. The soldiers left in Guadalcanal—some one hundred thousand of them— found themselves without food, fighting a hopeless defense. One survivor, Watanabe Shigeru, recalls the cruel torments of hunger and malnutrition that the Japanese soldiers suffered.

> If we were able to get even enough rice for a single rice ball, we did not eat it all at once. Rather, we would cook it in a full bowl of water, and only drink the water. We'd re-cook it like that around four times. Since we didn't know when the next ration would come, we'd try and make it last as long as we possibly could. . . . Of the four comrades with whom I was sharing a tent, two died of malnutrition. Their cheeks became sunken and hollow, skin and bones in which only their eyes glowed brightly. One of my comrades became sick from malaria and was unable to move. I tried to share my own ration with him, but he didn't even have the strength to eat that. I'd tell him "eat, eat—if you don't eat it will be curtains." But he would say, "I've eaten," even though he hadn't touched it. He rambled on to himself until late at night about his wife and kids at home, about his childhood, and his parents. One morning, when he didn't move I called out to him, but he had quietly died. I cried for him like a baby. I thought I would dig my comrade a grave, but I didn't have the strength, and in the end it was all I could do just to sprinkle some earth over him.[63]

Everyone who remembers Guadalcanal remembers the flies. They were an evil yellow color, and three times the size of a normal housefly. They settled on the dead and even on those who were merely weak, and began devouring their eyes, noses, and mouths. And they bred maggots by the tens of thousands. Koyama Motoyasu, who was hiding out on the Mamara River, recalls:

> I was sent to the ration depot to pick up food. It took one day to get there, and two to return carrying the food. During these three days, at least fifty or sixty of the one hundred and thirty men in my unit had died. The soldiers who I had left alive but too weak to move were bleached bones by the time I returned. The flies and maggots ate them down to the bone within two days. . . . Even the men who were still alive but couldn't move were smothered around their eyes, noses and mouths with flies and maggots. It was truly a terrible sight.

Miyano Kihiro was in a field hospital the day after the offensive, when a man lying on the ground next to him died.

> He was a man in my unit. He had been shot, and the wound had festered. Gradually he lost the strength to fight off the flies, and his condition got worse and worse. We didn't know what to do for him, so we carried him

to a spot in front of the clinic in the hope that a doctor would see him whenever one was available. The next morning, someone came and told us "someone from your unit has died, so please bury him." When we went to see, we found him lying dead in his blanket. When we took off the blanket, we saw that his entire body in one night had become covered with flies and maggots. It was awful.

Rikichi's death was not very different. After the war, a comrade who had been with Rikichi near the end came to Kosugi to return Rikichi's watch and o-*mamori* (a talisman carried for protection). The comrade told the family that Rikichi had been weakened by hunger and disease. At the end, he had lost the strength to walk. His unit had been forced to move, and they left the wounded and sick to take care of themselves. Rikichi begged them to take him with them, but he was already on the verge of death. In a cruel detail, the comrade mentioned that even as they left Rikichi, he was already being devoured by the voracious flies. Rikichi was one of thirteen men from Yokogoshi who died on Guadalcanal.

After a long and ominous silence, the Sakaue family heard of Rikichi's death in July 1943, when a tersely worded telegram arrived at the village office: "On January 8 1943, at Esperance in Guadalcanal, Solomon Islands, at 1:30 P.M., Sakaue Rikichi died of malarial fever." The family was informed that Rikichi's ashes were awaiting pickup in Sendai, a city in northern Japan. In the midst of their grief, Toshié with her father, sister, Rikichi's wife, and a representative from the village office, traveled to Sendai by bus and train to pick up the box of ashes. They returned with Masu wearing the box tied by a cloth to her chest. They returned to Yokogoshi and held a funeral ceremony, which the entire village attended. They did not tell any of the attendees that when they had opened the box of ashes to perform the ritual of passing around the charred bones, they had found the box empty.

Toshié's family removed the plaque attached to their house labeled "family of honor" (indicating serving soldiers in the family) and replaced it with one labeled "Yasukuni family" (indicating sons who had given their lives).[64] The death of their first-born was a cruel blow to the Sakaue family. Masu, his wife who had barely known him, was inconsolable at the loss of her husband and, perhaps, with the fear of what might now befall her. In an attempt to make things right with her, Kurakichi proposed that she should marry her husband's brother, Takeharu. She consented. Kurakichi wrote to his surviving son who was fighting in Indonesia, and after an interval Takeharu sent back his agreement to marry

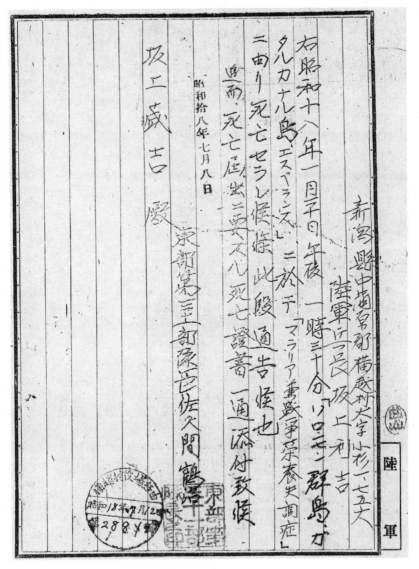

Figure 9. Telegram informing Toshié's family of the death of Rikichi, of malaria, on Guadalcanal (Courtesy, Sakaue Toshié)

Masu, if he survived the war. Toshié now invested all her hopes in the survival of her brother. Of all her siblings, he was the one she cared for the most.

But the cruel machinery of war continued to lay waste to human bodies. Takeharu was sent overseas soon after his conscription in 1942. The family received postcards from him from Malaya, Indonesia, and Burma. The cards were never informative about the conditions of his life or the dangers he suffered—such material would have been censored anyway. Since he did not come home on leave, Toshié never had a chance to hear about his experiences in person. Then, late in 1944, the postcards stopped coming. For a long time there was an ominous silence. The worst was finally confirmed by a telegram informing them of Takeharu's death on the island of Sumatra, from beriberi.

Late in 1943, word came that the government was looking for workers for the docks in Niigata. The departure of all the men for the war had left critical labor shortages, and they had to be filled by women, youths, and anyone else that the government could recruit. But it was not from motives of patriotism that Toshié went. The pay was excellent. The government was paying five yen per day for work on the docks with overtime, an almost unheard-of sum for a day of casual labor. Toshié's father urged her to go. "It will help us a lot," he said.

Every morning, a truck pulled up on the gravel road running on top of the levee and picked up a group of a half-dozen women. Toshié was one of them, as was her sister-in-law, Masu. They stood in the back of the truck while it lurched over the rough roads, picking up more people on the way. It was an hour's drive to the Yamanoshita docks at Niigata.

Toshié was assigned to a work gang unloading supplies from the ships. A mountain of coal had accumulated on the dockside as ships unloaded their cargoes. Toshié and the other laborers worked at the face of that mountain, hacking away at the congealed sides and loading the coal onto railcars, whence it would be delivered to the factories feeding Japan's war effort. Their tools were primitive: spades for loading the coal, and panniers on bamboo poles for carrying it. Toshié and Masu would stagger under the weight of a fully laden pair of panniers, but they managed to carry them to the waiting truck.

The variety of people at the docks was astonishing. Japanese, Koreans, Chinese, and Americans were working in gangs side by side. The Chinese and Americans were prisoners of war, the Koreans (presumably) forced laborers. Yet all were working together on the same urgent task: to feed the insatiable machinery of war. The foreigners were ragged and thin and worked under armed guard. It was the first time Toshié had ever seen westerners.

At lunch, the gang broke for thirty minutes. Black with coal dust, they sat on the hard concrete of the dockside and ate the rice balls that they had brought from home. A vendor sold them tea. The one comfort amid the exhaustion was to have other girls from Toshié's village around her. They gossiped about village affairs while they sat amidst the nightmarish activity of the docks.

By the evening, Toshié was utterly exhausted, but she was not able to go home until late in the evening. "It will help us a lot," her father had said, and she knew that she must work the overtime hours to earn the full wage of five yen. Anyway, she could not return home until the truck was ready to take her—and all the other members were working overtime. Her day, including overtime, lasted from eight in the morning until eight at night. She came home, had supper, and crawled into bed.

Without ever desiring such an outcome, Toshié had become a manual laborer, like her parents and her ancestors. Her brother, Takeharu, had been the only one with any prospect of escaping this destiny. Toshié was to continue to work as an unskilled manual laborer hired by the day for the next twenty years. As a child, she had been considered weak, and her parents had worried that she would not be able to do the heavy work of a farmer. But somewhere she had found the strength to work at even more arduous tasks.

In the early months of 1945, the skies around Yokogoshi took on a new and ominous aspect. Night after night, a deep drone could be heard in the distance, and on some nights it was possible to make out the silhouettes of masses of large aircraft lumbering overhead. The sky now flickered with the glow of searchlights, and the flash of antiaircraft guns toward Niigata. The war had finally reached the mainland. The U.S. planes—B-29 bombers—were using the Allies' newly acquired bases in Saipan, Guam, and Okinawa as takeoff points for the mainland. During the second three months of 1945, they launched powerful attacks on Niigata and Nagaoka, which was almost totally destroyed in one raid. The villagers of Yokogoshi lived in terror of air raids, especially after a stray American fighter strafed the village with machine gunfire (there were no casualties).

On July 19–20, shortly after midnight, a farmer called Meguro Keiichi was watching a spectacular night show, as a group of eight B-29s dodged roving searchlights and antiaircraft fire. Suddenly, he saw flames spurting from the rear of one aircraft, followed by an explosion that violently rocked the aircraft. Then he watched as it peeled away from its comrades and banked into a steep dive that seemed to be taking it right to the spot on which he was standing.

Meguro was a resident of Yakeyama, Yokogoshi's outlying hamlet on the far side of the Agano River. As he watched, the plane steepened its dive and slammed into the ground in a field no more than half a mile from Meguro's home. He immediately ran to the spot, along with a dozen other residents of the hamlet. The aircraft was on fire, and it was impossible to get close to it. The villagers watched the plane burn for a long time before they could get close enough to search for survivors. They found none. The front of the plane was deserted, but in the back cockpit they found a gruesome sight: four dead bodies, two of them burned beyond recognition, the others burned and scarred. By now the local police and other officials had arrived on the spot. Acting for the village, Sato Junichi of the village office ordered Meguro and his companions to drag the bodies from the plane, and under Kenpeitai (military police) orders Sato, Meguro, and others began digging graves for them on the spot. They dug five-feet deep and placed the bodies in the grave. Later, Meguro would erect a wooden inscription over the grave, stating "Grave of Unknown American Airmen." [65]

By early morning, the village of Yokogoshi was seething like an ant's nest. At first light, virtually everyone in the village rushed to get a first-hand look at the unprecedented event. The river was jammed with small boats ferrying villagers across the river, and large crowds were gathered at the crossing points and at the site of the crash. The excitement and the crowding resulted in a tragedy. A boat that was crossing the river crammed full of passengers suddenly overturned, tossing the villagers into the swift-moving water. Ten villagers were drowned.

Meanwhile, members of the local civilian defense forces quickly rounded up the seven surviving crewmembers, all of whom had parachuted from the falling plane. Four of them had landed in the neighboring village of Kyōgase. They hid as best they could, but the villagers flushed them out from various hiding places during the course of the night. The villagers treated them roughly—perhaps not surprisingly given the terrible loss of life that American bombing was inflicting within the prefecture and throughout the country. One crewmember later testified:

> Japanese civilians captured me and beat me with sticks and stones until I was unconscious. During the course of this beating, they made use of a long pole which had a small carved knife in one end, and as a result I received

three knife wounds. I do not have any noticeable scars, even though I never received any medical aid. Upon regaining consciousness, I learned that a Japanese soldier rescued me from these civilians. During the early hours of this morning, I heard many screams and a few weapon discharges, but I could not identify the person or persons, or the reasons for these screams.[66]

Members of the Kenpeitai arrived from Niigata soon after the plane crash, and by 4:30 A.M. four of the seven crewmen were in the Kyōgase village office, where a Kenpeitai officer questioned them. Since the officer spoke no English, the questioning did not proceed very far. At 6:30, the crewmen were transferred by truck to Niigata, where they were questioned in earnest (a local high school teacher acted as interpreter). That same night, they were sent by special train under heavy guard to Tokyo.

After the event, there were rumors that the villagers had committed atrocities against crewmembers of the plane. One woman, Imai Kimiko, went to the American authorities after the war and claimed that crewmembers had been tortured and beaten by villagers. One of the crewmembers was told at the time by a Japanese officer that one of his fellow crewmen had been beheaded. Another man, Shimada Yonerō, sent a letter from Tokyo to the American authorities, accusing eight Japanese soldiers of atrocities in the incident. Shimada claimed the soldiers "brutally murdered and robbed three airmen who landed by parachutes at this time." When the American authorities disinterred the four buried crewmembers, they found that all four had ropes around their necks. Meguro insisted that the ropes were attached in order to drag the bodies to the grave he had prepared, but the Americans went to Meguro's house to question him at least a dozen times. Nevertheless, since all the crewmembers were accounted for other than the four who died in the crash (who appeared to have died of injuries from the crash), the U.S. authorities found no evidence of atrocities. They discounted Shimada's letter and concluded that Imai was insane. The surviving airmen were perhaps lucky—execution of captured airmen was common in Japan, which considered them to be war criminals.[67]

The crash of the B-29 was a moment of vivid excitement in an otherwise bleak existence. The loss of both their sons had plunged the Sakaue family into darkest grief. The war was taking a harsh toll on their daily lives, too. Everything was in short supply, and with each year the demands on the villagers were harder to bear. Moreover, hanging over all of the villagers was the dull certainty that the glorious war, which was to secure Japan's position in Asia for generations to come, could not now be won. To the contrary, all of the reports on the radio and in the maga-

zine *Ie no Hikari* now urged the Japanese to prepare for a bitter and desperate defense of the homeland. Together with her fellow Women's Defense Association members, Toshié practiced attacking invading Americans with a sharpened bamboo stave. The future was uncertain and
terrifying.

But nothing prepared Toshié for the shock of August 15, 1945. On
that day, Toshié went as usual to the local defense headquarters for military drill. There, she heard that there would be a special broadcast
at noon. By the time she got home, more than a dozen neighbors were
gathered around her father's radio to listen to the broadcast. An unfamiliar, reedy voice began intoning a message using the formal, stilted
language of the imperial family. The emperor himself was talking to the
entire nation.

> To our good and loyal subjects:
> After pondering deeply the general trends of the world and the actual
> conditions obtaining in our Empire today, we have decided to effect a
> settlement of the present situation by resorting to an extraordinary mea-
> sure. . . . Despite the best that has been done by everyone—the gallant
> fighting of the military and naval forces, the diligence and assiduity of our
> servants of the State and the devoted service of our one hundred million
> people—the war situation has developed not necessarily to Japan's advan-
> tage, while the general trends of the world have all turned against her inter-
> est. . . . It is according to the dictates of time and fate that we have resolved
> to pave the way for a grand peace for all the generations to come by endur-
> ing the unendurable and suffering what is unsufferable.[68]

None of them understood the ornate language used by the emperor,
but most followed the import of the message. Some began to cry. Others refused to believe what they were hearing. They were too accustomed
to hearing of the coming fight to the last man, woman, and child. Toshié
has never forgotten the profound sense of shock, betrayal, and despair
as she grasped the meaning of the emperor's speech.

CHAPTER 4

Rural Life Under the Occupation

On August 14, the day before the announcement of Japan's surrender, Toshié turned twenty. For a woman, it was not a good age to be expecting the arrival of hundreds of thousands of foreign soldiers. Messages from the village office—via the neighborhood associations—warned young women to stay indoors at all times. Families were also cautioned to bury food in case the enemy soldiers requisitioned all the supplies. Who were they, these enemy men who were about to take over Japan? The only westerners Toshié had ever seen had been prisoners on the docks at Niigata. They had looked hostile, half wild. Would they be out now for revenge?

The work on the docks stopped. No money came in. Toshié stayed at home and waited. The endless village meetings also ground to a near halt. The youth school suspended its activities. The air raid team disbanded. The Women's Defense Association quietly ceased to exist. Only the neighborhood groups and the hamlet association continued to meet: the issue of rations and the requisitioning of food went on as before. For a while, the only duty was to survive.

The fields, however, would not wait for the harvest. Kurakichi had been able to purchase almost no fertilizer that year. The crops were poor. The year before he had taken his rice fields beside the river out of commission (there was little point in growing rice when it was all taken away by the government) and planted beans instead. Now the crops must be brought in. Shorthanded as the family was, Toshié could no longer stay indoors hiding. Toshié, her mother, her father, Masu, and even her un-well sister joined in the heavy work of picking and hauling the beans.

The fear did not last. Radio broadcasts reassured listeners that the occupying army was not out to commit violence. Everyone would be treated well, so long as they obeyed the rules. In mid-September, word came that a contingent of Americans had arrived in Niigata. But there were only sixteen of them, and the local newspaper reassured readers that their leader, a junior officer called Ben Dicksen, had informed the governor of Niigata that Americans investing the prefecture would not take any food from Japanese citizens, would not billet in schools or hospitals, and would observe the Japanese custom of driving on the left.[1] For the most part, the Americans were as good as their word. Over the next few months, several thousand Americans were to take up stations in Niigata prefecture. Most of them were stationed in the prefecture's major cities—Niigata, Shibata, Takada, and Muramatsu. Only two groups came to Kosugi, one to research *tsutsugamushi* disease, and the other to investigate the impact of the land reform. The Americans were polite, scholarly, and unthreatening.

Not long after the surrender, Toshié took the train into Niigata to visit her cousin, Kimié. Kimié was now working as a geisha. Her father, Niichirō, had sold her at the age of ten into a geisha house to work as a servant and train in the profession. Subsequently, she had gone to Tokyo to work in the Kagurazaka entertainment district as a trainee geisha. She had returned to Niigata fully qualified, and now belonged to an *okiya*—a geisha house—in the city. Toshié had remained close to Kimié as a child—after her first visit in the depths of the depression, Kimié had been a frequent visitor at the Sakaue house in Kosugi. Her life in Niigata seemed a fantasy to Toshié. Beautiful as ever, Kimié was in demand by Japanese businessmen, who would summon her to private rooms in elegant restaurants, where she would entertain them with songs, music, jokes, and games. She had beautiful clothes, wore her hair in an elaborate Japanese coiffure, but made up her face with a distinct touch of Western glamour. Toshié and her cousin went for a walk in the grounds of the Hakusan shrine—one of the leisure spots of Niigata. Here, in the grounds of the shrine, Toshié saw American servicemen strolling together, some with their comrades and others with Japanese girls. The occupying conquerors looked very different on this day from the bedraggled, hungry bunch she had seen working on the Niigata docks during the war. Well-fed, happy, relaxed, they seemed to be out for only one thing: to enjoy themselves, preferably in the company of pretty Japanese girls. Toshié, in her simple kimono and tied-up hair, felt distinctly drab next to her glamorous cousin. She noticed that her cousin was attracting a good deal of attention from the wandering Americans, several of whom whistled at them and called out in English to Kimié. Kimié—who spoke no English—responded gracefully, laughing and firmly moving on.

Fear of the Americans was replaced by anxiety about food. Japan in 1945 faced its greatest food crisis in more than a century. Farm families on average grew more than enough to feed themselves; the problem was how to feed the huge urban population that was dependent on their produce. And as always in such situations, the government did not leave this problem to the free market; rather, it resorted to compulsion to force farmers to share their supplies.

From March 1946, the government began falling behind in deliveries even of the meager rations allotted. By mid-1947, rations for Hokkaidō were arriving one and a half months behind schedule; Kyūshū was running two weeks late; Ōsaka was twelve days; and Tokyo was running a week late. Urban Japanese were literally desperate to find food wherever and at whatever price they could, and from the closing months of 1945, packed trains headed for the countryside with passengers hanging on to the outside windows and sitting on the roof became a common sight. The police did what they could to control this black-marketeering. Uniformed and plain-clothes detectives boarded trains to search people for contraband food. But the hunger of city people, and the fact that the police themselves must have been as dependent on the black market as anyone else, mitigated the effectiveness of these efforts. Newspaper editorials called for the police to distinguish between ordinary citizens and professional profiteers, as the following article in the Asahi newspaper suggests:

> Groups of pernicious black market operators are as usual strutting around on the trains making ordinary passengers frightened to move in the face of their violent behavior. . . . In these times when the rations are late and there is nothing to eat in the cities, it is important to note that people should not be prosecuted for bringing home a little [edible] souvenir; but that is exactly the kind of permissiveness that these pernicious operators are looking for. It is necessary to think of ways to distinguish clearly between food for travel or souvenirs, and food purchased by professional scavengers.[2]

City dwellers brought money, valuables, furniture, and clothing to offer farmers in exchange for a bag of rice or potatoes. It is not surprising, given the prevalence and necessity of the black market, that many farmers could not resist the temptation to profit at the expense of the official delivery quota. Buyers, moreover, could be very persuasive; newspapers reported that black market gangs were even "boasting that they have been buying rice from young farmers through the use of threats." [3]

Certainly, urbanites were very aware of the profits many villagers were making out of urban hardship. Most farmers above a certain level of production probably participated in the black market to some limited extent, and some certainly profited handsomely. But the reality of harsh quota requirements and strict penalties including fines and imprisonment ensured that the majority of farmers did their best to meet their legal obligations, suffering a degree of hardship as a result. For example, a 1949 survey of farm families found that 41 percent had found the previous year's quota "very hard" to meet, while another 51 percent had just "managed somehow." [4] In addition, the villages continued to suffer from a surfeit of population, as urbanites remained with their rural families after repatriation or until the situation stabilized in the cities; and farmers continued to feel the effects of shortages of skilled manpower, animal power, and fertilizer.

For the most part, the greatest profits went to larger-scale farmers; in many cases, they were able to meet their quota requirements and still had rice or other crops left over to sell—often at many times the "official" quota price. Small farmers, on the other hand, usually had little or no surplus to sell after setting aside food for quotas and for their own needs—indeed, the evidence is that many ran a deficit. One newspaper article quotes a farmer who grew a tiny plot of potatoes:

> Although the amount I grow is not enough even for my family, even for my tiny plot I am forced to cough up a quota of twenty *kan* [seventy-five kilograms]. After collecting [potatoes] from the fields, selecting the best ones to pass inspection, processing, and crating them, I deliver them to the agricultural association. Since the association is only small in scale, it must wait until it has collected a large amount before delivering in turn to the public food company. The food company distributes rations to consumers on a fixed day, but due to the rough treatment they have received, many of the potatoes are damaged by that time, and due to improper processing many are also rotten. Moreover, the farmers get paid in "new" yen three or even four months late. By contrast, large-scale farmers sell hundreds of kilos of potatoes directly from their fields to companies, factories and others who come in small trucks to pick up the produce, and pay ten times the official price, in cash. The farmer need not process, crate, or transport, and the buyer is able to deliver fresh produce to its employees—a very different situation from the public food company. [5]

A 1949 bureau of justice report on economic crimes is frankly sympathetic with the plight of the farmers:

In the confusion [accompanying the end of the war], the food that they delivered in the midst of their poverty "for the sake of victory" melted away
into private stores, but the people who commandeered it show no sign of
being punished, and the food has now turned into a high-priced black market commodity. The money that they deposited in response to calls for "patriotic savings" has been frittered away. And people who, believing the government's promise for compensatory rations, turned in 100 percent of their
quotas—though this meant turning in their own family supply—had to
suffer when the promise was broken and rations never came. Meanwhile,
those who did not meet their quotas have suffered nothing. With their sons
in the army, farmers' labor disappeared, but an ox they were forced to sell
for ¥350 now costs several tens of thousands. They were forced to make
great sacrifices for the sake of the nation, and the lesson that they learnt is
that honest people are losers.[6]

For Toshié and her family, the system was pernicious. The village allotted quotas to farm households without taking account of details such
as the differences in the productivity of one family's land versus another's. The majority of Kurakichi's rice land was on the reclaimed land on
the riverside of the levee. The productivity of this land was much lower
than that of good-quality rice land in the main part of the hamlet. Kurakichi was assessed as though his land was normally productive, and
his assessment therefore amounted to virtually the entire crop. Politically powerless as a member of the hamlet's lower class, Kurakichi nevertheless cared enough for his family's reputation that he could not re-
fuse to deliver his quota. He was well aware that anything he failed to
deliver would have to be made up by other families on top of their existing quota, for which they would of course resent the Sakaue family.

Late in 1946, word reached Kosugi that a great reform was to take
place in the Japanese countryside. General Douglas MacArthur himself
had announced his intention to "remove economic obstacles to the re-
vival and strengthening of democratic tendencies, establish respect for
the dignity of man, and destroy the economic bondage which has en-
slaved the Japanese farmer for centuries of feudal oppression."[7] After
some prodding, a partially willing Japanese government had enacted a
far-reaching land reform that was to be one of the major legacies of the
Allied Occupation.

The prevailing analysis among American policy advisors on Japan
was that latent "feudalism" had been a major contributing factor to Japanese ultranationalism and aggression. In the countryside, according
to this argument, "the low status of the Japanese farmer over the years
had created among that group a feeling of hopelessness and restlessness.

Agrarian unrest in turn provided no small part of the stimulus to Japan's imperialistic foreign policy. Tenants particularly, and farmers generally, were in a large measure sympathetic to the extremist political movements led by Japan's militarists."[8] At the same time, rural reform had long been a cherished goal of liberal Japanese intellectuals and bureaucrats who shared the widespread perception that the countryside was in a state of crisis and who felt a strong human sympathy for the oppressed condition of tenant farmers. Many of the leading bureaucrats in the Ministry of Agriculture shared this liberal background—influenced no doubt by left-wing academics who taught agricultural affairs in the elite universities. These men had spearheaded a number of previous attempts at creating basic reforms in the countryside, and it is not surprising that they saw the fluid period at the end of the war as an opportunity for another such attempt.

Arrayed against these forces were the landlords themselves and their supporters in the political parties and bureaucracy. These were by no means an insignificant group; the landlord class was the backbone of prewar political parties, which until 1925 relied on a very limited electorate for their votes, and landlords remained a powerful conservative influence within the political parties even as politicians moved into the arms of wealthy entrepreneurs for their financial support. Indeed, since much of the capital for Japan's early industrial development came from the landlord class, the links between conservative landlordism and industrial capitalism were deep. Even within the United States, conservative policy makers led by the long-serving ambassador to Japan, Joseph Grew, tended to favor the landlord and capitalist classes, who they perceived as having opposed militarism (and many of whom were among their personal friends). However, as a result of the prolonged agricultural depression in the 1920s and early 1930s, and the sustained assaults on landlord privilege by military-supported bureaucrats during the war, by 1945 the landlord class had been substantially weakened and was no longer able to mount the kind of powerful conservative campaign needed to stave off radical reform.

The law provided for compulsory purchase of land by the government, to be resold by farmers. Subject to purchase were:

1. All tenant-operated land owned by absentees
2. Tenant land in excess of one hectare per resident (four hectares in Hokkaido)

3. Owner-operated land that could not reasonably be managed by one family, defined as three hectares (twelve in Hokkaido)

4. Corporate-owned land not essential to the corporation's principal business

5. Idle agricultural land.

Dry field lands had similar criteria but different limits. Reclaimable land was also subject to the law even if not farmed. Only forest and wastelands were excepted.

The process set up by the Land Reform Law called for the creation of committees at the prefectural and village levels. Prefectural committees were composed of ten tenant farmers, six landlords, four independent farmers, and five "impartial" members—in practice, usually schoolteachers.[9] In Niigata, each of the 395 cities, towns, and villages elected a land reform committee, each composed of ten members of whom landlords were two, independent farmers three, and tenants five. Village committees had considerable leeway in setting the terms of land reform, but the prefectural committee had to ratify their decisions. The aggressiveness of the village committees was determined to a great extent by how bold the tenant representatives were willing to be, and how much the independent farmer representatives supported the tenants. On the whole, Niigata was known for its radical committees. For example the prefectural committee set a guideline price of no more than twenty-five times the rent of the land (thirty times for nonpaddy fields). Even by national standards, this was a low price, and eventually the Ministry of Agriculture, forests and fisheries, and the local U.S. commander pushed tenants to grant landlords a better deal. The new price was set at 31.7 times rent (thirty-six times for upland fields). This amounted to a price of ¥538.90 (less than two dollars) per *tan* for rice paddies, ¥256.90 for upland fields. Even this was some two hundred yen less than the standard price established at the national level. Landlords complained, "a *tan* [0.1 hectare] of land is worth no more than a straw mat."[10] There was a good deal of truth in this complaint. In 1937, one *tan* of good-quality rice paddy sold in Yokogoshi for ¥210 (about sixty dollars at the prevailing exchange rate).[11] By 1947, the consumer price index stood at roughly forty-five times its 1937 level.[12] Five hundred forty yen in 1947 was worth only twelve yen in 1937 money. By 1951, prices had increased another six times. Tenants were allowed to pay for the land over a period of fifteen years, and the price was not adjusted up for inflation. Landlords had to accept fifteen-year government notes in exchange for their land; the notes paid interest of only 3.6 percent.

The inflation, incidentally, had another important consequence affecting most farm families, regardless of their eligibility for land under the reform measures. Inflation effectively wiped out family debts. In the prewar period (and especially in the wake of the farm depression) these debts, which averaged about one year's income, were a major impediment to improvement of the material conditions of rural lives. However, the beneficial effects of the land reform were to some extent countered by a massive increase in taxes applicable to farmers. Tax increases under the 1947 Shoup Plan brought large numbers of formerly nontaxpaying farmers into the taxpaying fold. Taxes as a percentage of average total income increased from 6 percent in the mid-1930s, to 21 percent in the late 1940s, before declining again in the 1950s (by contrast, rents declined from 24 percent to less than 1 percent).[13]

The land reform was by no means implemented without opposition. The tactics employed by landlords were many and various, ranging from outright bullying and intimidation to more or less subtle legal maneuvers. Several landlords brought suits arguing the basic unconstitutionality of the Land Reform Law. After all, Article 13 of the new constitution guaranteed that "the right to own or to hold property is inviolable." For the most part, these cases were thrown out on narrow grounds. More frequently, landlords took their tenants to court for repossession of land prior to the implementation of the reform (if the land was no longer rented, it could not be forcibly sequestered), in the knowledge that the court system was likely to be more sympathetic to landlords than to land reform committees. For example, local occupation authorities reported in July 1947 that in Otawara, Tochigi prefecture, a court issued orders barring tenants from setting foot on the lands of fourteen landlords. None of the tenants was heard in the court cases, and the land reform committee had no money to appeal. The local branch of the Japan Farmers' Union was the only body to try to resist; but when the union took its case to local prosecutors, it was ignored. In other cases in Tochigi prefecture, the landlord had "simply taken over the land, by planting or putting his men on the land. In many cases, this is the end of the story. The tenant simply resigns himself to his fate."[14] In Utsunomiya, according to another complaint, more than four hundred tenants had filed complaints against landlords who were illegally reclaiming land, but "not a single case has been prosecuted or investigated by the prosecutor's office." The occupation authorities in Kyushu reported that landlords were forcing tenants off their land through a number of tactics, including attempts to infiltrate land reform committees and suppress tenant commissioners (according to the report, conservative forces "can muster sufficient pressure so that tenant commissioners, already cowed by a long tradition of subserviency, become ineffectual"); protests of land reform committee decisions (with the goal of delaying committee actions); organization into landlord associations for the purpose of concerted action and solidarity (tenants, the report points out, are seldom organized, and are not "adequately indoctrinated concerning their rights and prerogatives"); denouncing of land reform commissioners as "reds" to the military authorities; and exertion of undue influence over local newspapers that might otherwise help and inform tenants.

Nevertheless, the results of the land reform are indisputable. Tenant farmers radically changed their economic and social positions. The tenants who benefited the most from the reform were those who rented the most land: in other words, those who made their living mainly from farming as opposed to wage labor mixed with farming. Haga Yūkichi is an example of such a farmer in Kosugi. Haga was adopted into a poor tenant family in Kosugi in 1932. Virtually all of the two hectares of land that he farmed was rented. Haga grew rice, vegetables, and mulberry, and he rented patches of land from as many as seven different landlords. Some of these were local petty landlords, but Haga also rented from the Itō family—he remembers them as the best of the landlords he rented from, charging a low cash rent (he rented mulberry fields from them, so could not pay in kind) and supporting the hamlet's annual festival. With the land reform, Haga gained title to all of the land he had been renting. He was now one of the larger landowners in the hamlet. At the beginning of the 1960s, he was able to knock down the shabby peasant house in which he had been living and build a large and comfortable house on the family compound. Haga has devoted much energy over the succeeding forty years to cultivating a fine Japanese garden with unusual rocks, a pond, and painstakingly tended trees and shrubs. Today, a vigorous man of ninety-one, he still credits the land reform for all of his subsequent good fortune.

By contrast, Toshié's family benefited only slightly from the reform. Part of the reason is that farming was not their main economic activity. At the peak, they farmed 1.2 hectares of land, but by the end of the war this had declined to 0.7 hectares as Kurakichi sold off his tenancy rights to the part of the prefectural land that he no longer had the manpower

Figure 10. A farmer's house in Kosugi. The owner—a beneficiary of the land reform—is an aficionado of Japanese castles (Photo by the author)

to farm. The 0.3 hectares they rented from the prefecture was not subject to provisions of the reform, and could not be purchased. Kurakichi rented about 0.4 hectares in addition to this land, most of it from the Kofunato family. The relationship between the Sakaue and Kofunato families was a close one, but always based on the understanding that the latter were of higher standing, and that in exchange for providing favors for the Sakaue, the Sakaue in turn would recognize obligation to the Kofunato. There was also a family connection: Kurakichi's mother and the Kofunato family head's mother had been sisters. Thus before the land reform came into effect, when the Kofunato family head asked for the return of most of their land, Kurakichi felt that he had to comply. Toshié tried to dissuade Kurakichi, but he felt that the rental arrangement was only one part of a relationship that encompassed many ties and obligations—and that to fight the rental issue would be to threaten the entire relationship. Moreover, Kurakichi argued to his daughter that he now had no sons to pass the land on to. In the end Kurakichi returned three-quarters of the land. He gained 0.1 hectare through the land reform. By the end of 1947, the Sakaue family was farming only 0.4 hectare of land—0.3 hectare of rice, and a vegetable plot. This was enough for the family to retain its official and subjective identity as "farmers"; but the land reform nevertheless placed Toshié's family even more firmly into the class of those who must perform wage labor to get by.

For no one did the land reform mean more than for the house of Itō. Over generations of frugal management and opportunistic purchase, the Itō family had built their holdings from a few tens to almost two thousand hectares. As one of the largest landowning families in Japan, they were a symbol for the land reform. With some three thousand tenants tilling their land, they were seen as the embodiment of the feudal system. Now the end had come.

In fact, the collapse of the Itō family's empire was not as sudden as the idea of the land reform suggests. For the past fifteen years, tenant activism and government policy had reduced the attractiveness of land as an investment. Most wealthier landlords had diversified into commercial investments—particularly in joint stock companies. The Itō had invested substantially in banks, breweries, and railway companies, and the majority of these investments weathered the postwar chaos to become valuable sources of wealth for the family (the exception was their investment in the South Manchurian Railway, which became worthless).

The Itō family lost close to two thousand hectares as a result of the land reform. Unlike smaller landlords who could negotiate with tenants to return part or all of the land, the Itō were too big and too visible to play such games. The family instead had to develop a strategy to make the best of what they were left with. This included some thirteen hundred hectares of woodland, which was not subject to the land reform, as well as homes in Niigata, Tokyo, Zushi, and Karuizawa. By placing managers on site and entering into joint ventures, Bunkichi rapidly began turning his woodland holdings into a money-producing asset, which was to be an important component of the family's income in the years to come. The family's efforts to maximize woodland income were to cause problems, though, as some managers had the idea of growing buckwheat and sweet potatoes in the woods, opening themselves to the charge that the land was actually farmland and thus subject to forced sale under the land reform (one lawsuit on this issue dragged on into the late 1960s).

At home, meanwhile, Bunkichi increasingly saw his grand landlord's home as a liability. He had been deeply impressed by the Russian revolution and its aftermath, and he had become convinced that a similar revolution was inevitable in Japan. He had indeed come to believe that the trappings of a great landlord were potentially fatal in the postwar environment (his view was not totally unreasonable: landlords in neighboring China were routinely being shot in villages taken over by the communists). Already by the end of the war, Bunkichi's house had become a semipublic institution; its outbuildings were being used as a workshop for disabled workers, a shop to benefit Japanese refugees from Manchuria, and an official storage depot for government-controlled rice.

Bunkichi was deeply committed to leading the life of a "man of culture." He had been collecting art objects since his return from America, and he had formed close ties with local and national cultural organizations, particularly the Tokyo Arts Club, an elite club patronized by the leading museum managers and craftsmen of the capital. Thus, Bunkichi developed a plan to turn his house into a museum, a plan that he put into operation within a few months of the surrender. This plan had the further advantage that it would protect his house from onerous postwar taxes and possibly from hostile claims under the land reform legislation (Bunkichi's compound was so large that parts of it could be interpreted as "farm land").

In addition to his family heirlooms and objects of historical interest, Bunkichi took advantage of the postwar economic chaos to add large numbers of newly purchased art objects to his museum's collection. In the first decade after the war, Bunkichi's friends in Tokyo also arranged for his museum to host special exhibits of art objects from the national museum. Bunkichi's Northern Culture Museum opened in January 1946. Bunkichi and his family continued to live in a wing of the house, and Bunkichi became director of the museum, a position that his son (Bunkichi VIII, known by his foreign friends as Bunny) still holds today. The Itō family has continued to invest substantial sums of money in the house and gardens.

With the land reform, Bunkichi was forced to lay off much of his administrative staff, including his ten managers. But he was able to use his influence to secure important jobs for them in the agricultural cooperative, in the village office, and, in two cases, as mayors of Yokogoshi. The last in particular may seem strange in an era when mayors must be democratically elected, but in the earlier postwar years the Itō still had considerable say over village affairs, including over issues such as which candidates would and would not stand in mayoral elections. By the mid-1960s, however, a noticeable change occurred in the political environment of the village: villagers were much more likely to elect a candidate they thought would bring economic benefits to the village than to accept a candidate imposed on them by tradition. From that time, the political influence of the Itō has declined substantially, though by no means completely.

The Occupation brought a new face to Japan. In the cities, jazz music, cabarets, and Hollywood movies flourished amidst the ruins. The countryside, too, was affected by the wave of Americanization: spontaneously at times, and as a result of Occupation policy at others. The fashions and customs of America portrayed in American movies filtered down to the villages, through the media of books, popular magazines, and the radio. Even the staid rural magazine *Ie no Hikari* reflected the new ambiance. Beginning in 1947, the magazine offered features such as "How to make a Neckerchief," portraying women dressed entirely in American-style clothes (not just Western dresses, which had been popular before the war too, but dresses in the vogue of the time: wasp-waisted and full to the knees).[15]

The permanent wave, or perm, seems to have taken rural Japan by storm at the turn of the 1950s. Before the war, these hairstyles were quite common among fashionable women in the big cities, but virtually unknown in the countryside. Toshié had seen one once, when she was living with the Yamazaki family in Nishiyama. A woman who worked in Tokyo was back visiting her family. Toshié's fellow child minders agreed that it looked like a sparrow's nest. During the war, perms were proscribed as extravagant, unnatural, and (worst of all) American. Thus, most rural women had seldom if ever seen a permanent wave by the opening years of the Occupation. But in 1952, the Tanaka hairdresser in Yokogoshi acquired the sadistic-looking machinery necessary to administer the perm, and by the mid-1950s rural Japanese housewives felt incomplete without their neat bunch of curls.

Rural wives were also exposed to American culture through the new foods that specialists from the home life extension department were recommending as a way to improve their diet. Bread, potatoes, milk sauces, and cheese were all promoted as tasty and nutritious alternatives to the repetitive rural diet of rice and other grains flavored with morsels of pickle or fish. In part, these new food ideas emanated from research carried out at the Ministry of Agriculture by its new home life extension department—an Occupation-mandated initiative, which sent seven hundred specially trained young specialists on green bicycles pedaling through the Japanese countryside to spread the word on nutrition and family health.[16] Experiments in bread making gave rural families a sense of new beginnings, more tangible than the abstractions of democracy and the revised Civil Code.

The Occupation also provided an important stimulus for welfare in Japan through the passage of key laws—notably the Social Welfare Law

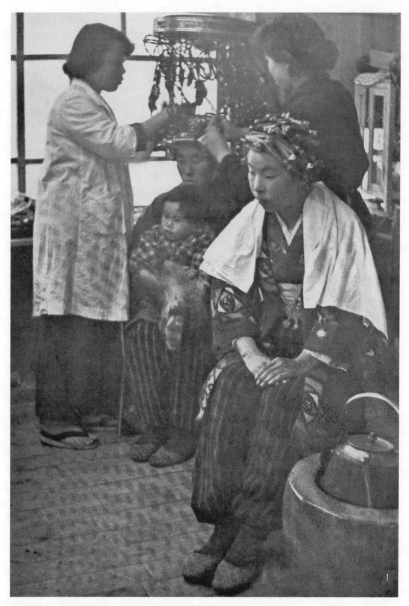

Figure 11. A rural hair salon, c. 1950, with equipment for permanent waves (Photo by Kumagai Motoichi, courtesy Iwanami Shoten).

of March 1951—and through the inclusion in the constitution of the principle that "the State shall use its endeavors for the promotion and extension of social welfare and security, and of public health." [17] Henceforth, the provision of welfare was to be a right of the people and an obligation of the state, rather than an act of benevolence to the deserving needy. In response to the new law, prefectures set up social welfare offices to administer benefits, staffed with social workers qualified under the new system. American officials also provided technological assistance in the form of medicines, pesticides, new fertilizers, and the most comprehensive soil surveys ever performed in Japan. The cumulative effect of wartime and Occupation welfare and technical assistance policies was a rapid improvement in the health conditions of rural Japan—though much of the effect of this was not seen until the early post-Occupation years.

The war was over, Toshié's brothers dead, her father a shadow of his former self, but life must go on. Masu, Rikichi's bride, returned tearfully to her family, vowing that she would run away and return to live again with the Sakaue family. A year or two later, however, she remarried, and she continued living in Kosugi until her death in 1997. Meanwhile, Toshié had turned twenty-two, and it was time for her, too, to get married.

The nation's new constitution had been promulgated in the previous year, and it gave important new rights to women, including the right to vote, the right to inherit equal shares of property, the right to retain property after marriage, and the right to set up independent households. But in rural Japan in 1947, it did not replace the father's customary right to choose a bride for his daughter. The negotiations to select a husband for Toshié were carried out almost entirely behind her back. The candidate selected by Kurakichi was a relative of the Kofunato family—former landlords of Kurakichi, with whom the Sakaue family remained close. The prospective groom's parents had contacted their Kofunato cousins, who in turn approached Kurakichi.

If Toshié had had living brothers, then Kurakichi would have sought an affluent groom for Toshié, ideally an eldest son. Toshié would go as bride to live with her husband's family and share their fortunes. But since Toshié was effectively an only child, Kurakichi must look for a *muko* for Toshié—a groom who would come to live with, and be adopted into, the Sakaue family as heir. In this case, a poorer candidate was appropriate: generally a younger son with no prospects of his own, who would welcome the opportunity to make good as caretaker of the Sakaue family property. However, the candidate should be hardworking and capable, since the Sakaue family fortunes—such as they were—were to be placed in his hands.

Hideshirō—the selected candidate—was a younger son in a large but poor family. He had lost his mother as a child, and his father had sent him to work as a boy with a farming family within the boundaries of Niigata city. He appeared to be hardworking. Kurakichi decided to accept him as groom and arranged with another relative to act as middleman in the negotiation of a wedding settlement. The negotiations were more formality than substance: Hideshirō had nothing to bring to the Sakaue family but his hands and his body, while Kurakichi settled on a small sum to give Hideshirō's parents as a wedding gift.

Toshié had noticed the unusual activity as the middleman came and went during the course of these negotiations, but she had received no hint of what it was all about. It therefore came as a bolt from the blue to learn that her husband had been chosen for her. She knew Hideshirō. Until his departure for Niigata, the two had been in the same year at elementary school. But they had scarcely exchanged a word. Since graduation, Hideshirō had been away, first as a farmworker and then in the military. The sexes had not mingled much at school. More recently, the two had attended a school reunion together, where she had been somewhat struck by Hideshirō's antics as he fooled about with his friends. But the man she was to marry was a virtual stranger to Toshié.

At first Toshié's attitude was one of rebellion. She would not marry this clown! But the obedient habits of a lifetime quickly reasserted themselves, and Toshié meekly assisted in the preparations for her wedding. Her next reaction was furious embarrassment. She virtually stopped going out because she was so scared that she would bump into him. The humiliation of meeting him while she was with her friends was what particularly tormented her. Nevertheless, in spite of her instinctive resistance, Toshié accepted the decision of her parents. She accepted it not only because she had no choice, but also because such acceptance was a part of village culture. Once again, her feeling of belonging to the rural community outweighed considerations of personal preference.

In a more fortunate age, Toshié might have had the opportunity to experience romantic love, and perhaps even to marry a man she loved. Such marriages were at least possible. Haruko, the protagonist of Gail Bernstein's portrait of village life, married a man who was passionately in love with her at roughly the same time.[18] In Kosugi, love matches as well as premarital sexual encounters were not unknown, though the lat-

ter were highly frowned upon (attitudes toward premarital sex seem to
have varied greatly from region to region and even village to village; in
some villages, "trying each other out" before marriage was said to be an
accepted part of courting). But whatever the prevailing morality in Kosugi, Toshié was prevented from experiencing romantic love by the absence of all the able-bodied men during the period when she might have
been most open to such encounters. Fifty years later, Toshié looks back
wistfully on romantic experiences she might have missed, but she has
clearly built an enduring relationship with her husband.

The wedding itself was a simple affair. Since Hideshirō was to be
a *muko* there was none of the ceremony that normally accompanied a
bride's departure from her family home. Hideshirō came to the Sakaue
house with no fanfare, and Toshié greeted him wearing an ordinary
kimono. The wedding celebrations extended to a meal for the twenty
or so wedding guests, but this was certainly not one of the extravagant
weddings that reformers so inveighed at. Toshié was busy most of the
time in the kitchen, helping with the meal. She was silent throughout the
simple ceremony. And then the guests were gone, the dishes washed and
returned, and the family was once again alone—with its new member.
Toshié and Hideshirō were given the upstairs room, where they began
their married life together.

There was no honeymoon. The very next day, the families of the hamlet were gathering by the river to cut rushes for use in roof thatching and
basket making. The rules of the hamlet allowed such cutting only on
specified days, and those who did not go would not get their allotment
of rushes. Representing her family, Toshié went down to the river and
worked all day amidst the rushes. Hideshirō, meanwhile, went out
salmon fishing on the river with his fellow members of the Kosugi fisher-
men's union. Then on succeeding days, Hideshirō quietly took up his duties. He took over much of the farmwork from Kurakichi, and on holidays he went fishing on the river, the place where he was happiest.

The following year, Hideshirō bought a boat and began trawling the
river for gravel. The business of Japan was rebuilding, and building materials of all kinds were in demand. The layer of gravel on the bottom of
the Agano was allocated by hamlet. Prices were high, and the rewards
were good for anyone with the stamina to haul the gravel up. Collecting
the gravel in the boat was not so difficult. But from the boat, Hideshirō
had to fill a bamboo basket with gravel and heft it up onto his shoulders
as he staggered up the slope with it wearing straw sandals that he had
made for himself in the winter.

After a marriage come children—or such was the case with all of Toshié's friends. But Toshié's joy when she found she was pregnant was soon dashed as she miscarried. The next year, she had another miscarriage. Then, nothing. No matter how hard she tried, she could not get pregnant again. Toshié watched her close friends giving birth and reveling in their new lives as mothers, and she felt a bitter envy. The doctor in Kameda sent her to a specialist in Niigata, who examined her and could find nothing wrong with her physically. Perhaps she was working too hard—but in her family's economic circumstances, that was something she could not avoid.

Japan had lost the war after its leaders had promised victory. Toshié had lost both her brothers in the vain struggle. Many in Japan and abroad blamed the emperor, Hirohito, for Japan's warmongering and defeat. Some said he should be tried and hanged as a war criminal. But Toshié had been brought up to love and respect the emperor, and it is hard to change the habits of a lifetime. Moreover, the emperor who she read about in magazines now was very different from the emperor of the war years. The latter had been a remote, awesome figure in his military uniform, mounted on a beautiful white horse. Now, the emperor was traveling around the country wearing a plain dark suit, raising his hat to the people he met, and making himself visible to as many of his people as possible. His legal status had of course changed. No longer the supreme ruler of the nation, he was now its "symbol." For Toshié, he appears to have symbolized a simple and naive patriotism that transcended the betrayals of the war.

In early 1948, Toshié set out by train to visit the Imperial palace in Tokyo. She went as part of a large group from Kosugi and nearby hamlets in order to donate voluntary labor restoring the palace grounds.

There was a craze for doing such work in the early postwar years. A youth group from Miyagi prefecture first broached the idea. In October 1945, the group requested permission to enter the palace grounds to perform maintenance work on a volunteer basis. Normally, visits by outsiders to the massive palace compound in Tokyo were strictly forbidden. But the condition of the grounds was quite dilapidated after the depredations of the war. Although the palace was only partially affected by the bombings, the lack of manpower had led to a decline in maintenance. Given this fact, and the desire to put the emperor on a new footing with his subjects, the palace officials decided to allow the visit. A group of sixty youths arrived in November, bringing their own tools and food from their village. They worked for three days, staying in a hostel off the grounds. On the third day, the workgroup assembled in front of the palace where the emperor greeted them.

The news of this group was widely reported, and shortly thereafter the palace was flooded with requests from other village groups to perform similar services. For the next two decades, some twenty thousand people per year visited the palace to perform labor in the grounds. Three-quarters of them were women.[19]

It was only the second time in her life that Toshié had been on a long train journey (the first was to Sendai, to collect her brother's "remains"). She had never before been to the capital. The group traveled third class, sleeping on the train on the long, mountainous route to Tokyo. The journey took a total of twenty-four hours. The group took with them plenty of food, since they had been told that supplies were still short in the city. Indeed, they had been requested to bring extra as gifts for imperial household staff and the organizers of their stay. Arriving at Shinjuku station, Toshié was struck by the shabbiness and obvious poverty of Tokyo. Many buildings were still bombed-out hulks. There were thousands of people living on the streets. The people looked pinched and hungry. For the first time in her life, Toshié felt well-off compared to her fellow countrymen.

The group stayed in a hostel in Shinjuku and early the next morning took the train to Tokyo station, from where they walked to the Imperial palace. That day and the next, they worked hard on the banks of the palace grounds overlooking the inner moat. At the end of the second day, they received their reward. Together with other groups, they assembled in front of one of the palace buildings. After a long wait, the emperor and his wife came out to greet them. They were a very small couple, an ordinary middle-aged gentleman and his slightly dumpy wife. But they were also familiar from the magazine photos, a part of Toshié's imaginative world. And this was the emperor to whose image she had bowed every day of her school life! As the assembled group sang the national anthem (a hymn to the emperor, the words of which begin, "Your reign shall last for ten thousand generations"), Toshié felt tears running down her face.

After they finished the song, their group leader stepped up and made a prepared address to the emperor. The emperor then spoke to the assembled crowd. He spoke in informal Japanese, not at all like the strange language he had used in his surrender address, but not quite like an or-

Figure 12. A work group from Yokogoshi rests on the Imperial palace grounds, 1948 (Courtesy, Sakaue Toshié)

dinary Japanese either. He told the people assembled that he knew many of them had lost loved ones in the war. They must do their best to soldier on. He was asking them personally. And he thanked them. His voice was hard to catch in the large space, but Toshié was nevertheless profoundly moved by the event. She has treasured it in her heart ever since.

For the first three years after her marriage, Toshié worked at whatever odd jobs she could find. Her mother was taking in piecework weaving baskets and knitting sweaters, and Toshié helped her out with these. She also helped her husband and father in the fields. But the work was irregular, and the family depended mainly on Hideshirō's gravel collecting on the river. Hideshirō was able to get a good income for this— about one thousand yen per day, equivalent to a good day's labor wage. Toshié gained a little extra income from farming. Although she only cultivated a small amount of land, the prices she received for her delivery quotas were improving every year, and by the beginning of the 1950s the quotas were largely removed. But the family still was living hand to mouth.

In October 1951, Niigata prefecture embarked on a second massive works project on the Agano River. The prewar river works, which had straightened the course of the river and narrowed its banks, had led to unintended consequences. As a result of the works, the flow of the river speeded up significantly, and this in turn led to a deepening of the river channel as silt was swept downstream by the accelerated flow. The deeper, lower, faster-running channel was weakening the foundations of the levee in some places. Moreover, as the overall water level sank by 1.2 meters, many of the irrigation pumps installed along the river were pumping dry air. The new project was intended to reverse the outflow of silt and to raise the water level by some two meters. From the end of 1951, Toshié began working on this project. The work was close to home, so she was saved the rattling truck rides required for day labor in farther-off places. But the work took place in and out of the river regardless of rain or snow. Wearing rubber boots, baggy trousers, and a padded cotton jacket, she worked with a team of twenty or more men and women using simple materials to control the flow of the river. Their basic technique was to build a container composed of several frames of straight sapling branches, piled on top of one another and tied together with rope. Into the container they then hurled large stones, eventually sinking it to the bottom of the river. In this way they could create obstructions to the flow of the river and channel it in the direction the engineers wanted. It was freezing-cold, often wet work, and there were bleak winter days when Toshié thought of nothing but how to warm her chilled limbs. In the evening, after dark, she would trudge for two miles back to Kosugi through piled-up snow, her tired legs hardly able to move one in front of the other. She finally arrived home to a cold and draughty house. Hungry for warmth as well as food, she would huddle by the *kotatsu* with its meager charcoal glow. The family still depended on driftwood and brush from the riverbank for its fuel needs, and the effort of gathering this made it a precious commodity to be used as sparingly as possible. Her father, now in his late sixties and no longer feeling strong, had little energy left after taking care of the fields. After dinner, prepared by her mother and waiting for Toshié and Hideshirō on their return, Toshié would long for a hot bath. But more often than not the effort and expense of bringing water and heating it was too much, so she crawled under her bedcovers for warmth instead. Even these were too meager, though, and she could barely sleep for her freezing feet. In the morning, still cold and tired, she dragged herself up for another day of labor.

Always, in the back of her mind amidst these hardships, was her worry about her sister Kiyomi. Day in and day out, Kiyomi's unpredictable behavior caused her family nights of missed sleep and days of anguish. During the day, when she was under her mother's watchful eye, Kiyomi was generally subdued and obedient. At times, she was even capable of helping with the never-ending chores. But the other, the sick, Kiyomi had become a creature of the night. Once the family was all asleep she would sneak out of the house and begin her nightly wanderings, regardless of cold and regardless of her appearance, through the streets of the village, and farther if the opportunity arose. For Kiyomi, the increasing traffic on the road along the levee was a godsend, for now she could flag down a truck or a handcart on its way to a dawn market in a neighboring town, and talk the driver into taking her along. Usually it was not long before her companion realized that there was something strange about her, and he would hasten to set her down. But then she would flag down the next comer, until by morning she could be miles away from Kosugi. Kiyomi's family would awaken to discover her absence, but after a tour of the village to establish Kiyomi was nowhere nearby, there was nothing they could do but wait for the inevitable call from the police. This normally took the form of a message, relayed by telephone from the police who had picked up Kiyomi to the town hall in Yokogoshi, who would then send a messenger to Kosugi with the news that Kiyomi was safe. (After the end of the 1940s, Kosugi was equipped with telephone connections between the village office and the Kosugi school. Later still, every house in the hamlet was connected via an intravillage telephone system.) The embarrassment of the family had no end in sight. Toshié, her mother and father would do their best to keep an ear open in their sleep to make sure that Kiyomi did not sneak out. But controlling and caring for their sick family member was wearing them all down.

One evening in the midst of this existence, Toshié had a visit from a neighbor, Mrs. Nishikawa. Everyone in Kosugi knew that Toshié had suffered miscarriages, and most understood her anguish at not being able to produce children. Mrs. Nishikawa had a proposal. She had a relative, a common laborer who lived in a nearby village. This man was burdened by his love life. He had both a wife and a mistress. He had five children by his wife, and had just had a second by his mistress. He was unable to support his large family and was looking for a good family to take in one of his children. Would Toshié consider adopting his two-year-old daughter Keiko?

Keiko's family situation was obviously impossible. Without even seeing the girl, Toshié agreed to adopt her. Within a week, Toshié's new daughter was delivered to her, and she set about filing the necessary paperwork to adopt the child legally.

Keiko was a large, good-natured child, who obviously found life in Toshié's household far preferable to the hardships of her natural family. For Toshié, motherhood was a welcome diversion from her own hardships, though she could not allow it to divert her from her main activity: working to earn enough money to make ends meet. Indeed, the presence of Keiko imposed that much heavier a responsibility. Without a pause, Toshié continued with her daily labor on the river, while her mother took care of Keiko. Still, it was a comfort to hear the cheerful little voice in the evenings, to admire the progress Keiko made in walking and talking, and to play with her daughter on holidays.

However, Toshié was not to be allowed to enjoy the comforts of a happy family life. Yet another sadness was waiting for her just around the corner. In the middle of 1952, her father began complaining of a loss of appetite, and he began to lose weight. Although he still went out to the fields, he was becoming noticeably slower. He was evidently in pain. His wife, Tsugino, began to help him out more and more in the fields, but she could not stray too far from where Keiko was sitting and playing. Eventually, they decided to take Kurakichi to consult the doctor at the new clinic in Yokogoshi hamlet. The doctor ordered an X-ray to be taken of Kurakichi's chest and abdomen. The next time they went to the doctor, he ordered Kurakichi into the treatment room for an injection. While the nurse was preparing him, the doctor took Tsugino aside and told her that her husband had inoperable stomach cancer. He would probably be dead within six months.

The doctor ordered Kurakichi into the hospital, and the same day he was carried by ambulance from Kosugi to the hospital in neighboring Kameda town. He spent three months in the hospital before the doctors released him to die. The entire hospital stay was at the family's expense. Kurakichi lived for another three months. He was never told that he had cancer, and the doctors, as well as his family, constantly reassured him that he was getting better. On his death, the doctor said, "Well, it's a good thing he enjoyed a long life." He was seventy at his death, well above the average for peasant farmers of his generation. Today, though, he would be considered a young man.

Kurakichi had experienced the hardships of peasant life to the full. A lifetime of harsh labor, periods of near-desperate poverty, the death of both sons, a mentally ill daughter with no hope of treatment, a government that took far more than it gave, the slow sale of land, and the decline into indebtedness; all these had been his lot, with few indications of relief to come. He would perhaps have been astonished if he could have seen the remarkable changes that were to take place in Kosugi in the next ten years.

CHAPTER 5

Red Carpets and Whisky

The fifteen years from 1955 to 1970 was a period of extraordinary change in both urban and rural Japan. Throughout this period, the Japanese economy grew by an average 10 percent per year—an unprecedented growth rate, and one that inevitably led to rapid social change. For the most part, the causes of the boom lay in the cities; industrial concerns poured money into new plants and equipment, stimulating and stimulated by a prolonged surge in consumer spending (and, from the 1960s, export demand). By 1960, newspapers and government analysts were talking of a consumer revolution sweeping the country as urban families poured money into purchases of high-value consumer products such as cameras, television sets, washing machines, and refrigerators. Late in the 1950s, analysts began talking wryly of the new "three sacred treasures": traditionally, these were the imperial regalia of mirror, sword, and jewels, but in the new secular age, they were taken to apply to the most sought-after consumer durable goods: television, washing machine, and refrigerator.[1]

At first, many were afraid that the countryside would be left behind by the transformation of lifestyles that was sweeping over the cities. After all, rural productivity was growing at a fraction of the pace of the booming industrial sector, and Japanese villages continued, in the eyes of many, to be mired in the past—held back by inadequate infrastructure, "feudal" family structures, and a culture of thrift and penny pinching. In 1956, a book on rural lifestyles included a detailed analysis of the state of rural toilets. The typical specimen was lamentably unhygienic; the need to store human waste for use as fertilizer in the fields meant that the toilet became a breeding ground for flies, mosquitoes, and bacteria. Even worse, since most farmers had intestinal parasites, the habit of spreading their manure over the fields meant that the parasites would inevitably remain in the food chain, even spreading to the urban families that purchased the farmers' produce. Yet the book concluded that given the current state of the farm household economy, it was impossible to expect farmers to give up using their waste as fertilizer. The book calculated that the average annual cost to replace the human manure with equivalent values of chemical fertilizer was two thousand yen ($5.56 at the prevailing rate of exchange). Expecting farmers to bear that cost was "impossible at the present time."[2]

Other pessimists focused more on cultural barriers to rural consumerism. For example, one retailer commented in a discussion forum on the unlikelihood of rural families joining in the boom in electrical household goods purchases: "Even if a young wife is thinking about buying a washing machine, the old folks will say 'that's because she wants to make things easy for herself' or 'typical of a daughter-in-law, she's planning to waste our assets.'"[3] Another reported having been told by a farmer: "We have two daughters, but if I let them use an electric washer, then when they get married they won't be able to do the washing." Yet another commented that farmers "believe that if a person does not suffer he can not gain merit, and that ease is the cause of a fall from grace."[4]

It is hard to assess how much validity these arguments had. Toshié had shown extreme deference to her father in important questions such as that of her marriage, but her household's financial management seems to have been both pragmatic and egalitarian. Toshié and Hideshirō pooled their earnings and Toshié managed them, consulting with Hideshirō about any significant expenditures. Toshié's mother had her own income—the pensions of her dead sons—which she did not feel obliged to make available to the family head. Indeed, Toshié had to resort at times to borrowing from her mother, who apparently treated her like any other debtor. Family "feudalism" was hardly an issue when it came to buying consumer goods. The main problem in their particular case was low income.

To some extent, the insistence by consumer goods companies on "feudal" and "irrational" rural values was self-serving. By creating an image of an irrational and backward society, companies could play up their role in bestowing "culture" on that society. A Matsushita executive commented, "It is very important to do [rural] consumers the favor of teaching them what they want through education and promotion."[5] The advertising and promotional activities of consumer goods companies heavily emphasized the "rationality" and modernity of their products, and usually in the context of a "democratic," Western-style nuclear family. In promotional activities aimed specifically at the countryside, companies tended to downplay the more frivolous aspects of the consumer lifestyle that might have appealed to urban consumers and to emphasize instead the worthier goals of reducing the burden on women, creating economic benefits, and "raising the level of culture."

In reality, thanks to a mixture of government protection and spillover from the industrial boom, rural and urban spending by the mid-1950s were not nearly as far apart as the gloomier analyses suggest; average monthly nonfood expenditure in 1955 was ¥13,048 (thirty-six dollars) for urban worker households versus ¥11,225 (thirty-one dollars) for rural households.[6] Given that the cost of a television was some one hundred thousand yen ($277) and a washing machine thirty thousand yen (eighty-three dollars), it might be fair to conclude that both rural *and* urban residents were poor—but (as events were shortly to attest) not so poor that they could not be induced into buying washing machines or flush toilets.

In spite of the growing disparity in production, the trend to equalization of urban and rural incomes continued throughout the 1950s and 1960s, and by 1970 the incomes and expenditures of rural families had caught up with and indeed overtaken those of urban families.[7] There were two major causes: protection and subsidies provided by the government and the diversification of rural incomes.

The government became a loyal protector of the countryside at the expense of urban consumers, ostensibly for reasons of social equity and food security. But at the heart of the policy was the political power acquired by the rural sector, as powerful agricultural groups forged an enduring alliance with the Liberal Democratic Party, which governed Japan continuously from 1955. This alliance became if anything stronger over time; since redistricting failed to keep up with the changing demographics of rural versus urban Japan, the value of rural votes became greater and greater. For example, in the 1972 lower house elections, a Liberal Democratic Party candidate was able to win a seat in Gifu prefecture with 37,258 votes, while a Socialist Party candidate lost in Tokyo in spite of gaining 144,415 votes. At the peak, a rural vote was worth more than five times as much as an urban one.[8] From the end of

the 1950s, the government committed to a policy that was already operating de facto: farm products would be subsidized to ensure income
parity with the industrial sector. To this end, the government turned the
system of government purchases that had oppressed farmers so much
during the war and occupation years into a mechanism of subsidy; the
government purchased rice and other crops from farmers at fixed prices
that increased annually based on the growth in industrial productivity
and sold the rice to retail distributors at a *lower* price. This was to turn
into an immensely costly program that burdened the government for
decades and arguably prevented much of the rural sector from ever becoming economically self-sufficient. In 1970, the price support program
cost the government ¥417 billion: close to 50 percent of all agricultural
programs, and some 6 percent of the entire national budget.[9] Since the
end of the 1960s, the government has also been paying farmers *not* to
grow rice, reflecting the surplus accumulated as a result of the government's price incentives.

Even more significant than the effect of government support for the
farm sector was the diversification of farm family incomes. As had always been the case in the past, those with sufficient land were able to
make a living solely from farming, and the extensive subsidies available
to the farming sector helped them keep their incomes close to those of
middle-class urbanites. But the number of families in this situation was
small. In 1960, only 4.1 percent of farm families outside Hokkaido
farmed more than two hectares, which for mainstream crops is considered the minimum size for economic self-sufficiency.[10] One of the ironies
of the land reform is that it did nothing to alleviate the basic fact of Japanese rural life: too many families on too small an area of land. The land
reform shuffled ownership of the larger holdings, but it did not significantly increase their number.[11] The majority of farm families who managed to remain on the land did so by family members taking outside
jobs, and the booming industrial sector provided an abundant source of
such jobs. Increasingly, even family heads and eldest sons went out to
work, leaving the farming activities to grandparents, women, and children—or doing the work at weekends. From the mid-1950s onward,
the proportion of farm families' incomes coming directly from farming
plummeted. In 1959, for example, families farming 0.5 to 1.0 hectare
earned ¥157,000 from nonfarming work, and ¥184,000 from agriculture, a ratio of 0.85 to 1.0. By 1970, families in the same group earned
¥942,000 from nonfarm labor, and only ¥354,000 from farming—a ratio of 2.7 to 1.0.

The consequences of the rapid increase in rural incomes were far reaching. Through the end of the 1950s, urban consumers had led the boom in domestic consumer spending that fed economic growth and propelled some Japanese manufacturers into positions of international competitiveness. By the end of the decade, though, rural consumers were supporting continued growth in industries that were already approaching saturation in urban markets. For example, from 11 percent in 1960, rural television ownership grew to 89 percent by 1965. During the same period, 10 percent of rural households acquired washing machines per year, bringing total penetration from 9 percent to 59 percent.[12] In spite of initial pessimism by consumer goods retailers, rural families appear to have made these purchases based on similar considerations to urban families: durable consumer goods made their lives easier and more entertaining. For example, when UNESCO ran a pilot television broadcasting project in rural Japan in the early 1950s, showing farm informational programming to communal viewers in village halls, the response was lukewarm at best. But when the Tokyo Olympics aired on television in 1964, rural viewers flocked to buy television sets.

Consumer product manufacturers had to overcome formidable practical obstacles in order to achieve this rapid market growth. Rural distribution systems for high-ticket items such as television sets or washing machines were primitive or nonexistent. For example, the typical retailer to rural families was an electrical shop in a provincial town. In many cases, these were small, family enterprises that made a living by sales and repairs. With the introduction of television, many small retailers did not even have the capital to purchase a display model; nor did most have the skills to repair such a complex piece of equipment. At the end of the 1960s, the majority of rural communities still lacked running water, making it much harder to make a case for the convenience of washing machines (manufacturers recommended placing the machine outside the house, near the well). Most important of all, the credit arrangements needed to sell big-ticket items were not yet institutionalized. At least until the 1950s, rural families had taken on debt primarily as an act of desperation, when they could not make ends meet in any other way. Now consumer goods manufacturers must persuade rural consumers that it was not wrong to borrow money to buy a convenience or entertainment product—and in many cases they must also provide the money. These obstacles were only overcome through huge investments in distribution networks, retail support and training programs, the establishment of lending subsidiaries, and marketing and demonstration. But overcome they were, and in this they were no doubt aided by a healthy desire on the part of farm families for the comforts of the consumer age.

Those families that bought television sets early often paid a very high price, both in absolute terms and in terms of the trade-offs that they made. Hasegawa Kikuyo, who lived in a rural part of Saitama prefecture, recalls that the ¥190,000 ($527) her husband paid for a large television set dashed forever her dreams of owning her own house. At the time, she recalls, a house could be purchased in her village for under one hundred thousand yen.[13] Fukuda Kiku, who came from a landlord family in a village in Fukushima prefecture, recalls that her family was the first in the village to purchase a television set, in 1955. But having bought it, they were unable to receive any signal. Eventually they had to work with the electrical retailer and the local broadcasting company to get relay antennas placed high up on a nearby mountainside. It took them several months, and considerable expense, before they were finally able to enjoy their purchase.[14] However, the majority who waited until the end of the 1950s benefited from steep reductions in the price of television sets—due to economies of scale and intense competition, prices fell as low as thirty thousand yen for a fourteen-inch black-and-white set— and from the improvement of broadcast facilities. Rural consumers were also able to get better use of their washing machines as, increasingly, villages invested in mains water supplies.

Toshié bought both television and washing machine at the end of the 1950s, at the same time that she and Hideshirō rebuilt their home. Toshié paid cash for the washing machine, but the television she bought on credit, paying installments of two thousand yen a month over a period of almost three years. It is worth pointing out that buying a television set was not, for Toshié, an unprecedented purchase. Toshié's father Kurakichi had bought a radio at a time when that expenditure was also high relative to his income. Since then, radio had been an integral part of Toshié's daily life. She was a consumer of broadcast news, entertainment, and sports before she bought a television set. Moreover, the postwar years had seen a rapid increase in the commercialization of the mass media. The Occupation had ordered the launch of private radio stations, and by the early 1950s Niigata had both national and private radio broadcasting. Meanwhile, monthly and weekly magazines, particularly those aimed at women, flourished during the 1950s. Both private radio and magazines carried extensive advertising, much of it for national brand goods, including consumer durables. Rural consumers had come a long way since the monolithic message-making of the wartime media.

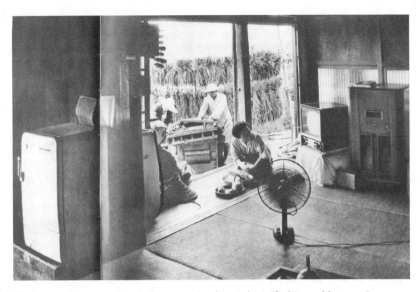

Figure 13. A promotional photograph of an "electrified" rural home (Courtesy, Mainichi Shinbunsha)

By 1970, the consumer boom in the countryside had transformed the contents of the rural home and many of the habits of everyday life. Families that had previously huddled around a central hearth where they parsimoniously burnt firewood they had gathered by their own labors now warmed their knees at kerosene stoves (owned by 70 percent of farm households by 1970) and their feet at electric *kotatsu* foot-warmers (owned by 73 percent of families). Although they were a little late in acquiring them, by 1970 the vast majority of farm families owned the "three sacred pieces of treasures" of the 1950s: 83 percent owned refrigerators, 91 percent owned washing machines, and almost 100 percent owned television sets. Other objects of convenience and entertainment included vacuum cleaners (48 percent ownership) and cameras (45 percent). Meanwhile, a significant minority of farm families owned the accoutrements of a typical Western-style home: interior carpets (18 percent), dining tables and chairs (16 percent), beds (13 percent), stereos (19 percent), couches (14 percent), and stainless-steel kitchen sinks (33 percent).[15] It was perhaps these families that prompted a worker in the cause of rural "lifestyle improvement" to comment (with strong disapproval) that:

Suddenly [villagers] were buying electrical products, cars, even trucks. In front of my eyes, thatched roofs were replaced by tiles. In the heated rooms there was no more than an empty kettle on the bubbling paraffin stove: even in mid-winter, people slept wearing only a nightshirt. They drank coffee, they watched television until midnight, and they bought luxurious three-piece suites of furniture to put on their red carpets. They kept high quality whisky in their beautiful sideboards. They bought stereos, and listened to them while they drank their whisky.[16]

The transformation of rural homes did not apply only to their contents. During the later 1950s and 1960s, the villages of Japan resounded with the sounds of the hammer and drill as homes themselves were torn down and rebuilt. It is hard to find statistics on construction activity specifically in villages, but indirect evidence of an unprecedented building boom is abundant. Until 1959, spending by farm families on new construction fluctuated with the vagaries of the rice harvest. After the bumper harvest of 1955, for example, spending on new construction jumped. However, after 1959, the expansion of spending became sustained and was no longer tied to the quality of the harvest. Whereas in 1959 the average family spent ¥13,556, or 6.2 percent of total cash expenditures, on new construction, by 1965 they were spending ¥53,600, or 10.4 percent of total expenditure.[17] Moreover, spending on repairs and maintenance—indicating a commitment to maintaining an older dwelling rather than rebuilding—grew at a much slower pace, declining from 7.1 percent of total expenditures in 1956, to 6.0 percent in 1965.[18]

In their 1959 work *Village Japan*, three American ethnologists described the process of home building in the village of Niike where they had lived on and off for four years from 1950 to 1954. According to the authors, the majority of building materials used in new Niike homes were local, wherever possible from land owned by the farmer building the house. Thus, wood generally came from a nearby pine grove, the walls were stitched in with bamboo and mud, and the roof was of thatch made from local rice straw. According to the authors, the only parts of the house that required purchased materials were the tatami and shōji for floors and interior partitions; and special woods used for the more ornamental parts of the house—the ceiling posts, and the external veranda, traditionally made of superior wood.[19]

By the end of the 1960s, this account of home building already seemed rather quaint. Thatched roofs disappeared from the building agenda with dramatic abruptness in around 1955. From that point on, tile was virtually the only material used in roofing. The use of local materials also declined steeply. With the availability of mass-produced lumber, cutting and processing one's own wood became much more expensive than buying it from a lumberyard. Indeed, the process of building a house became closely integrated with the urban housing market from this time.

The process of rebuilding appears to have cut across socioeconomic boundaries. In many cases the wealthiest families saw no need to rebuild, as they already had comfortable homes. Indeed, from this point on, the thoughts of the most privileged villagers turned toward the question of preservation, as their homes came to be the sole remaining witnesses to the "old" way of life. In an extreme case, the Itō family mansion, the home became a museum. However, the homes of poorer villagers were often the most in need of replacement.

Toshié and Hideshirō participated in this transformation, even as they continued to struggle with inadequate land, hard daily labor, and low wages. From 1955, both Toshié and Hideshirō began working on a day laborer basis for the Kumaki group, a labor contractor that hired manual workers from villages in the Niigata area. They were to work for Kumaki for the next ten years. For the most part they worked on the public works projects that were slowly changing the landscape and the local economy in Niigata prefecture: road building, river management, laying of telephone and electric lines, and harbor work. For Hideshirō, the turn to regular paid labor was a change from his life of the past several years as an independent collector of gravel from the river bottom. The gravel was becoming harder and harder to find as demand increased with the growing economy, and as works on the river affected the composition of the riverbed. For Toshié, work in the Kumaki was little different from the kind of labor she had become accustomed to over the past ten years. She continued to be hired by the day; most of the work was unmechanized and involved heavy lifting and hauling; she worked outdoors in all weathers and the pay remained low.

Nevertheless, the Kumaki provided the family with steady work, and day laboring jobs indeed became readily available from this time on; the family never had to worry about finding work so long as they were willing to put their backs into it. The pay from Kumaki was around one thousand yen per day for Hideshirō, six hundred yen for Toshié. Together, if they both worked full time, they might make as much as forty thousand yen per month, more than the salary of a typical urban office clerk. In practice, Toshié took time off when necessary to work on the fields (since they were hired by the day they were free to work or not as they wished), and their income from Kumaki was generally between fifteen and twenty thousand yen per month in the latter part of the 1950s.

In addition to her work in the Kumaki, Toshié was now the main person in charge of what was left of the family farm. The family land had by this time been further reduced. The river works of the 1950s had caused the river to overflow its prewar banks, taking with it some of the land that the family had reclaimed with such effort in 1937. Toshié, faced with continuing demands on her time and with money shortages, sold the tenancy rights to another piece of land during the 1950s. Still, the land that remained amounted to a great deal of work for a woman working largely on her own, and carrying on a more or less full time job at the same time. During the six months from April to September, Toshié got up at four every morning, seven days a week, to work on the fields, managing a couple of hours before going home for breakfast and catching the van that took them to work on the current Kumaki project. In the longer summer days, she went to work in the fields after coming home from the Kumaki, too (Hideshirō often stayed with the work group to do overtime, sleeping over in a tent near the work site). She worked during these years as hard as at any time in her life.

From the mid-1950s, the income of Toshié's family was augmented by an unaccustomed source: government largesse. In August 1953, the Diet voted after a heated debate to restore military pensions to the families of the war dead. The government in the past had always paid such pensions, but after Japan's defeat, the U.S. Occupation authorities banned the payment of pensions, both as an economic measure and as a gesture of retribution. Small allowances continued to be paid out only to dependent widows and survivors who were in clear distress, but the majority of survivors—including Toshié's parents, who under the wartime system qualified for pensions for their dead sons—got nothing. Since more than two million servicemen died in action, the restoration of pensions implied an enormous financial commitment by the government; for the next decade, the pension payments amounted to close to 10 percent of the central government's budget. For Toshié's family, the new law meant that Toshié's mother—the qualifying relative—would get pensions for both Rikichi and Takeharu. At their reinstatement in 1953, the pensions were set at ¥26,765 per year. For the two brothers, then, this amounted to a total of some forty-five hundred yen per month. This could scarcely be considered a princely sum. Young female workers in the textile mills made more than five thousand yen per month, and that was about the lowest wage that Japan afforded in the early 1950s. At the time, Toshié's husband could make about one thousand yen in a single day of work. But the forty-five hundred yen made the difference between a scrabbling existence at the bare subsistence level, and the ability to save and build plans for the future. For the most part, the family allowed the pension money to sit in a post office account and grow.

And the pension itself grew, too. By 1958, five years after its implementation, the annual amount had grown to ¥53,200. The family was now receiving almost nine thousand per month for the two dead brothers—a substantial increase, even accounting for inflation. Rikichi and Takeharu died miserable deaths in far-off countries, in the cause of a lost war. For their family, little could alleviate the grief and resentment at their loss. But the resumption of pensions on their behalf was nevertheless the beginning of a kind of redemption.

The resumption of pensions was one manifestation of a surge in government-sponsored projects to improve the material welfare of rural Japanese. Many of these programs were kick-started by the Occupation authorities. Others had their origins in the welfare policies of the wartime government. But it was only with the substantial increase in available funds during the 1950s and beyond that the programs began to have a significant effect on the health and welfare of villagers.

With the Kumaki money added to Toshié's brothers' pensions, Toshié and her mother decided that they could afford to put Kiyomi in the hospital, where they desperately hoped not only to relieve themselves of the burden of her care, but also to find a cure for her. In early 1957, Kiyomi went into the new mental asylum in Niitsu, six miles away from Kosugi. They visited her once or twice a month, and they were impressed with the progress that she seemed to be making in the hospital. Perhaps this was to be the solution to their troubles. The cost of Kiyomi's hospitalization was steep, however; at around ten thousand yen per month, it amounted to between one-quarter and one-third of their total family income. The new village health insurance program covered doctor's visits, but not hospitalization.

In September 1958, just after she had brought the harvest in, Toshié found herself feeling queasy at times during the day. She wondered if she was sickening. With mounting disbelief, she noted that her period did not come that month. A visit to the hospital confirmed the unbelievable: after twelve years of marriage, two miscarriages, and ten years with no signs of anything at all, Toshié was pregnant. Her doctor worried that she was a "high risk" pregnancy, but it was economically impossible for Toshié to stop working, so she continued doing heavy labor through the months of her pregnancy. Only after the eighth month did she stop working. She spent the last month of her pregnancy sewing clothes out of old rags. For the birth, Toshié hired the local taxi to take her to Sōmi, where there was an obstetrician. Under normal circumstances she would have used the midwife in Kosugi, who still presided over most deliveries (she was the wife of the village priest, and the daughter-in-law of Mrs. Yamazaki, who had delivered Toshié). Toshié gave birth to a daughter without incident. They called the baby Ayako. For two months after the birth, Toshié rested at home and took care not to do heavy lifting work. After that, she left Ayako together with Keiko (now in the fourth year of elementary school) in the care of her mother, and rejoined the Kumaki labor gang. Toshié's family was growing again.

Unlike the babies of a generation earlier, Ayako's prospects for survival through infancy were excellent. As a result of hygiene and disease control measures implemented during the war and occupation, the ratio of deaths to births in infancy in Yokogoshi had drastically declined, from 20 percent in 1928 to 10 percent in 1950. Yokogoshi's death rate had also declined; during the prewar period it hovered around 2 percent of the village population per year, but in 1950 it fell to 1.4 percent and thereafter it continued to decline. The birthrate also fell, from a prewar average of 4 percent of the village population per year, to 3.2 percent in 1950 and only 1.3 percent by 1970.[20] The speed at which these improvements came about is particularly striking. Effective disease prevention and birth control programs were implemented even before high economic growth brought large increases in government spending. The speed and early effectiveness of the campaigns testifies to the importance of initiatives by the wartime and Occupation governments.

And the initiatives continued. Niigata prefecture established a total of 232 day care centers by 1954, primarily as a welfare measure to allow needy mothers to go out to work. Niigata also participated in a national campaign to reduce the incidence of tuberculosis, which surged at the end of the war. Niigata prefecture mobilized its seventeen health centers (which were a legacy of the wartime welfare system) to visit schools and factories for group check-ups. From 1951, the national government began paying 50 percent of medical expenses for tuberculosis treatment. Deaths from tuberculosis in Niigata declined from 3,580 in 1950 to 993 in 1955, and 408 in 1965. Niigata also led steps to reduce the incidence of contagious diseases, particularly dysentery, which reached epidemic proportions in the early 1950s (in 1951, there were 6,094 cases in the prefecture and 362 deaths). The key to reducing the incidence of dysentery was hygiene. Niigata encouraged the establishment of local organizations for the promotion of hygiene, of which there were 1,096 by 1955. The prefecture also developed ambitious plans to increase the availabil-

ity of running water, seen as essential to improved hygiene, and participated in national campaigns to eliminate flies and mosquitoes. By the
early 1960s, dysentery had been virtually eliminated as a health problem (there was one death in the prefecture in 1965).[21]

Yokogoshi also made decisive progress against the *tsutsuga* insect that
had caused so much suffering in the village. After the war, researchers
found (with American research assistance) that the American drug chlo-
romycetin was effective in curing the disease that the insect caused. In
1951, researchers finally identified the specific insect—Trombicula In-
telmedia—that caused the disease, and from the end of the 1940s the
prefecture began (again, with Occupation assistance at first) spraying
the riverbanks with U.S.-supplied benzine hexachloride (BHC) disin-
fectant. In addition, residents of Yokogoshi who were going to work by
the river were sprayed in advance with pesticide. In 1951, for the first
time in recorded history there were no deaths from *tsutsuga* disease in
Yokogoshi.[22]

The village of Yokogoshi also participated in an area-wide project,
with major government funding, which resulted in decisive improvements to the agriculture of the village. The project was originally planned
during the war, as part of the government's initiative to increase food
production. It was closely related to the river management projects,
which included large pumping stations that could be used for irrigation.
The plan, which was largely implemented in the postwar years, called
for consolidation of some thirty-four small pumping stations into three
large ones, one of them being in the hamlet of Sōmi. The water pumped
out was then channeled into a system of newly dug irrigation channels.
The improvement project eventually encompassed the building of roads
between fields, regularization of fields, and laying down of irrigation
pipes. The total cost of the project was in excess of thirty billion yen,
shared between the national and prefectural governments, and the direct
beneficiaries of the project, who paid (and continue to pay) annual fees
for use of the facilities. The project brought controlled irrigation to almost five thousand hectares of rice fields and is the major contributor to
the impression a visitor has today of a sea of perfectly cultivated rice in
identically shaped paddies.[23]

By the end of the 1950s Toshié and Hideshirō, like many others in the
village who had endured years of economic hardship and privation accompanying the war, decided that the time had come for them to rebuild
their house. Although they were still living on very restricted means,
Toshié and Hideshirō managed to find the resources between 1960 and

1962 to rebuild completely. The differences between the old home and the new were startling. While the old house had nothing but rush mats scattered on the floor, the new house was floored throughout with tatami. Living on tatami had been unthinkable to Toshié just a few years earlier. The wooden bathtub in the kitchen was replaced by a proper bathroom, with tiled floor and a gas-fired metal tub. The homemade toilet with a container underneath for collecting precious manure was replaced by a porcelain flush toilet. There was also a men's urinal. In both cases, the toilets flushed into a holding tank that was emptied periodically by a truck sent by the village—sewage lines would not come to Kosugi for several more decades. But the days of collecting ordure for use in the fields were forever gone. The old roof of gray cement tiles was replaced by a fine, glazed tile roof. And the new kitchen was equipped with a gas stove, an aluminum sink with running water, and vinyl flooring. Moreover, as soon as the house was erected, Toshié and Hideshirō invested in an electric washing machine and a black and white television.

The house was not all built at once. The builder, from Niigata, was a cousin of Toshié's, and he worked with them to build only what they could afford. For several years, they lived without proper walls or ceilings. Nor did her cousin insist on full payment up-front. So long as they came up with the money for building materials, he was happy to wait for payment of his fee. But the basic house structure, plus initial equipment, cost them in the range of one million yen (twenty-eight hundred dollars at the then-prevailing rate of exchange), including ¥260,000 for wood.

Ever since the immediate postwar years, Toshié kept a careful accounting of her daily income and expenses, using the *kakeibō* (household account books) provided each year to subscribers of the farmers' magazine *Ie no Hikari*. Many of these have since disappeared, including those from the crucial years 1960–61. But Toshié's account books from 1962–64 survive, and from these it is possible to construct a detailed picture of her household economy.

The family's income as recorded in the account books came from farming and day labor, with the much larger amount coming from the latter. In 1962, Toshié and Hideshirō's combined income from day labor was ¥263,000 (an average twenty-two thousand yen per month). Farm income was seventy-seven thousand yen, but against this must be set the direct expenses of farming activities, which amounted to seventy-eight thousand yen. Farming did not therefore contribute directly to the cash economy of the household, although it did probably provide rice and vegetables for the family for much of the year. The picture for 1963 is

similar: laboring income of ¥318,000 (¥26,500 per month), with farming more or less at break-even. Not included in these income figures are
the pensions for Toshié's dead brothers, which were kept by Toshié's
mother, who at age seventy-four was still living with the family. Although
this was clearly delineated as the mother's income and not Toshié's, Tsugino was willing to make the accumulated savings available for the purpose of rebuilding. The income amounted to around ¥120,000 per year.

Against this income must be set the expenses of the family. Apart
from building and farming expenses, these totaled ¥238,000 (twenty
thousand yen a month) in 1962 and ¥267,000 (twenty-two thousand
yen a month) in 1963. The surplus excluding pensions was thus slim indeed: twenty-four thousand yen for the entire year in 1962, and fifty-
one thousand yen in 1963. However, of this amount, Toshié was placing forty-eight thousand yen per year in a long-term insurance plan, as
well as contributing twenty-seven thousand yen in 1962 and thirteen
thousand yen in 1963 to a savings plan. Pension money aside, the
Sakaue household was running a negative cash flow in 1962 and 1963,
and indeed this seems actually to have been the case, as both years saw
substantial withdrawals from savings (eighty-four thousand yen in 1962
and ¥166,000 in 1963).

From month to month, the household finances appear to have been
quite unstable. In some months, the labor gang that they worked for did
not pay them (payment was usually made up in the following month).
In others, there were substantial irregular expenses that could not be
covered from ordinary income—for example, in October 1962 Toshié
paid thirty-two thousand yen for farm help, with no farm income to
compensate. At times like these, Toshié resorted to a time-honored ex-
pedient: she borrowed from her neighbors and family members. During
the two years, Toshié borrowed money on six separate occasions. The
amounts ranged from one thousand to thirty-five thousand yen. In addition, Toshié paid off debt during the two years totaling ¥109,000 more
than she borrowed—indicating that during previous years she had accumulated an even higher level of debt.

All of this indicates a family that was barely managing to make ends
meet. Toshié did pay some construction expenses during the period,
but only a total of thirty-four thousand yen. The key to building the
new house, then, does not lie in the family economy as shown in the account books. It must, rather, lie in the pensions that Toshié's mother was
receiving.

Toshié herself affirms that the pensions were crucial to being able to

Figure 14. Toshié's house, late 1990s (Photo by the author)

afford the new house (other important factors were the builder's willingness to defer payment and the family's willingness to delay completion
of the details of the house until their finances were replenished). Toshié
recalls that the family spent everything they had saved from the pensions
(although those savings had been depleted by Kiyomi's hospitalization
expenses), and that Hideshirō worked heroically to make the additional
cash needed to make key payments, such as that for the wood.

The house faced its gravest threat just weeks after its structure went
up. In 1961, a massive typhoon swept down the Japan Sea coast, bringing winds of 120 miles per hour to Kosugi. Toshié remembers it as the
most terrifying day of her life, worse even than the air raids at the end
of the war. The new house creaked and groaned in the fiercely violent
winds. Pillars that had been nailed together just days before now bent
and swayed in the storm. Terrified for their lives, Toshié and her family
fled to the school building across the street. But they were luckier than
some: their new house survived the storm unscathed.

The family that moved into the new house was almost as big as Toshié's
family had been at the peak in the years before World War II. Toshié and
her husband lived with their adopted daughter, Keiko, their natural
daughter, Ayako, Toshié's mother, Tsugino, and Toshié's sister, Kiyomi.

Kiyomi had come home in early 1961, as Toshié and Hideshirō acknowledged that they could not continue paying for her hospitalization and finance the new house. For the next twelve years, Kiyomi continued to be a daily worry for the family. It was during these years that Kiyomi got into some of her most notorious scrapes, seriously threatening at times the family's position in the village. Worst of all was the time when Kiyomi started a fire in the garden of one of the prominent houses in the village, threatening to burn the entire house down. Luckily, the owners quickly saw the blaze and were able to put it out, but from that time on, Kiyomi was generally acknowledged to be a menace to the village. Kiyomi was also a threat to the stability of the family at times. The only people who could manage her were Toshié and her mother. Kiyomi was abusive to Hideshirō, never accepting him in spite of her living with him for more than twenty years.

By the mid-1960s, Toshié and Hideshirō had gained many of the trapping of the consumer lifestyle: a brand new house, a television, a flush toilet, a washing machine, and many other unaccustomed comforts. But the realities that had characterized Toshié's life since her childhood—hard work, manual labor, limited cash, and unyielding soil—continued unchanged. Indeed, the cost of the expensive purchases made by Toshié's family at the beginning of the 1960s ensured that she and Hideshirō had to work as hard as they possibly could. Because Toshié's landholdings were so small, she was among the last to benefit from another great wave of change that affected rural life: farm mechanization.

Beginning in 1957, the arrival of mechanized farming was as rapid and startling as the rural consumer boom a year or two later. In 1950, total production in Japan of motorized cultivators—the product that was to define mechanized farming through the 1960s—was less than three thousand per year; by 1962, 484,000 cultivators were being manufactured.[24] In 1955, one farming family in one hundred owned a cultivator; but by 1960 the ratio had climbed to one in seven, and by 1965 it was one in two.[25]

The arrival of mechanized farming depended on both economic and technological factors. Until the early 1950s, there was no inexpensive, lightweight cultivator on the market. Japanese companies had been making motorized farm equipment for some thirty years. But until the end of World War II, the industry was highly localized, centered on a few small manufacturers, primarily in Okayama prefecture. This was a prosperous rural area, and the manufacturers were catering mainly to local demand, much of it from landlords. The total market penetration by the

1930s was in the hundreds rather than thousands of machines. Prewar machines tended to be very bulky, complex, and expensive—at around two thousand yen (equivalent to about five hundred thousand in 1955 money), the prices far exceeded the incomes of all but a tiny fraction of farmers.

The farm machinery industry underwent drastic change in the early postwar years. In a literal exercise in turning swords into plowshares, several munitions manufacturers turned to agricultural equipment in an attempt to diversify out of an industry in which demand had dropped to zero overnight. Although in their desperation munitions companies turned to all sorts of exotic activities (manufacturing frying pans, for example), agricultural tools were an attractive market because many farmers were beneficiaries both of the postwar food shortage and of the land reform, and they used their windfall gains to purchase much-desired equipment that had been unavailable during wartime. The first implement to boom was a motorized thresher, which quickly reached the one million mark.[26] The result was to bring powerful new competitors, such as steel manufacturer Kubota and industrial giant Mitsubishi Heavy Industries, onto the scene. The new giants entered the market with experimental power cultivators, but their machines continued to be bulky and expensive, until they were exposed to the powerful stimulus of foreign competition. This came in the form of a product called the Merry Tiller, which took the Japanese market by storm starting in 1953.

The Merry Tiller was a lightweight and simple-function machine manufactured by the American company MacKissic. Similar in appearance to a walking lawnmower, the tiller had one front wheel and a pair of handlebars on which clutch and accelerator were mounted. The company introduced the machine into the Japanese market in 1953, and it was an instant success. The advantages of the Merry Tiller were its moderate price and its light weight: thirty-eight kilograms, compared to sixty for the lightest Japanese model.[27] The Merry Tiller was a small, practical, hand-pushed implement that could be hitched to a plow or used to carry loads. It was adapted for sale in Japan with an attachment to use the current ox-drawn plows. Although it could not handle very heavy burdens (such as, for example, plowing a sodden rice field), it was useful for a variety of other applications, including field maintenance, and plowing of dry fields. Probably its main attraction, though, was the price; at between eighty thousand and one hundred thousand yen, it was substantially cheaper than either the Japanese machines on the market or than imported tractors. The Merry Tiller was an instant hit, and provided the major stimulus to local manufacturers to produce competing products.

Japanese manufacturers were quick to reverse-engineer the Merry Tiller, and to provide lighter-weight products of their own. By 1957, the Merry Tiller had been relegated to minor player status, while Kubota, Iseki, Yanmar, and Mitsubishi dominated the market. From this point on, Japanese companies took the lead in innovation for the unique conditions of the Japanese market. Japan was among the first wet-rice producing countries to industrialize, so Japanese companies were forced into a pioneering position in the development of appropriate cultivators, rice transplanters, and combine harvesters.

Japanese manufacturers first turned their attention to producing a cultivator with the light weight and low price of the Merry Tiller, but suitable for rice paddies. The challenge was to produce wheels that would not stick in the mud and a blade that could turn the sodden earth of a flooded rice field. The motor also had to be protected from water damage, as the machine would operate in fields with up to a foot of standing water. Kubota launched its first model meeting these specifications in 1957, and the wet-rice cultivator became the standard type of cultivator by the end of the decade.[28]

The development of less expensive, lightweight cultivators suitable for paddy fields made them extremely attractive to Japanese farmers. But at roughly one hundred thousand yen (plus various attachments that could easily double the price), a cultivator was no small investment for a farmer. Total agricultural income for the median 0.5- to 1.0-hectare farmer in 1959 was ¥184,000. A cultivator for a farmer in this range therefore cost between six and twelve months' agricultural earnings. Not surprisingly, the earlier buyers of cultivators tended to be those with larger holdings—typically, farmers with two hectares or more, many of whom had gained their land through the land reform. In addition, some farmers with smaller holdings justified their purchases on the grounds that they could repay some of the cost by hiring out their services to farmers who did not yet have cultivators. A number of farmers contributed "success stories" of this nature in the pages of *Mechanized Farming (Kikaika nōgyō)*.[29]

In fact, the principle of some form of communal use dominated discussion and purchases of motorized cultivators in the early years. In 1960, for example, only 21 percent of farmers using cultivators owned their own machines. Nine percent were communally owned, while 61 percent hired a cultivator and associated labor.[30] Since a cultivator was typically used only a few weeks of the year, notably at plowing time, some form of communal use seems an eminently sensible idea. But as it turned out, the focus on communal use was short lived. By 1967, communal ownership had declined to 6 percent while personal ownership had grown to 55 percent. By 1970, essentially all farmers with holdings over 0.5 hectares owned their own cultivators.[31] The trend away from communal use was to continue even as farmers invested in much more expensive machinery such as mechanical rice transplanters and combine harvesters.

This movement away from communal ownership even as the economics of farming went from bad to worse is ironic and needs some explanation. It seems that for some decades, everyone had agreed in theory that communalization of tasks such as plowing, planting, cooking, and child care were desirable, both from the point of view of "rationality" and for the preservation of the spirit of communalism that was held by many to be the essence of Japanese rural tradition. Communal activities were a frequent theme in discussions of "lifestyle improvement" from the 1920s right through to the 1960s. And, faced with severe labor shortages during World War II, many hamlets did in fact implement communal plowing, cooking, and day care. This was, of course, on top of a variety of activities that had always been communal: notably rice transplanting, roof raising, thatching, fire fighting, and irrigation. It was not without justification that analysts referred to the *kyōdōtai* (gemeinschaft) nature of the Japanese village. Sentimentalists—who were in the mainstream during the era of fascist influence in the 1930s—extolled this spirit as one that should be extended to the entire nation.

But in the postwar period, both older and more recent communal activities quite rapidly disappeared. Communal thatching went out together with the use of thatched roofs, roughly in the mid-1950s. Communal rice transplanting lasted a little longer, until done away with by the arrival of mechanical rice transplanters in 1970. Communal cooking does not seem to have survived beyond the immediate postwar years. Fire fighting and day care survived, but they were integrated into the bureaucratic village administration. Other popular ideas, such as communal laundry, never caught on at all, it seems.

Underlying these piecemeal retreats from communal activity was the more fundamental breakdown of the extremely delicate and sensitive system of mutual ties and obligations that prevailed in the prewar Japanese hamlets. This system was based on relatively fine gradations of wealth and patronage and might involve the ties between branch and main family, between patron and client (either in the present generation or in

some prior generation), or between neighbors. The degree of cooperation expected, and the compensation provided (whether cash, entertainment, or the promise of future reciprocity), depended on the nature and
grade of those ties. Those ties—and particularly the issue of compensation—were delicate and problematic at best, and the postwar social and
economic order placed much of the system on its head. The land reform
placed tenants on an economic par with their former landlords; the availability of outside jobs made patron-client relations irrelevant; and the
declining importance of land as a measure of wealth tended to weaken
branch-family/main-family ties. Moreover, the ideology of the postwar
era strongly favored individual equality, individual pride—and individual consumption.

The ideology of individual consumption was undoubtedly promoted
by manufacturers, whether of farm machinery or of consumer goods
(television broadcasting had been launched in 1953 based on the prem-
ise that most watching would be communal, but that idea, too, did not
last).[32] The unit of consumption on which advertising invariably focused
was the family: advertisements from the late 1950s, for example, tend to
dwell on images of happy, Western-dressed young farm wives pushing
their mechanical cultivators, presumably while their men folk are out at
work earning salaries. But it seems that farm families did not need much
convincing about the disadvantages of communal ownership. Memories
of the delicate and time-consuming task of maintaining the prewar network of mutual ties were evidently enough to put many off.[33] In addition, a host of new problems emerged with the early experiments in
communal use or hiring of farm machinery. The most common issue was
availability of the machinery. Most farmers tend to plow and harvest at
roughly the same time; thus, even if a machine were only used for one
week a year, all the farmers would want the machine in the same week.
Another problem was maintenance: Who would be responsible, and how
would the group react if one coowner damaged the machine? Another
was operation: Should the group have only one (highly skilled) operator,
or should all be free to operate the machine (in which case there was
a risk of damage by unskilled operators). How would the operator be
compensated? Between them, these issues were enough to persuade most
farmers that they should buy their own machine if they could possibly
afford it. Paradoxically, the worry that communal ownership might lead
to conflict and damage the harmony of the community led many into the
culture of individual consumption.[34]

Perhaps even more than its use in plowing and tilling, farmers valued the cultivator for its use in hauling. Carrying, particularly carrying crops from the often-distant fields, was the greatest physical burden that farmers faced. Most cultivators permitted a hook-up to a trailer, which allowed the farmer to walk or even ride while the cultivator did the work of hauling. The narrow streets of the village, which heretofore had seldom had to accommodate more than a bicycle, now hummed with the progress of slow-moving cultivators carrying the morning's haul back to the work shed. Moreover, once they understood the convenience of these vehicles, farmers began using them to go further afield—to carry vegetables to the market to sell, or to the farm supply shop to buy fertilizer, or even to take the whole family to the cinema. The sudden spread of these vehicles caused unanticipated problems. Most farmers had never driven anything but a bicycle or a horse or ox in their lives before. They were unaccustomed to the complexities of gears, accelerators, and steering mechanisms. The number of accidents on rural lanes suddenly shot up, and it was not long before the police took note of the fact that cultivators used in this way fell within the category of wheeled motor vehicles. Farmers would have to get drivers' licenses. The situation remained ambiguous for some time, as farmers resisted being drawn into the network of rules and regulations governing roads and safety. But slowly the police became firmer in their insistence on properly licensing operators of cultivators or tractors that were used on the roads.[35]

By the end of the 1960s, Japanese farm equipment makers had their sights set on some much more glamorous products than the workaday cultivator. By 1970, they were ready to launch two of the holy grails of Japanese agricultural mechanization: mechanical rice transplanters and paddy field combine harvesters. Each of these had exercised the maker's ingenuity and originality to the full. Indeed, their stories make an excellent rebuttal to the often-repeated observation that Japanese companies in the 1960s were imitative, not innovative. For example, the rice transplanter had to be capable of taking the tiny, delicate shoots grown in seed beds in a warm part of the hamlet and inserting them one at a time in the paddy without breaking or mangling them. Italian engineers had succeeded in making a machine that did an excellent job of planting the shoots—but they had to be carefully inserted one at a time into a magazine. It was said that the Italian machine needed three people to operate and fifty to work behind the scenes preparing the magazines. The Japanese solution was to plant rice seeds in a special box, which, once the seeds had germinated, could be placed directly onto a tray mounted on the rice transplanter. The boxes were designed so that the transplanter could extract one shoot at a time and place it in the ground.[36] The combine harvester overcame problems of traction in wet rice fields—it used a caterpillar track—and of top-heavy rice stalks, which tended to bend or flatten in rough weather (the combine featured a scoop to straighten stalks before cutting them).

These pieces of equipment were far more expensive than the (now) humble cultivator. A rice transplanter cost from two hundred thousand yen and up in the early 1970s, while a combine harvester started at six hundred thousand.[37] Yet penetration of transplanters and combines was even more rapid than that of cultivators. And farmers also bought a variety of other lesser (some, such as riding tractors, not so lesser) pieces of machinery. As a result of these purchases, by 1975 Japan was the most heavily mechanized farming nation in the world. To take one example, in 1978, Japanese tractor horsepower per hectare was twelve times the U.S. level, six times that of Britain, and double that of West Germany.[38]

But in the process, Japanese farming also became the most inefficient among the world's industrialized nations. Rice, for example, sold in 1998 for thirteen times the price in Japan compared to the United States, although Japanese farmers still lost money growing it.[39] At the same time, farmers have labored under an increasing burden of debt, needed to pay for the increasingly expensive machinery they have purchased. The debt service cost for an average farm family with 0.5 to 1.0 hectare rose from ¥2,430 in 1959 to ¥28,200 in 1969.[40] The heavy indebtedness of many farm households has led to the "theory of mechanized poverty," which is now recognized as an integral part of the postwar farming "crisis"— a crisis that has dominated discussion of postwar Japanese agriculture even though virtually all of the problems that defined the prewar farm "crisis" (notably poverty, overpopulation, and an excessive burden of labor) have been resolved.

Toshié, too, benefited from mechanization, although not through the direct purchase of expensive machinery. At 0.4 hectares, Toshié's holdings were too marginal to justify such purchases (even applying the contorted logic used by the promoters of mechanization)—and the family was already as stretched as it could go financially. Hideshirō invested in a small motorcycle, which he was then able to hook up to a trailer, relieving him of much of the heavy burden of hauling. That in itself was a major saving of labor. Toshié continued to do much of her farm labor by hand. But from the mid-1960s, she began paying a neighbor to do the plowing for her with his mechanical cultivator, and from this point on she relied increasingly on machinery and hired help to relieve herself of the heavier burdens of farm labor. Toshié's accounts from the beginning of the 1960s make it abundantly clear that she was not farming for profit. Her farm provided her with rice and vegetables for the year, which must have been a significant contribution to her household economy; but on a cash basis, the operation barely broke even. However, the steep increases in the price of rice during the 1960s—the result of government support—placed a small surplus in Toshié's hands, and she used this to relieve the burden of her and Hideshirō's labor by hiring help with her farm.

By the early 1960s, the road on top of the levee above Toshié's house began to sound very different from before. The prefecture metaled the surface in 1960, and the volume of motorcycles, automobiles, trucks, and buses steadily increased. By 1965, more than half of Japan's farm families owned motor scooters, and from that point on they increasingly began investing in automobiles and light trucks. Rural ownership of convenience goods tended to lag behind the cities, but ownership of cars outpaced urban Japan from the start. Meanwhile the cows that had previously been driven up the road hauling loads on trailers disappeared, as did the frames of vegetables and rice left to dry on the side of the road. When the larger trucks went by they made the ground shake as if a minor earthquake was shaking the house. One day near the end of the 1960s, it suddenly came to Toshié that the noise of passing traffic on the road had become constant, a new background sound in her life that showed no sign of fading away. Nor was it only farm equipment and trucks that changed the way that the village sounded. Machinery of all sorts increasingly came to define the sounds of village life: from electric equipment for the host of side occupations that farm families undertook in addition to their agricultural work, to stereos blaring out the sounds of Western and Japanese pop music, to the village broadcasting system that transmitted morning music to every house in the hamlet at eight o'clock sharp.

Meanwhile, the animals that had been quiet companions of many Kosugi families gradually disappeared. Almost all families had kept a few hens, generally in order to sell the eggs. But rising incomes, combined with the spread of mass-production chicken farms, made the hens more trouble than they were worth. Goats, too, were no longer needed for their milk, which could much more easily be purchased in the grocery store. And draft animals—cows and horses—were rapidly made redundant by the arrival of farm machinery. Those who owned cows (Toshié never did) had treated them as part of the family—in many cases, the animals lived in stalls inside the family home. But now that their economic value had declined, farm families were glad to be rid of the animals, which needed care and attention and attracted flies and dirt into the house. The population of farm animals (excluding specialized rearing operations, which experienced strong growth) declined precipitously from the late 1950s. Between 1955 and 1965, almost two million cows ceased to exist—a population decline of 63 percent. The attrition in the goat population was even more extreme, with the population falling from 650,000 to a mere twenty thousand.[41]

The smells of the village also changed. Gone was the pervasive odor of manure, hoarded and guarded by each family and spread lovingly on the fields after being carried through the village lanes. With growing prosperity, chemical fertilizers came within the reach of most families; they built new toilets with flush mechanisms, sending down the drain material that had previously been carefully conserved. Gradually, the dense smells of wood smoke, sent up in a haze by every house in the village before the morning and evening meals, disappeared as charcoal or paraffin burning heaters replaced wood-burning *kamado* stoves. And the rich smells of home preserved food—powerful-smelling pickled daikon, fomenting *miso,* and boiling soy sauce—were slowly replaced with new smells: frying meat, curry, and yeast.

Of course, the appearance of the village changed too. Thatched roofs disappeared at such a pace that within a few years there were no more than a dozen or two left in the hamlet. In their place, bold roofs of ornamented red, ochre, and blue tiles adorned the new houses that were being built all around the village. There were fewer people out in the village lanes, now, as more and more went by motorcycle, automobile, or tractor-cart. The children no longer played in the grounds of the temple—nowadays they bicycled into the larger hamlet of Yokogoshi where they went shopping, read magazines in the bookstore, or visited their friends' homes to listen to their stereos. As a result, the temple looked increasingly cold and forlorn.

Forlorn, indeed, was the state of much of rural Japan as the industrial boom of the 1960s drained villages of manpower, or swallowed them up in encroaching industrial suburbs. Economic growth brought opportunity, but it also spelled decline and even dissolution for areas of society that were unable to keep up with it. In parts of Japan during the 1960s, the rural population began abandoning the villages at an alarming rate. The problem was most severe in the mountain villages, which found

their populations inexorably declining even as the booming cities became global watchwords for overcrowding. The residents of mountain
villages were hit in a variety of ways by changing economic circumstances. First, they tended to be far from urban or industrial areas, making it impossible for the residents of many mountain villages to commute
to factory or office jobs while managing their farm on the weekends—
as more and more of those who lived closer to cities were doing. Since
this combination of factory or office work and weekend farming was the
most common strategy for farm families to survive and even prosper,
mountain villages were at a major disadvantage. In addition, the traditional activities of the residents of mountain villages—forestry, charcoal
manufacture, and the cultivation of grain crops such as wheat and barley—were all hit to a greater or lesser degree by the consequences of
rapid economic growth. Charcoal, for example, was almost totally replaced by kerosene as a heating fuel within the space of just a few years;
Japan's total consumption of charcoal dropped from 2.2 million tons in
1957 to just sixty thousand tons in 1979.[42] Wheat and other nonrice
grains, though seldom grown as cash crops and never very profitable in
the first place, were hit hard by the government's policy of large-scale
importation of cheap American grains. And forestry, in spite of extraordinary growth in demand, was also a victim of large-scale, cheap foreign
imports. However, urban labor markets beckoned with ever greater demand for unskilled labor. From the mid-1950s, rapidly growing elec-
tronics and textile companies began snapping up female middle school
graduates, recruiting them even before they finished their schooling. By
the 1960s, demand was so intense that recruiters and their agents were
scouring the countryside for any available hands. The perennial problem of rural overpopulation—cited by many as one of the justifications
for Japan's entry into World War II—suddenly reversed itself, as second
and third sons, daughters, and eventually whole families joined the exodus to the booming cities.

In 1970 the government, recognizing the problem of exodus from
mountain villages, passed the Mountain Village Promotion Law, which
identified 776 distressed villages—those that had lost more than 10 percent of their population in the past ten years. In three prefectures—Shi-
mane, Ōita, and Kōchi—more than 60 percent of towns and villages
qualified.[43] Many villages looked to tourism as a potential savior from
the problems of declining agricultural profitability and declining village
population. High economic growth brought a surge in domestic tourism, which grew from ¥1.2 trillion in 1963 (fifty-six thousand yen per

family) to ¥3.8 trillion by 1980 (¥112,000 per family).[44] Increasing urbanization brought with it a new wave of nostalgia for the countryside and a desire for rural space for leisure pursuits such as skiing, tennis and fishing. But tourism is a notoriously difficult business. Tourists must not only visit, they must also spend. In spite of the huge outflow of urbanites on weekends and holidays, only a relatively few rural communities have succeeded in exploiting tourism as a major economic lifesaver. These include the ski resorts within reach of major cities, famed scenic or historical sites such as the area round Mount Fuji, and, more recently, specially developed rural theme parks.

At the other extreme, villages close to major cities or to designated industrial areas found themselves becoming rapidly engulfed by industrial development and suburbanization. Edward Norbeck, an American anthropologist, visited the island village of Takashima in 1950 and reveled in the sheer beauty of its landscape in the island-studded Inland Sea. "There are too many picturesque islands," he wrote. "No such tranquil sea could exist. It is a Japanese painting."[45] When he returned to Takashima in 1970, after it had been absorbed into the new Mizushima industrial complex, he was appalled at the changes he saw:

> Before me stretched a maze of industrial plants, all gray and looking grimly functional. A haze of smoke filled the air and extended to the horizon in all directions. . . . Only the nearest of Takashima's neighboring islands were visible, dimly, in the haze. After some moments of inspection, I recognized Takashima as a hilly eminence arising from a sea of industrial plants where once a genuine sea had existed. . . . The small pines that remained stood in ragged, small patches or in isolation amidst low vegetation, the red-brown needles of many of the trees announcing sickness or coming death. A long procession of large tankers and freighters was visible in the sea at both ends of Takashima, sailing in nearly single file in opposing directions.[46]

Through a mixture of policy and circumstance, Yokogoshi avoided both the extremes of depopulation and excessive urbanization. A number of factors contributed to this stability. First, Yokogoshi was a rice farming community, and, thanks to government support, rice farming remained economically viable. Thanks to the size of many pre–land reform tenant holdings, landholdings in Yokogoshi tended to be larger than average, enabling the majority of farm households to remain farmers, even if they increasingly supplemented their incomes with other activities.[47] Overall, the number of farm families in Yokogoshi (including part-time farmers) declined from 1,054 in 1960 to 963 in 1970, a much smaller decline than in many other communities.[48] Farmers did diversify their farm activities to cater to the demands of a more affluent market. Although rice farming remained the principal business of Yokogoshi farmers (remaining above 50 percent of all farm income), pig rearing began growing rapidly as a secondary occupation. The number of pigs on Yokogoshi farms increased from 485 in 1970 to 5,650 in 1980, by which time pig farming accounted for 13 percent of agricultural income. On a smaller scale, dairy farming (7 percent of agricultural income by 1980), pear orchards (5 percent), and tulips (2 percent) also became important secondary farming activities.[49]

Second, Yokogoshi was only ten miles from a fast-growing urban center, the city of Niigata. With the improvements in communications, residents of Yokogoshi were increasingly able to access the Niigata market for sales and, more important, employment. Since nonfarm employment was increasingly to become the dominant factor in farm family finances, this was a vital factor enabling families to remain on their farms. The number of full-time farm families declined from 511 in 1960 to only 123 in 1970. By 1980, there were only ninety-eight full-time farm families, and more than half of the village's farm families reported that their non-farm employment income exceeded income from farming. Of twenty-eight hundred Yokogoshi residents who worked outside their homes in 1975, 1,240 worked in Niigata, while another 662 worked in the neighboring towns of Niitsu and Kameda.[50]

Third, even as younger sons and daughters left the farm to take up more attractive opportunities in Niigata or further afield, Yokogoshi selectively opened itself up to settlement by nonfarming commuters, most of whom worked in Niigata. The population of Yokogoshi declined during the first two postwar decades—from a high of 9,700 in 1950 to a low of 8,100 by 1970. But the number of households actually grew slightly, indicating that much of the population loss was due to the declining birthrate and the emigration to the cities of younger sons and daughters. From 1974, the decline in population actually reversed itself, as more and more newcomers came to live in Yokogoshi (in 1995, Yokogoshi's population was 10,009).[51] The village authorities designated a part of the central hamlet of Yokogoshi for "new town" development.

Fourth, Yokogoshi took a conservative stance with regard to opening up rural land to urban development. Rural land was protected from development by a battery of national laws, many of them originally designed to protect the gains of tenant farmers in the land reform. Opening up land to urban-style development required an extensive application and approval process. But the village of Yokogoshi wanted to focus on agriculture as a matter of policy, and thus it willingly complied with the restrictions. The majority of the land in Yokogoshi remained restricted to rural uses. Most of the population growth in Yokogoshi was concentrated in what is now the town center. Kosugi (which has remained a "pure" farming community, though its residents have shared in the advantages of ready communication with Niigata) remained stable in terms of number of households, while declining slightly in absolute numbers.

Toshié's life of hard physical labor came to an abrupt end one winter day in 1965, when the truck carrying Toshié, Hideshirō, and several others to a work site slipped in the snow and collided head on with another truck headed in the other direction. Luckily, none of the occupants was seriously injured, but Toshié received a nasty head wound that required a dozen stitches. The doctor, an unsympathetic type, shaved off half of Toshié's hair before applying the stitches, and what with the pain (she had headaches for weeks after the accident) and the shame of her appearance (Toshié bought a wig to hide it), she stayed away from work for the next several weeks. She ended up never going back. At forty years old, she was finding the effort of manual labor more and more taxing, and, with the house largely paid for, the family's economic burdens were no longer so daunting. Tsugino, now seventy-nine, was lonely and increasingly in need of care. Toshié went to work part-time making school lunches for the elementary school across the road, but after a couple of years the school decided to hire a permanent cooking staff (they offered Toshié the job, but she declined), and from that time on, Toshié never went back out to work, although she remained busy taking in piecework, which she continued to do at home until the 1990s. For seven years, Toshié spent five to eight hours a day winding thread onto spools for a textile company. When she was not busy with piecework, Toshié had to take care of the remaining family fields. She continued to get up at four in the morning to make the fullest use of the day until, in 1979, she followed a path increasingly being taken by those either too small or too busy to deal with the chores of farming: she hired a professional to work her rice fields for her. He is a neighboring farmer, well equipped with machinery that leaves him with spare time from his own fields. Toshié pays him in cash, twice yearly, for working her fields. Today, Toshié continues to cultivate a vegetable field (0.1 hectare) that provides food, gifts, and a little income for her family. Of the thirteen hundred kilograms that her rice fields produce, she is able to sell some 250 kilograms after paying the farmer who works her fields and meeting her own needs.

In 1967, a rope-making company in Niigata for which Hideshirō had

been working on and off as a day laborer offered him a full-time job, with
benefits. Jobs were plentiful at the time. The Niigata earthquake of 1964,
which left twenty-seven dead, combined with the prolonged economic
boom sweeping the whole country, making labor scarce and able-bodied
men in high demand. In spite of his middle age and his lack of skills, Hideshirō found secure employment until he reached the company's official retirement age of fifty-five, in 1981. On his retirement, he was able to
claim a company pension—a considerable improvement on the standard
national pension and a major contribution to the security of the family
for the following decades. Even then, Hideshirō did not stop working.
He found a job in an auto parts company for three years, and then, in
1984, he was taken on by the Northern Culture Museum (the former
home of the Itō family) as night watchman. The work is part time—only
two nights a week. Hideshirō leaves at 4:30 P.M. and returns at nine the
next morning. Much of the time he is able to sleep on a portable bed in
the museum office. He continues to work at the museum today.

In 1963, a group of Toshié's friends decided to form a travel club.
They made regular contributions and met once a month to discuss plans
and enjoy each other's company. In 1964 they made their first trip, to
Atami, a hot spring near Tokyo. The money for that first trip seemed
a needless extravagance, and Hideshirō was opposed to it. But Toshié's
mother encouraged her and promised to help from the pension money
she received. She said that she wanted Toshié to enjoy the pleasures in
life that she could never have. The pension money, indeed, continued to
provide the funds for nonessential and consumer purchases until Tsugino's death in 1979, at the age of ninety-three. The pension died with Tsugino, but her long life assured the family that her sons' legacy was used
to the full. Since that first trip, Toshié has traveled with her group every
year. In the earlier years, the trips tended to be closer to home, but in recent years they have branched further afield, traveling to Okinawa most
recently. They have never ventured abroad, however, probably from lack
of confidence more than from financial reasons.

In 1973, Toshié was finally able to put her sister into permanent care.
After Kiyomi had proved that she was a real threat to the security of the
hamlet, Toshié persuaded the village authorities to cooperate with her in
preparing an application for welfare relief. She was helped by major ex-
tensions in the Japanese social welfare program that extended medical
benefits to hospitalization. Kiyomi went into the Niitsu mental hospital,
where she was cared for at state expense until her death in 1993 at the
age of seventy-six. Although Toshié visited her regularly, she believes that

Figure 15. Toshié at age 75 (Photo by the author)

Kiyomi was happier at the hospital than at home, and that her previous life with Toshié's family became increasingly remote to her.

Toshié has come full circle from her family's early days as poor tenant farmers at the bottom end of the village social scale. As one of the senior residents of the hamlet—and a survivor of the long chain of depredations on the hamlet society, including the war, the lure of factory jobs, and the difficulties of making a living in a small rural community—Toshié enjoys a position of quiet authority in Kosugi today. In recent years, she has been able to enjoy to the full the benefits of her commitment to the hamlet: her large and relatively comfortable home (much larger and better appointed than the homes of urban workers of equivalent social status); a caring local community and substantial financial support from the state; and, above all, the company of friends who have been by her side through all of the trials and tribulations of the past seventy years. In spite of the hardships she has endured, Toshié believes the blessings of her life outweigh the suffering. Her biggest worry today is the future of the Sakaue family. For generations, the Sakaue were able to preserve their name and their home in Kosugi in the face of the constant challenges of poverty and infertility. Now, in the midst of relative affluence, those assets are at risk. With the birth of Ayako, Toshié's adopted daughter Keiko was relegated to subordinate status in the succession order. Keiko married shortly after leaving middle school and was a grandmother while still in her mid-forties. Ayako went out to work in the neighboring town of Kameda after graduating from high school, and has been with the same company ever since. Ayako chose her own husband. Toshié did her best to help find a marriage partner for her daughter, arranging countless introductions *(omiai)*. None of them worked out. Finally, Ayako met her husband through a dating service, and the two are happily married. Ayako's husband agreed to be adopted as a *muko,* so the future of the Sakaue family name, at least, is assured. The couple have two small children, who attend the Kosugi day care center so that Toshié can pick them up in the afternoon and take care of them until Ayako fetches them after work. But Ayako does not live in Kosugi. Although Toshié and Hideshirō invested a large amount of money during the 1980s in rebuilding the work shed into a substantial house with a garage/work shed on the ground floor, Ayako has never lived on the second floor as Toshié intended. Instead, she and her husband rent an apartment in Kameda, where they can more readily enjoy the conveniences of urban life. Toshié wonders if her daughter will ever come back to Kosugi to take on the responsibilities of the land, the family home, and the graves of the Sakaue ancestors.

Conclusion

The story of Toshié's life resonates in many compelling ways with larger narratives of Japan's twentieth century, as told in countless popular history books, television documentaries, and life histories. Toshié was born in the first year of the Showa era—the year of accession of the emperor Hirohito. Popular histories tend to divide this long reign into two distinct halves—the first including the war years, and the second beginning in the late 1940s and progressing through successive phases of consumer well-being to the emperor's death in the boom years of the 1980s. As Carol Gluck has analyzed these accounts, the years to 1945 are generally portrayed in terms of war, the state, militarism, and domestic terrorism: there is "no mistaking the image of prewar Showa as a period of war and darkness." [1] Moreover, many accounts portray the events of these years as driven by a fanatical militarism in which the majority of ordinary Japanese did not participate: in other words, many Japanese people saw themselves as victims of the war, almost as much as the Asian populations against which the Japanese military was engaged. Gluck also points out that the state is an ineluctable presence in the popular histories of the prewar and war years.

By sharp contrast, after an Occupation interregnum—a period that is often portrayed as a preparatory phase for the economic growth and prosperity that followed—popular accounts tend to portray the postwar years in terms of "democracy and prosperity," "peace and world economic power." Gluck points out that the state virtually disappears from accounts of the postwar: "ever-improving livelihood, not the march of politics, provided the story line." Accounts tend to dwell on a progression of consumer items that are seen as emblematic of the recovery and well-being of the Japanese people: the "three sacred treasures" of the 1950s, the "three C's" of the 1960s, the "my car" and "my home" phenomena of the 1970s and 1980s. Indeed, the story of postwar Showa is a "bright" one in which the "light of economic well-being and national pride" shone on a population of whom 95 percent identified themselves as middle class. Not discussed by Gluck, but clearly a part of this story, is the gendered nature of the "bright" postwar life; while the menfolk went to work in the factories and offices of Japan's resurgent corporate machine, women stayed at home as guardians and managers of the consuming household, enjoying increasing leisure as a result of the acquisition of labor-saving household appliances.

In spite of the obvious exaggeration inherent in this "tale of two Showas" (as Gluck points out, "personally, socially, or nationally, history does not begin again"), there is much here that is recognizable in Toshié's story.[2] The first twenty years of Toshié's life fit the stereotyped image of "dark" Showa in a variety of ways. First there was the darkness of poverty and labor. Toshié's family lived in a cold, dark house in a region known for its bitter winters. Even minimal comforts—a pair of rubber boots for the winter, a good book to read on a rainy day, a soft mat to sit on the floor—were denied her. Toshié's parents were forced to work long hours at any employment they could find in order to earn the cash necessary for subsistence. Their own crops were only brought forth with the expenditure of immense amounts of painstaking physical labor. Even then, Toshié's parents were in debt and frequently harassed by creditors. And this stern necessity of work was not limited to the adult members of her family. Toshié was put to work from an early age as babysitter and household helper, and, like her sister and eldest brother, she was sent out to work full-time while still a child. From the age of eighteen, Toshié was again forced out into the workforce, this time as a manual laborer. Toshié was made to work in bitter conditions on the Niigata docks, alongside chain gangs of prisoners of war. Poverty prevented Toshié from getting an education beyond the sixth grade; it prevented her from traveling beyond the confines of the nearest city; and it prevented her from realizing her simple dream of working at a clerical job in nearby Niigata.

Allied to this was the darkness of the social system into which Toshié was born. Born into a tenant family, her life appeared to be permanently separated from the privileged lives of the landlord class. Landlord families belonged for the most part to a hamlet aristocracy that had its origins in the Tokugawa era: a club of families that might shrink as its members experienced economic decline, but that was hard for new members to enter. Tenancy required Toshié's father to give up a large percentage of his crops to the owners of the land that he worked, thus helping perpetuate the unequal economic relations. And the "dark" social system was not only external to Toshié's family. Within the family, too, Toshié was forced to obey the dictates of the family head, even after she reached adulthood. Toshié's parents selected a husband for her, and—as she recounts it—she had no choice but to acquiesce.

Then, special to Toshié's family, but still "dark," was the illness of her sister Kiyomi. Although this was a personal affliction with little apparent relevance to the larger circumstances of village and nation, the dark cloud of mental illness that descended on Kiyomi may well have been linked to the harsh circumstances of her childhood: custom and economic necessity induced her father to send Kiyomi away from her family at the age of ten, to work as a maid. Moreover, once it was apparent that Kiyomi was ill, the family's poverty prevented it from seeking effective treatment for her. The social and economic dictates of the era forced Toshié's family to endure the burdens of care giving, anxiety, and shame that Kiyomi's illness brought, with little hope of relief.

And, last but most extreme, there was the darkness of the war. The war—which for Toshié's family began in 1937 with the outbreak of full-scale war against China—killed Toshié's two precious brothers. It forced the family to give up the majority of its produce to the state in return for unreliable and inadequate rations. It demanded onerous "volunteer" labor and community service of Toshié. And, as the war situation deteriorated, it brought with it the anxiety and fear of bombing and invasion.

As in the popular histories of the "dark" Showa era, the state played a large role in Toshié's early life. Toshié's education was explicitly designed to make a loyal and obedient citizen of her. Her schooling made it clear to her that she was above all else a loyal servant of the emperor; that her duties to her country and family were not a matter of choice but of sacred obligation. The state demanded, and gave the family no choice but to provide, the bodies of Toshié's brothers, the produce of the family smallholding, and any other small surplus of labor or wealth that the family might yield. Indeed, seen from Toshié's perspective, the limits of her choices are striking. Toshié did not choose to be sent to work at twelve. She did not choose to become a manual laborer. However she may have been passively supportive, she did not actively promote the entry of Japan into war. She did not choose to lose her brothers. She did not choose the man she married. Seen in this light, Toshié could well be forgiven for sidestepping all personal responsibility for the war, for the cult of the emperor and imperialism, and for Japan's aggression in Asia.

A visit to Toshié today offers a vivid contrast to this dark picture of involuntary sacrifice, want, and suffering. Toshié is enjoying her retirement in a comfortable and spacious home—far larger than the average urban dwelling—fully equipped with modern conveniences. Although she still works her vegetable fields, she has entrusted much of the work on her small farm to a contract farmer, who pays her a share of the crop—an extraordinary reversal of her early days as a tenant farmer. As a result, she has ample leisure to take care of her grandchildren, to meet with her friends in the hamlet—many of them of more than seventy years' standing—and to share her memories with a visiting researcher. She enjoys frequent outings, including at least one major tourist excursion per year. And she and her husband benefit from government and company pensions and a state-funded medical system that give them a measure of financial and physical security that they could never have expected five decades ago. Compared with the crowded and often overworked lives of Japanese city dwellers, Toshié's spacious and leisurely life surrounded by old friends seems enviable. Toshié does indeed seem to have enjoyed a "bright" postwar.

But a little deeper investigation reveals significant ways in which Toshié's story also departs from the established narrative; and from these deviations and departures we can perhaps gain some insight into the diverse experiences that are often obscured by this "master narrative" of twentieth century Japanese history. First, and perhaps most obvious, is the long period after the end of the war during which Toshié's life remained anything but "bright."

Narratives of rural life often tell of the liberation of the Japanese countryside after the end of the war by the land reform and by the provision of new rights for women. Here, the experiences of Toshié's family seem to depart markedly from the mainstream. The land reform provided Toshié's family with a mere 0.1 hectare of land—not enough to make any significant difference in its household economy. The case of Toshié's family illustrates that the land reform was a lopsided initiative that benefited a subgroup of tenant farmers—those renting large amounts of land—far more than others. For Toshié and her family, the basic reality of marginal land holdings continued unchanged—and indeed the net result of the land reform was that they farmed even less land, since their landlord successfully demanded back some of the land he was renting to them.

Toshié remembers the ten years following defeat as being the hardest of her life. For much of this period, her family continued to be subject to confiscatory requisitions of its hard-grown produce. The loss of manpower with the death of her brothers brought an immense physical as well as emotional cost to Toshié's family members. The entire family continued to suffer from severe financial insecurity, and all able-bodied members had to work at any type of manual labor available in order to make ends meet. The family's living conditions, health care, real income, and community obligations (with the exception of home defense and military support activities) remained little changed from the war era. And the special burden of caring for Kiyomi was as fraught with care and anxiety as ever. Even during the following decade (from 1955 to 1965), conditions can hardly be said to have improved for Toshié. Although now in early middle age, she continued to work at outdoor manual labor jobs, hired on a daily basis and paid a minimal wage of under two dollars a day. In addition to the care of Kiyomi, Toshié also had to worry about the health of her mother, who was in her eighties. When the family decided to take advantage of new mental health facilities and hospitalize Kiyomi, they had to pay the entire cost from their own funds—a sum amounting to almost half of their monthly wages.

Granted, during this second postwar decade Toshié was able to build a new house and equip it with much of the equipment of the new and "bright" consumer age—tatami mats, television set, washing machine, stainless-steel kitchen fixtures, flush toilet, and tiled bathroom—but herein lies another twist on the conventional tale of the postwar "bright" life. For these new appurtenances were only acquired at an enormous cost to Toshié and her husband. Certainly, a large part of the cost of the house was paid for by the pensions of Toshié's dead brothers—a source that could be interpreted as recompense by the state for its implacable demands during the years of war. But in addition to the pension money, the house cost every penny of their savings, and they were only able to finance it by pulling Kiyomi out of the hospital and resuming her daily care, and by both Toshié and Hideshirō working doggedly and unceasingly to earn the cash to buy necessary materials. Although they were able to build the house without borrowing, Toshié resorted to installment plans to purchase her appliances. These costs and obligations had the effect of perpetuating the family's financial insecurity for close to a decade: Toshié had to borrow money on a monthly basis to make ends meet in the early 1960s, as her father had done in the 1930s.

Only from the mid-1960s, with the costs of rebuilding behind them and with Toshié retired from day labor, did her life begin to approximate the "bright" consumer lifestyle portrayed in the popular histories. By this time Toshié and Hideshirō were in their forties—an age when even in the prewar era they might have been thinking about passing on the family headship and the main burden of labor to a younger generation. And even during the following two decades, Hideshirō continued working as a factory laborer, while Toshié spent long hours at work on poorly paid piecework of various kinds. Arguably, it was not until they reached conventional retirement age that Toshié and Hideshirō were able to enjoy some of the leisure and pleasurable consumption that is frequently associated with the postwar era. Like most rural wives, Toshié never fit the stereotyped image of leisured housewife. Until her forties, she worked side by side with her husband as a manual laborer—about as far from housewifely leisure as one can get. Even afterward, Toshié remained a significant labor contributor to the household economy, through her piecework and her farm labor. Moreover, given her position as the wife of an adopted husband (muko), Toshié has always played a leading decision-making and management role within her own family.

And it is in this fact that we can get a hint of the ways in which Toshié's life diverged from the dominant narrative during the wartime and prewar eras, too. For Toshié's mother was also the wife of a muko, and she, too, played a dominant role in family decision-making and management. Wives of muko husbands are perhaps a special case, but they are also illustrative of the many variations based on region, class, and family circumstances in the position of women in the family and community. The "dark" prewar family with its autocratic male head and submissive women was, like the tales of ferocious mothers-in-law and abused brides, a generalization that failed to reflect the variety and complexity of human relations within families.

Similarly, the image of relentless obligation conjured up by the prewar era—obligation to state, to hamlet and village community, to emperor, to landlord, and to the family—is a generalization that needs qualification. Undoubtedly, Toshié and her parents were faced with stern obligations: to work with their hands to feed the family, to provide tribute to landlord and village tax collectors, to go through at least the outward motions of reverence for the emperor, and—during the war years—to offer up their produce, their labor, and their sons. But if To-shié and her family members had few choices in the big things in life—labor and tribute, for example—they appear to have enjoyed consider-able freedom in many of the smaller things. For all the hard work that they were forced to do, for example, Toshié's family members appear also to have enjoyed considerable flexibility to choose their hours and days of work. As day laborers, they (both Toshié's parents and, from adulthood, Toshié herself) were free to take a day off if there was some-thing they wanted to do about the house or the farm. Much of the work they performed—Tsugino's piecework, for example, or sandal and rope making in winter—was done in or about the home, and it gave ample time for family togetherness, conversation, and gossip. And the family always appears to have had time for friends and neighbors, who con-tinue today as during Toshié's childhood to drop in several times a day for a cup of green tea and a chat. As a rural family living without the con-strictions of office hours, train timetables, daily commutes, or crowded living quarters, Toshié's family appears to have enjoyed a relative free-dom and private space that were denied to many urbanites. Even work-ing in labor gangs on the riverbanks or at the docks, Toshié remembers with some fondness the camaraderie and easy conversation that she was able to carry on with her fellow villagers as they worked and rested.

Nor was the state, for all its demands, such an immediate presence that it denied Toshié and her family the enjoyment of their immediate community of family and friends. Toshié remembers her schooling not for the frequent lectures on obligation, nor for the moral training in the duties of a "good Japanese," nor for the emperor and his portrait in its shrinelike cabinet, but rather for friendship and play, and for the plea-sure of learning. And as much as she enjoyed school, she also looked for-ward intensely to the hours after school when she could—so long as she was able to avoid her mother's grasp—laugh and play with her friends in the grounds of the temple. Indeed, one of the most striking contrasts with the Kosugi of Toshié's youth is the absence today of the bright laughter and mischievous faces that must have animated the hamlet's outdoor spaces. Even during the exceptionally exigent years of the war period, Toshié's memories are not only of work, obligation, and loss. She is also able to remember with pleasure the fellowship of her female friends, the relative freedom and autonomy that resulted from the lack of men in the community, and the camaraderie and humor of some of the activities she helped organized, such as the annual hamlet entertain-ment. Toshié, indeed, is quick to say that in spite of all the hardships and losses of her childhood, she feels blessed for her ability from an early age to enjoy family, community, and friends.

It is important to note also that Toshié and her family were only tangentially affected by the events that fill many histories of prewar rural Japan. At the time of Toshié's birth, the tenant movement was the key issue in the countryside. Tenant unrest was caused by hardship—particularly in a world of declining commodity prices and threatened incomes—and by opportunism, and both were undoubtedly present in the protests within Niigata prefecture. Niigata was a relative hotbed of tenant unrest, the scene of several of the most contentious and bitter disputes of the tenant movement. Yokogoshi village was home to the Itō, one of the largest landholding families in Japan, so inevitably Yokogoshi was drawn into the conflict between tenant and landlord. In Sōmi, just three miles from Kosugi, there were violent clashes as angry tenants staked out the Itō family mansion.

The tenant movement was, at the time and since, seen as a defining moment in the history of rural Japan. It marked the rise to political consciousness of the tenant farmer class: educated and increasingly integrated into the national cash economy, tenant farmers were said to be aware of the inequities of their political position as never before. The tenant movement also marked the first major challenge to the system of landlordism in Japan, and, although landlords regained the upper hand as they successfully crushed many of the protests of the 1930s, the challenges were to continue until the system was effectively dismantled by the Occupation-mandated land reform. And the tenant movement reflected the breakdown of long-established hierarchical social structures in the Japanese village.

Toshié was in her infancy, and remembers nothing of tenant protests. But it appears that Toshié's father was not directly involved in any protests. Like many other tenants, he rented his small plots of land from a family that was related to him by close ties of marriage and obligation. Certainly, there were instances in 1920s Japan when such ties were upended by a new consciousness that pitted educated proletarian tenants against established hierarchies. But the available evidence—particularly the actions of Toshié's father during the time of the land reform—indicates no such trend in Toshié's family.

Indeed, the lack of direct involvement in tenant disputes reflects the majority experience in rural Japan in the 1920s and 1930s. All of the tenant disputes from 1918 until 1940 involved less than one million people combined—and this number must include many individuals involved in multiple disputes.[3] Since there were some three million tenant farmer families in Japan in the late 1920s, it is clear that the majority were not at any time involved in tenant disputes. The more subtle changes in landlord-tenant relations are harder to measure. Toshié's father may well have benefited from a general decline in rents compared to output during the 1920s—a decline that owed much to tenant activism. But the evidence is that he did not share in the increasingly confrontational politics of unionized tenants and their landlords during the 1920s.

The same is true of the farm depression of the early 1930s. Available statistics indicate that average farm family income declined from a high of ¥1,563 in 1925 to a low of ¥542 in 1931—a decline of roughly two-thirds. By contrast, the incomes of urban laborers declined by less than 20 percent—though this obviously does not apply to those thrown out of work by the depression.[4] During the same period, overall prices declined by 43 percent. Even allowing for serious deficiencies in the representativeness of government surveys, farm families clearly suffered a serious real decline in income. According to the statistics, at the turn of the 1930s the average farm family recorded a deficit of expenses over income of almost eighty yen.[5] While I have no information on the state of Toshié's family finances, I can safely assume that they were affected by falling commodity prices, certainly of silk. The effect of declining crop prices must have been much less, since the family consumed the vast majority of production that it did not turn over to its landlord. However, given the stability of Kurakichi's work on the river improvement project, it also seems safe to assume that he suffered less than many. Absolutely clear is the vast difference between Toshié's family experience of the rural depression and the experience of the mountain villages of northern Japan. While it would be wrong to claim that the depression did not affect Toshié's family, it appears to have been just one more episode in a more generalized financial instability that forced Kurakichi to resort to borrowing at some point in most years. Toshié remembers having to tell creditors her father was not home (while he hid in a back room) at many points in her childhood, and she does not distinguish the depression years as especially dire. And at least in their case, they were apparently better-off than their urban relative Niichirō, who came to Toshié's family to find refuge from the storm.

During the war years from 1937 to 1945, Toshié's family was caught up like everyone in the general mobilization of Japan. This mobilization included the military impressment of Toshié's brothers. The offering up of sons to the military was a near-universal condition of rural life in the war era. Given their lack of advanced skills, inevitably rural families sent more sons to the frontlines than their urban counterparts. Nor was Toshié's family's loss of both of its sons at all unusual. The death rate of those serving at or close to Japan's far-flung battle lines was extraordinarily high: 1.8 million, or 19 percent of all men in the fifteen-to-thirty age group in Japan in 1940 were dead by the end of the decade.[6] Villages like Yokogoshi suffered even higher death rates, of 30 percent or more. The farmers' magazine *Ie no Hikari* carried many stories of farm mothers stoically giving up three, four, or even more sons for the sake of emperor and country.

Toshié's memories of the war are of course embittered by the loss of her brothers, not to mention the other hardships that she and her family were forced to endure. She affirms that she had little interest in politics or international affairs, and the war was not something that she ever desired or promoted. Toshié also talks of her profound sense of betrayal at Japan's defeat. To this extent, her memories are consistent with a widespread sense among ordinary Japanese that they, too, were "victims" of the war. But Toshié is also quite honest about her wholehearted support for the war effort. She was convinced that Japan could not lose, and even today, it is the betrayal of the politicians and military leaders who promised victory—rather than the depredations caused by Japanese aggression—that stirs Toshié to bitterness. I conclude that the support of Toshié and other villagers for the war was genuine, it was passionate, and it was grounded in a long series of successful alliances between villages and the military, even if past wars and campaigns were less than "total." Did Toshié hesitate when she heard rumors of Japanese atrocities in China? She confirms that she did hear such rumors, but she seems to have successfully dissociated herself from feelings of complicity or guilt. An important factor to consider with respect to the commitment of Toshié and other villagers was that the war brought them important benefits in the form of high wages (in Toshié's job at the docks, for example), cash incentives for tenant farmers, and the extension of social welfare in the villages. The relative freedom and authority gained by women in the absence of men in the village was also an enjoyable new experience. However, the commitment of Japanese farmers seems to have run up against its limits when it came to activities farmers clearly saw as detrimental to their economic well-being: most notably, the forced requisition of rice and other foods grown by the sweat of their brows. Although the great majority complied with these demands, it was hardly with pleasure or joy, but rather out of a sense of duty to the nation, and a desire not to cause trouble for other families in the neighborhood group.

Finally, there is the question of the most striking feature of the "dark Showa," "bright Showa" dichotomy: the unnatural bisection of history into two distinct and starkly contrasting eras. During our many interviews, I often felt that in spite of the obvious contrasts between her life today and during the 1930s or 1940s, Toshié herself is unaware of any yawning gap between her postwar and wartime lives. The hamlet, she seems to feel, has and will go on much as she has always known it. Certainly, life has become much more comfortable, but this comfort was achieved gradually, and by no means followed immediately on the end of the war. Indeed, the landscape of Kosugi affirms this continuity: while many of the low-lying areas of Japan have been transformed into sometimes-terrifying industrial suburbs, Kosugi retains its bucolic charm and exudes a certain aura of timelessness. For Toshié, I believe, the hamlet community has always been more real, more important, and more fulfilling than the "external" communities of workplace, nation, or class. Her relations with family members, neighbors, hamlet and village have endured (though not, of course, without some change) even as the technologies and economics of daily life have been transformed. Indeed, my most enduring—and warming—impression of Toshié at seventy-six is that she has not in any important respect changed from the girl who, seventy years ago, stood hesitantly for the first time on the doorstep of the Kosugi elementary school.

Notes

PREFACE

1. Eugen Weber, *Peasants into Frenchmen: The Modernization of Rural France, 1870–1914* (Stanford: Stanford University Press, 1976), 14. Weber is referring to the French peasantry of 1914.

2. Here and throughout this book, I use the Japanese order in writing names: family name followed by given name.

3. Arthur F. Raper, *The Japanese Village in Transition* (Tokyo: Supreme Commander Allied Powers, 1950).

4. Yokogoshi Chōshi Hensan Iinkai, *Yokogoshi chōshi—shiryōhen* (Yokogoshi: Yokogoshimachi, 2000).

5. In 1925, 1.9 million out of 5.4 million farm households outside Hokkaido cultivated less than 0.5 hectare total, making this the median group in terms of size of operations. In the same year, 1.5 million households were pure tenants, while another 2.3 million combined tenancy with some level of land ownership. Sōmu chō tōkei kyoku, *Nihon chōki tōkei sōran,* 5 vols. (Tokyo: Nihon Tōkei Kyōkai, 1988), 2: 28, 32.

6. Simon Partner, *Assembled in Japan: Electrical Goods and the Making of the Japanese Consumer* (Berkeley: University of California Press, 1999).

CHAPTER 1: ON THE BANKS OF THE AGANO

1. Details here are extracted from Julie M. Rousseau, "Enduring Labors: The 'New Midwife' and the Modern Culture of Childbearing in Early Twentieth-Century Japan" (Ph.D. diss., Columbia University, 1998).

2. Yoshinaga Akira, "Echigo Sōmi sōdō no kenkyū," *Fukuyama daigaku ningen kagaku kenkyū sentaa kiyō,* Oct. 1997.

3. According to a 1933 source, the entire village of Yokogoshi produced 12,559 *koku* of rice on a land area of 7,410 *tan*. A *koku* is a unit of volume, not weight, but this translates roughly into two thousand kilograms per hectare (assuming ten *tan* per hectare, and 150 kilograms per *koku*). In Kosugi, land productivity was said to be from four to six *hyō* per *tan*. A *hyō* is roughly one third of a *koku*. Making the same assumption about the weight of one *koku*, five *hyō* per *tan* would also translate to roughly twenty-five hundred kilograms per hectare. See "Yokogoshimura nōson keizai kōsei keikakusho," in Yokogoshi Chōshi Hensan Iinkai, *Yokogoshi chōshi—shiryōhen* (Yokogoshi: Yokogoshi-machi, 2000).

4. Precise data on landholdings by family are lacking. The information cited is from "Yokogoshimura nōson keizai kōsei keikakusho" and "Nōchi kaihō kansui chōsa," in Chōshi Iinkai, *Yokogoshi chōshi—shiryōhen*, 677–94, 790–91.

5. This and the following details on family life in Yokogoshi are drawn from Toshié and from *Yokogoshimura no minzoku* (Yokogoshi: Privately published, 1973), 57.

6. Kären Wigen, *The Making of a Japanese Periphery, 1750–1920* (Berkeley: University of California Press, 1995), 235.

7. Nihon Sonrakushi Kōza Henshū Iinkai, *Seikatsu 3: kingendai,* vol. 8 of *Nihon sonrakushi kōza* (Tokyo: Yuzankaku, 1990), 10.

8. This description is adapted from Akiyama Takashi et al., eds., *Zuroku nōmin seikatsushi jiten* (Tokyo: Kashiwa Shobō, 1991), 84–91.

9. Kayō Nobufumi, *Nihon nōgyō kiso tōkei* (Tokyo: Nōrin Tōkei Kyōkai, 1977), 494–96. The average farm size in the survey was 1.7 hectares, of which 0.8 hectares were owned outright.

10. A survey of tenant farmers found average income to be ¥901 in 1929. The average farm size in the survey was 1.5 hectares, including rented land. Sumiya Mikio, ed., *Shōwa kyōkō : sono rekishiteki igi to zentaizō* (Tokyo: Yūhikaku, 1974), 293.

11. A 1934 survey of the village of Tayama in Iwate prefecture found an average income of eighty-eight yen. Admittedly this was in the midst of the farm depression, but villagers emphasized that the recent poor harvest was not the root cause of their poverty. Morioka Tomo no Kai, ed., *Tayama mura no seikatsu* (Morioka: Morioka Tomo no Kai, 1935), 97.

12. For plains villages, see Ōkado Masakatsu, *Meiji Taishō no nōsō n* (Tokyo: Iwanami Shoten, 1992), 18. For Iwate, see Morioka Tomo no Kai, *Tayama mura no seikatsu,* statistical tables.

13. Ōkado Masakatsu, *Meiji Taishō no nōson,* 19. The Engel coefficient is the ratio of food expenditure to total expenditure.

14. Isabella Bird, *Unbeaten Tracks in Japan* (London: Virago, 1984), 88, 99.

15. Zenkoku Tomo no Kai Chūōbu, *Nōson seikatsu gōrika undō Tōhoku settorumento no kiroku* (Tokyo: Zenkoku Tomo no Kai Chūōbu, 1989), 16.

16. Hani Tomoko, *Jiyū kyōryoku ai* (Tokyo: Fujin no Tomo Kai, 1963), 114.

17. Ella Lury Wiswell and Robert J. Smith, *The Women of Suye Mura* (Chicago: University of Chicago Press, 1982).

18. For Yumada, see Ōkado Masakatsu, *Meiji Taishō no nōson,* 13. For Yo-

kogoshi, see Takahashi Itsuo, *Waga kyōdo Yokogoshi* (Yokogoshi: Privately published, 1951) 112; and Chōshi Iinkai, *Yokogoshi chōshi—shiryōhen*, 645, 67.

19. For an example of such a village as late as the mid-1960s, see Sanson Shinkō Chōsakai, *Tosa kyūshun sanson no sugata to shinro: Kōchiken Kamigun Monobemura* (Tokyo: Sanson Shinkō Chōsakai, 1966).

20. Shakai Fukushi Chōsa Kenkyūkai, *Senzen Nihon shakai jigyō chōsa shiryō shūsei* (Tokyo: Keisō Shobō), 6: 1108.

21. Chōshi Iinkai, *Yokogoshi chōshi—shiryōhen*, 645, 646.

22. Nihon Kokuyū Tetsudō Sōsaishitsu, *Tetsudō 80-nen no ayumi* (Tokyo: Nihon Kokuyū Tetsudō, 1952), 18–19.

23. Tetsudōin, *Honpō tetsudō no shakai oyobi keizai ni oyoboseru eikyō*, vol. 12 of *Kindai Nihon shōhin ryūtsūshi shiryō*, ed. Shōhin Ryūtsūshi Kenkyūkai (Yamaguchi Kazuo) (Tokyo: Nihon Keizai Hyōronsha, 1916), 1616–20.

24. Nagatsuka Takashi, *The Soil: A Portrait of Rural Life in Meiji Japan*, trans. Ann Waswo (London: Routledge, 1989), 18.

25. Wigen, *The Making of a Japanese Periphery*, 254–55.

26. Tetsudōin, *Honpō tetsudō no shakai oyobi keizai ni oyoboseru eikyō*, 1606–9.

27. Taniguchi Zentarō, *Taniguchi Zentarō shū* (Tokyo: Shin Nihon Shuppansha, 1986).

28. Shimazaki Tōson, *Before the Dawn* (Honolulu: University of Hawaii Press, 1987).

29. Both cited in Ōkado Masakatsu, *Meiji Taishō no nōson*, 36.

30. Both cited in ibid., 42.

31. Calculated from Yūsei Shō, ed., *Yūsei hyakunenshi* (Tokyo: Teishin Kyōkai, 1971), 30, 361–62.

32. Ibid., 42.

33. Ōkado Masakatsu, *Meiji Taishō no nōson*, 15.

34. Sonrakushi Iinkai, *Seikatsu 3: kingendai*, 7–8.

35. See Richard J. Smethurst, *A Social Basis for Prewar Japanese Militarism: The Army and the Rural Community* (Berkeley: University of California Press, 1974).

36. There were in fact two lines of the Nakagawa family, a main family and a branch family. Sakichi was head of the branch family. But both families were economically and politically dominant in the hamlet.

37. For a full description of prewar village society (and comparison with the early postwar) see Tadashi Fukutake, *Rural Society in Japan* (Tokyo: University of Tokyo Press, 1980).

CHAPTER 2: THE MAKING OF A JAPANESE CITIZEN

1. Ann Waswo, "The Transformation of Rural Society, 1920–1950," in *The Twentieth Century*, ed. Peter Duus, *The Cambridge History of Japan* (Cambridge: Cambridge University Press, 1988), 576–83. See also Ann Waswo, *Japanese Landlords: The Decline of a Rural Elite* (Berkeley: University of California Press, 1977); and Yoshiaki Nishida, *Kindai Nihon nōmin undōshi kenkyū* (Tokyo: Tokyo Daigaku Shuppankai, 1997).

2. Ōkado Masakatsu, *Meiji Taishō no nōson,* 8.

3. Ōkado Masakatsu, *Meiji Taishō no nōson,* 39.

4. Quoted in Ōkado Masakatsu, *Meiji Taishō no nōson,* 46–47.

5. Niigataken, *Niigata kenshi,* 9 vols. (Niigata: Niigataken, 1988), 9: 93.

6. Chōshi Iinkai, *Yokogoshi chōshi—shiryōhen,* 653–60, 685–93.

7. Niigata Nippō Jigyōsha, ed., *Shin kenmin kikikakichō: sesō moyō—18 nin no jikakuzō* (Niigata: Niigata Nippō Jigyōsha, n.d.), 204–5.

8. Niigataken, *Niigata kenshi,* 9: 302.

9. Chōshi Iinkai, *Yokogoshi chōshi—shiryōhen,* 660.

10. Ibid., 729.

11. Yokogoshi Sonshi Hensanshitsu, *Yokogoshi sonshi ryakunenpyō,* Yokogoshi: Yokogoshi Sonshi Hensanshitsu, n.d.

12. Sōmu chō tōkei kyoku, *Nihon chōki tōkei sōran,* 4: 388–89; Sumiya Mikio, *Showa kyōkō,* 291.

13. For an example of the effects on a silk-dependent community, see Wigen, *The Making of a Japanese Periphery,* 221.

14. Sumiya Mikio, *Showa kyōkō,* 292.

15. Niigataken, *Niigata kenshi,* 8: 295.

16. Sōmu chō tōkei kyoku, *Nihon chōki tōkei sōran,* 3: 45. Rice imports were 46,000 tons in 1916, 85,000 in 1917, 697,000 in 1918, 696,000 in 1919, 71,000 in 1920, 239,000 in 1921, 457,000 in 1922, 265,000 in 1923, 490,000 in 1924, 771,000 in 1925, 345,000 in 1926, and 584,000 in 1927. Thereafter, imports declined substantially.

17. Sumiya Mikio, *Showa kyōkō,* 291–93. The average farm size was 1.5 hectares including rented land.

18. Ibid., 294.

19. Ronald P. Dore, *Land Reform in Japan* (London: Athlone Press, 1984).

20. Niigataken, *Niigata kenshi,* 8: 266–67.

21. Yamakawa Kin, "Tōhoku kiga nōson wo miru," *Kaizō,* Dec. 1934.

22. Fukushi Kenkyūkai, *Senzen Nihon shakai jigyō chōsa shiryō shūsei,* 6: 1106–7.

23. *Tokyo asahi shinbun,* Oct. 28, 1934.

24. *Akita sakigake shinpō,* Oct. 25, 1934.

25. For an overview of the traffic in human beings in Japan, see Mikiso Hane, *Peasants, Rebels and Outcastes: The Underside of Modern Japan* (New York: Pantheon, 1982).

26. Chūō Shokugyō Shōkai Jimukyoku, "Geishōgishakufu shōkaigyō ni kansuru chōsa" (1926), in Shakai Fukushi Chōsa Kenkyūkai, *Senzen Nihon shakai jigyō chōsa shiryō shūsei,* 6: 943–1028.

27. Ibid., 986–87.

28. Ibid., 991.

29. Ibid., 1108.

30. Ibid., 1109.

31. A detailed account of the relief effort, and of its effects in one village community, can be found in Kerry Smith, *A Time of Crisis: Japan, the Great Depression, and Rural Revitalization* (Cambridge, Mass.: Harvard University Press, 2001).

32. Quoted in Masao Maruyama, "The Ideology and Dynamics of Japanese Fascism," in *Thought and Behaviour in Modern Japanese Politics,* ed. Ivan Morris (London: Oxford University Press, 1963), 45.

33. Quoted in W. G. Beasley, *The Meiji Restoration* (Stanford: Stanford University Press, 1972), 360.

34. Monbushō, *A General Survey of Education in Japan* (Tokyo: Department of Education, 1926).

35. Kaigo Muneomi, *Shūshin,* vol. 3 of *Nihon kyōkasho taikei* (Tokyo: Kōdansha, 1962).

36. "Yoi Nihonjin," in ibid., lesson 27.

37. Ibid.

38. David John Lu, *Sources of Japanese History,* 2 vols. (New York: McGraw-Hill, 1974), 2: 70.

CHAPTER 3: THE VILLAGE GOES TO WAR

1. Niigata Shi Gappei Chōsonshi Henshūshitsu, ed., *Ishiyama sonpō ni miru senjika no nōson,* vol. 5 of *Niigata Shi Gappei Chōson no rekishi kenkyū hōkoku* (Niigata: Niigata Shi Gappei Chōsonshi Henshūshitsu, 1984), 112.

2. Yui Masaomi, *Sensō to kokumin,* vol. 8 of *Zusetsu Shōwa no rekishi,* ed. Shōwa no Rekishi Kankōkai (Tokyo: Shūeisha, 1980), 77.

3. Chōsonshi Henshūshitsu, *Ishiyama sonpō ni miru senjika no nōson,* 162. A similar list can also be found in Thomas R. H. Havens, *Valley of Darkness: The Japanese People and World War Two* (New York: W. W. Norton, 1978), 84–85.

4. Partner, *Assembled in Japan,* 29.

5. The quote is from a speech by the communications minister, Nagai Ryūtarō. Nihon Hōsō Kyōkai, *Nihon hōsōshi,* 2 vols. (Tokyo: Nihon Hōsō Kyōkai, 1965), 1: 476.

6. M. D. Kennedy, *The Military Side of Japanese Life* (London: Constable and Co., 1924), 51.

7. Masao Maruyama, "Theory and Psychology of Ultra-Nationalism," in *Thought and Behaviour in Modern Japanese Politics,* ed. Ivan Morris (London: Oxford University Press, 1963), 19. For a similar analysis, see also Yuki Tanaka, *Hidden Horrors: Japanese War Crimes in World War II* (Boulder, Col.: Westview Press, 1996), especially the concluding chapter entitled "Understanding Japanese Brutality in the Asia-Pacific War."

8. Iwate Ken Nōson Bunka Kondan Kai, ed., *Senbotsu nōmin heishi no tegami* (Tokyo: Iwanami Shoten, 1961), 57.

9. Quoted in Lord Russell of Liverpool, *The Knights of Bushido: A Short History of Japanese War Crimes* (London: Cassell and Company, 1958), 49–50. The author notes that the only information censored in this missive was the name of the town where the writer had been engaged in action.

10. See ibid.; Tanaka, *Hidden Horrors.*

11. Itō Keiichi, *Heitaitachi no Rikugunshi: Heiei to senba seikatsu* (Tokyo: Banchō Shobō, 1969), 107–9. See also Edward J. Drea, "Trained in the Hardest School," in *In the Service of the Emperor: Essays on the Imperial Japanese Army* (Lincoln, Neb.: University of Nebraska Press, 1998).

12. Katō Ken'ichi, ed., *Shōnen kurabu meisakusen*, 3 vols. (Tokyo: Kōdan-sha, 1966). See also Machida Shiritsu Hakubutsukan, ed., *Norakuro—Tagawa Suihō tanjō hyakunen kinen* (Machida: Machida Shiritsu Hakubutsukan, 1999). Norakuro's first life came to an end in 1944, when the home ministry banned all children's cartoons as lacking the seriousness called for in time of war.

13. Takahashi Itsuo, *Waga kyōdo Yokogoshi*, 134–35.

14. For wedding costs, see Yokogoshi Chōshi Hensan Iinkai, *Yokogoshi chōshi—shiryōhen*, 694.

15. These details are drawn from ibid., 938–42.

16. Chōsonshi Henshūshitsu, *Ishiyama sonpō ni miru senjika no nōson*, 120.

17. Ibid., 130.

18. Yui Masaomi, *Sensō to kokumin*, 65.

19. Niigata Shi Gappei Chōsonshi Henshūshitsu, ed., *Ishiyama sonpō ni miru senjika no nōson*, 172.

20. Ibid., 121.

21. Yui Masaomi, *Sensō to kokumin*, 63–65. The Japanese pejorative for Chinese was "*chankoro.*"

22. Chōsonshi Henshūshitsu, *Ishiyama sonpō ni miru senjika no nōson*, 120.

23. Ibid., 112; See also Yui Masaomi, *Sensō to kokumin*. Details in the following two paragraphs are from 40–41.

24. Ibid., 113.

25. Havens, *Valley of Darkness*, 80.

26. Chōsonshi Henshūshitsu, *Ishiyama sonpō ni miru senjika no nōson*, 123–25.

27. Yui Masaomi, *Sensō to kokumin*, 154.

28. Itagaki Kuniko, *Shōwa senzen senchūki no nōson seikatsu—zasshi "Ie no Hikari" ni miru* (Tokyo: Mine Shobō, 1992), 182.

29. Yui Masaomi, *Sensō to kokumin*, 154.

30. Quoted in Itagaki Kuniko, *Shōwa senzen senchūki no nōson seikatsu*, 214.

31. Sōka Gakkai Seinenbu Hansen Shuppan Iinkai, ed., *Kita no taichi ni namida shite: senjika no nōson*, vol. 18 of *Sensō wo shiranai sedai e*, second series (Tokyo: Daisan Bunmei Sha, 1984), 23, 30.

32. Itagaki Kuniko, *Shōwa senzen senchūki no nōson seikatsu*, 196–97.

33. "Yasei karamushi wo torō," *Ie no Hikari*, Nov. 1940; "Dare ni mo de-kiru zassōmen no tsukurikata," ibid., Aug. 1943.

34. "Tatakainukō kessen seikatsu," ibid., Apr. 1943.

35. "Machi ya mura wo mamoru shikyō fujin no katsudō zadankai," ibid., July 1940.

36. Sōka Gakkai, *Kita no taichi ni namida shite*, 18–19.

37. Chōsonshi Henshūshitsu, *Ishiyama sonpō ni miru senjika no nōson*, 169–74.

38. Itagaki Kuniko, *Shōwa senzen senchūki no nōson seikatsu*, 216.

39. Between 1941 and 1942, average height declined from 161 centimeters

to 160 centimeters. Average weight declined from 54.8 kilograms to 52.8 kilograms. Yokogoshi Chōshi Hensan Iinkai, *Yokogoshi chōshi—shiryōhen*, 755.

40. "'Seidō' no seikatsu seishin undō nōson ha dō uketorubekika ni tsuite," *Ie no Hikari*, Sept. 1939.

41. Itagaki Kuniko, *Shōwa senzen senchūki no nōson seikatsu*, 216.

42. Ibid., 217.

43. Ibid., 218.

44. Yokogoshi Chōshi Hensan Iinkai, *Yokogoshi chōshi—shiryōhen*, 756.

45. Ibid.

46. Chōsonshi Henshūshitsu, *Ishiyama sonpō ni miru senjika no nōson*, 132.

47. Ibid., 212.

48. Waswo, "The Transformation of Rural Society, 1920–1950," 604.

49. Ibid., 758; Chōsonshi Henshūshitsu, *Ishiyama sonpō ni miru senjika no nōson*, 115.

50. Sōka Gakkai, *Kita no taichi ni namida shite*, 27, describes such a ceremony in which a mother stood in front of the altar and said, "My son died for the emperor and for his country. That, surely, was your will."

51. Fujii Tadatoshi, *Kokubō fujinkai: hinomaru to kappōgi* (Tokyo: Iwanami Shoten, 1985), 181.

52. Smethurst, *Social Basis for Prewar Japanese Militarism*, 169–70. See also Fujii, *Kokubō fujinkai*, 181, for a breakdown of Women's Defense Association activities, including arranging lectures.

53. Chōsonshi Henshūshitsu, *Ishiyama sonpō ni miru senjika no nōson*, 136, 178.

54. Yui Masaomi, *Sensō to kokumin*, 157.

55. Ibid., 150.

56. Chōsonshi Henshūshitsu, *Ishiyama sonpō ni miru senjika no nōson*, 116, 151.

57. Fujii, *Kokubō fujinkai*, 181.

58. The villages were also the recipients of labor assistance. After labor conscription was introduced in 1941, students, schoolgirls, and children were sent into the countryside to help, especially with harvests and planting. Soldiers stationed in rural regions also were allowed home at planting and harvest time to help out in the busiest farming season—though by the end of the war the vast majority were committed overseas. Yui Masaomi, *Sensō to kokumin*, 143–45.

59. Chōsonshi Henshūshitsu, *Ishiyama sonpō ni miru senjika no nōson*, 147.

60. Yokogoshi Chōshi Hensan Iinkai, *Yokogoshi chōshi—shiryōhen*, 764–67.

61. Yui Masaomi, *Sensō to kokumin*, 129–32.

62. My (admittedly simplistic) assumption is that the village contained roughly five thousand males, equally divided into cohorts of some 714 per decade (with one cohort assigned to all those over sixty years of age). The twenty to thirty years age group would thus have 714 members (252 is 35 percent of 714).

63. This and subsequent quotes are from Sōka Gakkai Seinenbu Hansen Shuppan Iinkai, ed., *Aa, tsūkoku no shima Gadarukanaru*, vol. 20 of *Sensō wo shiranai sedai e*, second series (Tokyo: Daisan Bunmei Sha, 1985), 54–62; 13.

64. Chōsonshi Henshūshitsu, *Ishiyama sonpō ni miru senjika no nōson*, 141.

65. Details of this incident are drawn from U.S. military records collected by the village historian's office of Yokogoshi. The military government conducted an extensive investigation into the incident after the war ended.

66. "Investigation of Aircraft Lost in Niigata Raid, July 19, 1945," undated U.S. Army document.

67. Russell, *The Knights of Bushido*, ch. 4.

68. Lu, *Sources of Japanese History*, 176–77.

CHAPTER 4: RURAL LIFE UNDER THE OCCUPATION

1. Niigataken, *Niigata kenshi*, 9: 12.

2. Ibid.

3. Both quotes and preceding details are from "Haisengo no hanzai no jitsujō ni tsuite (keizai han no bu)," *Hōmu kenkyū* 37, no. 1 (1949): 57–58.

4. Kokuritsu Yoron Chōsajo, *Nōson yoron chōsa: kyōshutsu seido yo nōgyō kyōsai kumiai* (Tokyo: Kokuritsu Yoron Chōsajo, 1949).

5. "Haisengo," 58.

6. Ibid., 59.

7. Supreme Commander Allied Powers: Instructions to Japanese Government (SCAPIN) 411, quoted in Mark B. Williamson, *Agricultural Programs in Japan, 1945–51*, vol. 148, *Natural Resources Section Reports* (Tokyo: Supreme Commander Allied Powers, General Headquarters, 1951), 10.

8. Supreme Commander Allied Powers, General Headquarters, *History of the Nonmilitary Activities of the Occupation of Japan: Agriculture (September 1945 through December 1950)* (Tokyo: SCAP, 1950), 2.

9. Tanaka Keiichi, *Niigata-ken no rekishi* (Tokyo: Yamakawa Shuppansha, 1998), 308–11.

10. Ibid., 311.

11. Yokogoshi Chōshi Hensan Iinkai, *Yokogoshi chōshi—shiryōhen*, 693.

12. Sōmu chō tōkei kyoku, *Nihon chōki tōkei sōran*, 4: 347.

13. Ino Ryūichi, *Sengo Nihon Nōgyōshi* (Tokyo: Shin Nippon Shuppansha), 55.

14. Information and quotes in this paragraph are from Supreme Commander Allied Powers, Natural Resources Section, NRS 05423.

15. See for example "Karuyaka no natsu no fujin wanpiisu," *Ie no Hikari*, Aug. 1947, 42; and "Ichimai no nekkachiifu de dekiru samazama no yosōi," ibid., Apr. 1948, 41.

16. For a study of this department, see Simon Partner, "Taming the Wilderness: The Lifestyle Improvement Movement in Rural Japan, 1925–1965," *Monumenta Nipponica* 56, no. 4 (winter 2001): 487–520.

17. Quoted in "Social Welfare," in *Encyclopedia of Japan* (Tokyo: Kodansha, 1983), 211. The quote is from Article 25.

18. Gail Bernstein, *Haruko's World: A Japanese Farm Woman and Her Community* (Stanford: Stanford University Press, 1983), pt. 2.

19. Rekishi Hyakka Jiten Henshūbu, *Kōshitsu no hyakka jiten* (Tokyo: Shinjinbutsu Ōraisha, 1963).

CHAPTER 5: RED CARPETS AND WHISKY

1. See Partner, *Assembled in Japan*, 262n2.

2. Mizutani Yūji, *Minna de yaru seikatsu kaizen* (N.p: n.p., 1956), 196.

3. Ibid., 29.

4. Ibid., 29, 18.

5. Kimura Noboru, "Nōson hanbai seikō no hiketsu," *Nashonaru shoppu*, Aug. 1958, 26–29.

6. Sōmu Chō Tōkei Kyoku, *Nihon chōki tōkei sōran*, 5 vols. (Tokyo: Nihon Tōkei kyōkai 1988), 4: 548–49.

7. In 1970, average nonfood living expenditure in urban (cities over fifty thousand) workers' households was ¥57,175 versus ¥63,116 in rural households. Total aftertax household income was ¥105,715 for urban households versus ¥120,733 for rural households. See Sōmu Chō Tōkei Kyoku, *Nihon chōki tōkei sōran*, , 4: 490–509, 548–49.

8. See Aurelia George Mulgan, *The Politics of Agriculture in Japan* (London: Routledge, 2000), 329.

9. Ino Ryūichi, *Sengo Nihon Nōgyōshi*, 125.

10. Sōmu chō tōkei kyoku, *Nihon chōki tōkei sōran*, 2: 29.

11. Ibid. In 1946, 28 percent of all farms outside Hokkaido were more than one hectare in size. By 1954 (after the land reform) the percentage of farms over one hectare had actually declined to 25.8 percent.

12. Ibid., 4: 552–53.

13. Partner, *Assembled in Japan*, 164–5.

14. Interview with Fukuda Kiku, Feb. 9, 1996.

15. Sōmu Chō Tōkei Kyoku, *Nihon chōki tōkei sōran*, 4: 552–53.

16. Zenkoku Nōgyō Chūōkai, *Seikatsu Shidōin no Katsudō Kiroku* (Tokyo: Ie no Hikari Kyōkai, 1980), 8.

17. Nōrinshō Nōrinkeizaikyoku Tōkei Chōsabu, *Nōka keizai chōsa hōkoku* (Tokyo: Nōrinshō, 1955–65). Note that new construction, a capital expense, was not included in household expenditure. The percentage is provided only for reference.

18. Ibid. These percentages combine capital spending (not included under household expenditure) and noncapital spending on repairs, maintenance, and rent.

19. Richard J. Beardsley, John W. Hall, and Robert E. Ward, *Village Japan* (Chicago: University of Chicago Press, 1959), 90ff.

20. Takahashi Itsuo, *Waga kyōdo Yokogoshi*, 112; Yokogoshi Mura, ed., *Yokogoshimura tōkei shiryōshū* (Yokogoshi: Yokogoshi Mura, 1979), 80, 86.

21. Details on Niigata prefecture's activities are from Niigataken, *Niigata kenshi*, 9: 344–56.

22. Takahashi Itsuo, *Waga kyōdo Yokogoshi*, 114–17.

23. Details on the land improvement project are from Kamedakyō Tochi Kairyōku Yokogoshi Kōku, ed., *Yokogoshi no tochi kairyō jigyō* (Yokogoshi: Kamedakyō Tochi Kairyōku Yokogoshi Kōku, 1979).

24. Nihon Nōgyō Kikai Kōgyōkai, *Nichinōkō 35-nen no Ayumi* (Tokyo: Nihon Nōgyō Kikai Kōgyōkai, 1973), 212–17.

25. Nōka keizai chōsa, 1960 and 1966. The data are based on sample surveys.

26. Suzuki Shigeru, "Nihon nōgyō wo kaeru kōunki," *Kikaika nōgyō*, Mar. 1956, 37.

27. Kazuo Wada, *Kōunki Tanjō* (Tokyo: Fumin Kyōkai, 1979), 220.

28. Kubota K. K., *Kubota 100-Nen* (Osaka: Kubota K. K., 1990), 116.

29. See, for example, "Kōunki wo wagamono ni suru," *Kikaika nōgyō*, Mar. 1956, 13.

30. Chōsei Shichinoe, *Nōgyō Kikaika no Dōtai Katei* (Tokyo: Nōgyō Sōgō Kenkyūjo, 1974), 31.

31. In Niigata prefecture, 75.3 percent of farm households owned cultivators; 72 percent of households had holdings over 0.5 hectares. Hokuriku Nōseikyoku Niigata Tōkeijōhō Jimusho Niigata Shutchōjo, ed., *Yokogoshimura no nōgyō* (Niigata: Niigata Nōrin Tōkei Kyōkai, 1983), 30–31.

32. For the launch of television broadcasting in Japan, see Partner, *Assembled in Japan*, ch. 3.

33. For a discussion of some of these issues, see John F. Embree, *Suye Mura: A Japanese Village* (Chicago: University of Chicago Press, 1964), 133–35.

34. For discussions of communal ownership and its problems, see *Kikaika Nōgyō*, Jan. 1956, 41; Sept. 1957, 84; and Dec. 1957, 66; also Shimizu Hiroshi, *Nihon Nōgyō no Dokujisei to wa Nani ka* (Tokyo: Nihon Keizai Hyōron Sha, 1988), 35–40.

35. "Kōunki no unten menkyo," *Kikaika nōgyō*, Mar. 1957, 60–61.

36. "Saikin," 17–18; Shimizu Hiroshi, *Nihon Nōgyō no Dokujisei to wa Nani ka*, 15.

37. Kayō Nobufumi, *Nihon nōgyō kiso tōkei*, 544–45. A transplanter cost ¥159,000 in 1970, ¥240,000 in 1975. A combine cost ¥590,000 in 1970, ¥1,055,000 in 1975. The increase is partly due to inflation, presumably also partly to technological improvements.

38. Shimizu Hiroshi, *Nihon Nōgyō no Dokujisei to wa Nani ka*, 17.

39. In 1998, U.S. farmers sold their rice for an average price of $0.086 per pound. Japanese farmers sold at ¥17,410 per sixty kilograms, which equates to $1.09 per pound using an exchange rate of ¥120 to one U.S. dollar. See Sōmu chō tōkei kyoku, *Nihon chōki tōkei sōran*, 2: 238.; U.S. Census Bureau, *Statistical Abstract of the United States*, 119th ed. (Washington, D.C.: U.S. Census Bureau, 1999), 687.

40. Nōka keizai chōsa, 1959 and 1969.

41. Kayō Nobufumi, *Nihon nōgyō kiso tōkei*.

42. Morii Junkichi, *'Kōdo Seichō' to nōsanson kaso* (Kyoto: Bunrikaku, 1995), 26.

43. Ibid., 24.

44. Calculated from Sōrifu, *Kankō hakusho* (Tokyo: Ōkurashō Insatsukyoku, 2000), 20.

45. Edward Norbeck, *Country to City: The Urbanization of a Japanese Hamlet* (Salt Lake City: University of Utah Press), 1–2.

46. Ibid., 241–42.

47. Of 961 farm families in 1970, 629 (65 percent) had holdings over one hectare, and 249 (26 percent) had holdings over two hectares. By contrast, the national average was 30 percent over one hectare and only 6 percent over two hectares. Sōmu chō tōkei kyoku, *Nihon chōki tōkei sōran*, 2: 29.

48. Hokuriku Nōseikyoku Niigata Tōkeijōhō Jimusho Niigata Shutchōjo, *Yokogoshimura no nōgyō*, 22–23.

49. Ibid., 37.

50. Yokogoshi Mura, *Yokogoshimura tōkei shiryōshū*, 91.

51. Ibid., 86; Takahashi Itsuo, *Waga kyōdo Yokogoshi*, 16.

CONCLUSION

1. Carol Gluck, "The Idea of Showa," in *Showa: The Japan of Hirohito,* ed. Stephen Graubard and Carol Gluck (New York: W. W. Norton, 1992).

2. Ibid., 8.

3. Andō Yoshio, *Kindai Nihon keizaishi yōran,* 2nd ed. (Tokyo: Tokyo Daigaku Shuppankai, 1997), 107.

4. Overall industrial employment declined by only 219,000 from 1930 to 1932, although a greater number of layoffs must have been offset by new entrants to the labor force. See Sōmu chō tōkei kyoku, *Nihon chōki tōkei sōran,* 1:452.

5. Sōmu chō tōkei kyoku, *Nihon chōki tōkei sōran,* 4: 330; 2: 94–95; 4: 474–75. Salaried urban workers were worse affected than laborers, with an income decline of close to 40 percent.

6. Sōmu chō tōkei kyoku, *Nihon chōki tōkei sōran,* 1: 86.

Bibliography

Akiyama Takashi et al., eds. *Zuroku nōmin seikatsushi jiten.* Tokyo: Kashiwa Shobō, 1991.

Andō Yoshio. *Kindai Nihon keizaishi yōran.* 2nd ed. Tokyo: Tokyo Daigaku Shuppankai, 1997.

Beardsley, Richard J., John W. Hall, and Robert E. Ward. *Village Japan.* Chicago: University of Chicago Press, 1959.

Beasley, W. G. *The Meiji Restoration.* Stanford: Stanford University Press, 1972.

Bernstein, Gail. *Haruko's World: A Japanese Farm Woman and Her Community.* Stanford: Stanford University Press, 1983.

Bird, Isabella. *Unbeaten Tracks in Japan.* London: Virago, 1984.

Dore, Ronald P. *Land Reform in Japan.* London: Athlone Press, 1984.

Drea, Edward J. "Trained in the Hardest School." In *In the Service of the Emperor: Essays on the Imperial Japanese Army,* 75–90. Lincoln, Neb.: University of Nebraska Press, 1998.

Embree, John F. *Suye Mura: A Japanese Village.* Chicago: University of Chicago Press, 1964.

Encyclopedia of Japan. Tokyo: Kodansha, 1983.

Fujii Tadatoshi. *Kokubō fujinkai: hinomaru to kappōgi.* Tokyo: Iwanami Shoten, 1985.

Fukutake, Tadashi. *Rural Society in Japan.* Tokyo: University of Tokyo Press, 1980.

Gluck, Carol. "The Idea of Showa." In Stephen Graubard and Carol Gluck, eds., *Showa: The Japan of Hirohito,* 1–26. New York: W. W. Norton, 1992.

Hane, Mikiso. *Peasants, Rebels and Outcastes: The Underside of Modern Japan.* New York: Pantheon, 1982.

Hani Tomoko. *Jiyū kyōryoku ai.* Tokyo: Fujin no Tomo Kai, 1963.

Havens, Thomas R. H. *Valley of Darkness: The Japanese People and World War Two.* New York: W. W. Norton, 1978.

Hokuriku Nōseikyoku Niigata Tōkeijōhō Jimusho Niigata Shutchōjo, ed. *Yokogoshimura no nōgyō.* Niigata: Niigata Nōrin Tōkei Kyōkai, 1983.

Ino Ryūichi. *Sengo Nihon Nōgyōshi.* Tokyo: Shin Nippon Shuppansha, 1996.

Itagaki Kuniko. *Shōwa senzen senchūki no nōson seikatsu—zasshi "Ie no Hikari" ni miru.* Tokyo: Mine Shobō, 1992.

Itō Keiichi. *Heitaitachi no Rikugunshi: Heiei to senba seikatsu.* Tokyo: Banchō Shobō, 1969.

Iwate Ken Nōson Bunka Kondan Kai, ed. *Senbotsu nōmin heishi no tegami.* Tokyo: Iwanami Shoten, 1961.

Kaigo Muneomi. *Shūshin.* Vol. 3 of *Nihon kyōkasho taikei.* Tokyo: Kōdansha, 1962.

Kamedakyō Tochi Kairyōku Yokogoshi Kōku, ed. *Yokogoshi no tochi kairyō jigyō.* Yokogoshi: Kamedakyō Tochi Kairyōku Yokogoshi Kōku, 1979.

Katō Ken'ichi, ed. *Shōnen kurabu meisakusen.* 3 vols. Tokyo: Kōdansha, 1966.

Kayō Nobufumi. *Nihon nōgyō kiso tōkei.* Tokyo: Nōrin Tōkei Kyōkai, 1977.

Kennedy, M. D. *The Military Side of Japanese Life.* London: Constable and Co., 1924.

Kokuritsu Yoron Chōsajo. *Nōson yoron chōsa: kyōshutsu seido yo nōgyō kyōsai kumiai.* Tokyo: Kokuritsu Yoron Chōsajo, 1949.

Kubota K. K. *Kubota 100-Nen.* Osaka: Kubota K. K., 1990.

Lu, David John. *Sources of Japanese History.* Vol. 2. New York: McGraw-Hill, 1974.

Machida Shiritsu Hakubutsukan, ed. *Norakuro—Tagawa Suihō tanjō hyakunen kinen.* Machida: Machida Shiritsu Hakubutsukan, 1999.

Maruyama, Masao. "The Ideology and Dynamics of Japanese Fascism." In Ivan Morris, ed., *Thought and Behaviour in Modern Japanese Politics,* 25–83. London: Oxford University Press, 1963.

———. "Theory and Psychology of Ultra-Nationalism." In Ivan Morris, ed., *Thought and Behaviour in Modern Japanese Politics,* 1–24.

Mizutani Yūji. *Minna de yaru seikatsu kaizen.* N.p.: n.p., 1956.

Monbushō, *A General Survey of Education in Japan* (Tokyo: Department of Education, 1926).

Morii Junkichi. *'Kōdo Seichō' to nōsanson kaso.* Kyoto: Bunrikaku, 1995.

Morioka Tomo no Kai, ed. *Tayama mura no seikatsu.* Morioka: Morioka Tomo no Kai, 1935.

Mulgan, Aurelia George. *The Politics of Agriculture in Japan.* London: Routledge, 2000.

Nagatsuka Takashi. *The Soil: A Portrait of Rural Life in Meiji Japan.* Trans. Ann Waswo. London: Routledge, 1989.

Nihon Hōsō Kyōkai. *Nihon hōsōshi.* 2 vols. Tokyo: Nihon Hōsō Kyōkai, 1965.

Nihon Kokuyū Tetsudō Sōsaishitsu. *Tetsudō 80-nen no ayumi.* Tokyo: Nihon Kokuyū Tetsudō, 1952.

Nihon Nōgyō Kikai Kōgyōkai. *Nichinōkō 35-nen no Ayumi.* Tokyo: Nihon Nōgyō Kikai Kōgyōkai, 1973.

Nihon Sonrakushi Koza Henshu Iinkai. *Nihon sonrakushi kōza.* Vol. 8 of *Seikatsu 3: Kingendai.* Tokyo: Yuzankaku, 1990.

Niigata Nippō Jigyōsha, ed. *Shin kenmin kikikakichō: sesō moyō—18 nin no jikakuzō.* Niigata: Niigata Nippō Jigyōsha, n.d.

Niigata Shi Gappei Chōsonshi Henshūshitsu, ed. *Ishiyama sonpō ni miru senjika no nōson.* Vol. 5 of *Niigata Shi Gappei Chōson no rekishi kenkyū hōkoku.* Niigata: Niigata Shi Gappei Chōsonshi Henshūshitsu, 1984.

Niigataken. *Niigata kenshi.* 9 vols. Niigata: Niigataken, 1988.

Nishida Yoshiaki. *Kindai Nihon nōmin undōshi kenkyū.* Tokyo: Tokyo Daigaku Shuppankai, 1997.

Nōrinshō Nōrinkeizaikyoku Tōkei Chōsabu. *Nōka keizai chōsa hōkoku.* Tokyo: Nōrinshō, 1955–65.

Norbeck, Edward. *Country to City: The Urbanization of a Japanese Hamlet.* Salt Lake City: University of Utah Press, 1978.

Ōkado Masakatsu. *Meiji Taishō no nōson.* Tokyo: Iwanami Shoten, 1992.

Partner, Simon. *Assembled in Japan: Electrical Goods and the Making of the Japanese Consumer.* Berkeley: University of California Press, 1999.

———. "Taming the Wilderness: The Lifestyle Improvement Movement in Rural Japan, 1925–1965." *Monumenta Nipponica* 56, no. 4 (winter 2001): 487–520.

Raper, Arthur F. *The Japanese Village in Transition.* Tokyo: Supreme Commander Allied Powers, 1950.

Rekishi Hyakka Jiten Henshūbu. *Kōshitsu no hyakka jiten.* Tokyo: Shinjinbutsu Ōraisha, 1963.

Rousseau, Julie M. "Enduring Labors: The 'New Midwife' and the Modern Culture of Childbearing in Early Twentieth-Century Japan." Ph.D. diss., Columbia University, 1998.

Russell of Liverpool, Lord. *The Knights of Bushido: A Short History of Japanese War Crimes.* London: Cassell and Company, 1958.

Sanson Shinkō Chōsakai. *Tosa kyūshun sanson no sugata to shinro: Kōchiken Kamigun Monobemura.* Tokyo: Sanson Shinkō Chōsakai, 1966.

Shakai Fukushi Chōsa Kenkyūkai. *Senzen Nihon shakai jigyō chōsa shiryō shūsei.* Tokyo: Keisō Shobō, 1986.

Shichinoe Chōsei. *Nōgyō Kikaika no Dōtai Katei.* Tokyo: Nōgyō Sōgō Kenkyūjo, 1974.

Shimazaki Tōson. *Before the Dawn.* Honolulu: University of Hawaii Press, 1987.

Shimizu Hiroshi. *Nihon Nōgyō no Dokujisei to wa Nani ka.* Tokyo: Nihon Keizai Hyōron Sha, 1988.

Smethurst, Richard J. *A Social Basis for Prewar Japanese Militarism: The Army and the Rural Community.* Berkeley: University of California Press, 1974.

Smith, Kerry. *A Time of Crisis: Japan, the Great Depression, and Relief Policy.* Cambridge: Harvard University Press, 2001.

Sōka Gakkai Seinenbu Hansen Shuppan Iinkai, ed. *Aa, tsūkoku no shima Gadarukanaru.* Vol. 20 of *Sensō wo shiranai sedai e,* second series. Tokyo: Daisan Bunmei Sha, 1985.

———, ed. *Kita no taichi ni namida shite: senjika no nōson.* Vol. 18 of *Sensō wo shiranai sedai e,* second series. Tokyo: Daisan Bunmei Sha, 1984.

Sōmu Chō Tōkei Kyoku. *Nihon chōki tōkei sōran.* 5 vols. Tokyo: Nihon Tōkei Kyōkai, 1988.

Sōrifu. *Kankō hakusho.* Tokyo: Ōkurashō Insatsukyoku, 2000.

Sumiya Mikio, ed. *Showa kyōkō: sono rekishiteki igi to zentaizō.* Tokyo: Yūhikaku, 1974.

Supreme Commander Allied Powers, General Headquarters. *History of the Nonmilitary Activities of the Occupation of Japan: Agriculture (September 1945 through December 1950)* (Tokyo: SCAP, 1950).

Takahashi Itsuo. *Waga kyōdo Yokogoshi.* Yokogoshi: Privately published, 1951.

Tanaka Keiichi. *Niigata-ken no rekishi.* Tokyo: Yamakawa Shuppansha, 1998.

Tanaka, Yuki. *Hidden Horrors: Japanese War Crimes in World War II.* Boulder, Colo.: Westview Press, 1996.

Taniguchi Zentarō. *Taniguchi Zentarō shō.* Tokyo: Shin Nihon Shuppansha, 1986.

Tetsudōin. *Honpō tetsudō no shakai oyobi keizai ni oyoboseru eikyō.* Vol. 12 of *Kindai Nihon shōhin ryūtsūshi shiryō.* Ed. Shōhin Ryūtsūshi Kenkyūkai (Yamaguchi Kazuo). Tokyo: Nihon Keizai Hyōronsha, 1916.

U.S. Census Bureau. *Statistical Abstract of the United States.* 119th ed. Washington, D.C.: U.S. Census Bureau, 1999.

Wada Kazuo. *Kōunki Tanjō.* Tokyo: Fumin Kyōkai, 1979.

Waswo, Ann. *Japanese Landlords: The Decline of a Rural Elite.* Berkeley: University of California Press, 1977.

———. "The Transformation of Rural Society, 1920–1950." In Peter Duus, ed., *The Twentieth Century,* 541–605. Cambridge: Cambridge University Press, 1988.

Weber, Eugen. *Peasants into Frenchmen: The Modernization of Rural France, 1870–1914.* Stanford: Stanford University Press, 1976.

Wigen, Kären. *The Making of a Japanese Periphery, 1750–1920.* Berkeley: University of California Press, 1995.

Williamson, Mark B. *Agricultural Programs in Japan, 1945–51.* Vol. 148, *Natural Resources Section Reports.* Tokyo: Supreme Commander for the Allied Powers, General Headquarters, 1951.

Wiswell, Ella Lury, and Robert J. Smith. *The Women of Suye Mura.* Chicago: University of Chicago Press, 1982.

Yokogoshi Chōshi Hensan Iinkai. *Yokogoshi chōshi—shiryōhen.* Yokogoshi: Yokogoshimachi, 2000.

Yokogoshi Mura, ed. *Yokogoshimura tōkei shiryōshū.* Yokogoshi: Yokogoshi Mura, 1979.

Yokogoshi Sonshi Hensanshitsu. *Yokogoshi sonshi ryakunenpyō.* Yokogoshi: Yokogoshi Sonshi Hensanshitsu, n.d.

Yokogoshimura no minzoku. Yokogoshi: Privately published, 1973.

Yoshinaga Akira. "Echigo Sōmi sōdō no kenkyū." *Fukuyama daigaku ningen kagaku kenkyū sentaa kiyō* 12, no. 10 (Oct. 1997): 65–74.

Yūsei Shō, ed. *Yūsei hyakunenshi.* Tokyo: Teishin Kyōkai, 1971.

Yui Masaomi. *Sensō to kokumin.* Vol. 8 of *Zusetsu Shōwa no rekishi.* Ed. Shōwa no Rekishi Kankōkai. Tokyo: Shūeisha, 1980.

Zenkoku Nōgyō Chūōkai. *Seikatsu Shidōin no Katsudō Kiroku.* Tokyo: Ie no Hikari Kyōkai, 1980.

Zenkoku Tomo no Kai Chūōbu. *Nōson seikatsu gōrika undō Tōhoku settorumento no kiroku.* Tokyo: Zenkoku Tomo no Kai Chūōbu, 1989.

Index

Compositor:	G & S Typesetters, Inc.
Text:	10/13 Sabon
Display:	Sabon
Printer and binder:	Thomson-Shore, Inc.